POLICE

BRUTALITY

POLICE
BRUTALITY

An Anthology

Edited by

JILL NELSON

W. W. Norton & Company   New York • London

"Another Day at the Front: Encounters with the Fuzz on the
American Battlefront" by Ishmael Reed printed with the
permission of the author.

For information about permission to reproduce selections from
this book, write to Permissions, W. W. Norton & Company, Inc.,
500 Fifth Avenue, New York, NY 10110

The text of this book is composed in Berling
with the display set in Meta Normal.
Composition by Sue Carlson.
Manufacturing by Haddon Craftsmen.
Book design by Chris Welch.

Library of Congress Cataloging-in-Publication Data

Police brutality : an anthology / edited by Jill Nelson.
        p.   cm.
Includes bibliographical references.
ISBN 0-393-04883-7
1. Police brutality—United States. 2. Discrimination in law
enforcement—United States. I. Nelson, Jill, 1952–
HV8141.P567 2000
363.2'32—dc21   00-020532

W. W. Norton & Company, Inc., 500 Fifth Avenue, New York, N.Y. 10110
www.wwnorton.com

W. W. Norton & Company, Ltd., 10 Coptic Street, London, WC1A 1PU

1 2 3 4 5 6 7 8 9 0

Contents

POLICE
BRUTALITY

Introduction

JILL NELSON

Outrage. Disgust. Sadness. These were the emotions felt by most African Americans on February 4, 1999, when they heard that Amadou Diallo, a twenty-two-year-old immigrant from Guinea, had been shot at forty-one times, and killed with nineteen bullets by members of the New York Police Department's Street Crime Unit. Yet, while shocked by the magnitude of police firepower used to kill this unarmed young man, we were not surprised. In a wide range of communities of color, being harassed, or brutalized, or even murdered by the police has never been cause for surprise. Alarm, yes, but not surprise.

We felt similar emotions ten months later when the New York State Supreme Court's Appellate Division, an all-White panel of five judges, responding to a defense motion, moved the trial of the four officers indicted for the Diallo shooting from the Bronx to Albany, New York's state capital. The justification? That it would be impossible to find twelve impartial jurors in the Bronx or anywhere else in New York City had a jury trial taken place. The appellate justices decided in what is, regrettably, a much too predictable way, that it would be better to move the trial to upstate Albany, an overwhelmingly white county 150 miles removed from New York, than to keep the trial in the Bronx where the shooting took place. It was hardly a surprise then to learn that Albany County is a place where African Americans and Latinos combined make up less than 14 percent of the population, an area where even fewer people of color become potential jurors, and where roughly 100 percent of police officers who go on trial are acquitted.

Nor did it come as a surprise when on February 25 the four officers who shot Amadou Diallo were each acqutted of all six charges against them—from second-degree murder down to reckless endangerment—after the jury deliberated for two and a half days. A profound disappointment, yes, but not a surprise. We have seen this scenario played out too many times. The United States attorney in Manhattan, whose office has been monitoring the case, and the Civil Rights Division of the Justice Department will review the case to determine if any civil rights laws were violated. Diallo's parents plan to file a civil lawsuit against the city, and it is possible, though unlikely, that the officers could face administrative charges within the deparment.

Surprise. Shock. Disbelief. These were the emotions felt by most White Americans when they learned of Amadou Diallo's murder by the police. Theirs is a world of White privilege in which Whiteness confers not only power and opportunity but also a presumption of innocence and the right to protection. It is a world in which the police are, if not exactly friends, certainly not enemies, a world in which, more often than not, if the players are a Black person and a policeman, the policeman will receive the benefit of the doubt.

Standing on a street corner in Manhattan two days after Diallo's murder, having just come from a meeting of concerned citizens to plan an organized response, I was so filled with frustration and sorrow that I turned to the woman beside me waiting for the light to change and asked "What do you think about the cops shooting that man forty-one times?"

She looked startled, confused—could she not feel the palpable rage, pain, and fear that pulsed through the black veins of this city and other cities across this nation?

"I don't know. I have to wait until all the facts are in. I'm sure they had a reason," she finally responded.

Perhaps she saw the disgust and disappointment on my face. Stepping off the curb as the light turned green, she added, "I mean, he must have done *something*." She was gone before I could tell her that Amadou Diallo and thousands of others didn't do anything: his crime was being Black and leaving his apartment building to go get something to eat. And of course there was no time to ask her exactly what "something" any human being could possibly do to warrant being shot at forty-one times by officers hired, paid, and pledged to "serve and protect." She could not understand that the issue wasn't Amadou Diallo's behavior but the actions of the police. I was disappointed and hurt by her words, but I was no more surprised by her response than by Diallo's murder.

There is nothing new about these responses to police brutality, or about brutality itself. The Kerner Commission on Civil Disorders, appointed by President Lyndon B. Johnson to look into the cause of the urban rebellions of the 1960s, reported in 1968,

> We have cited deep hostility between police and ghetto communities as a primary cause of the disorders surveyed by the Commission. In Newark, in Detroit, in Watts, in Harlem—in practically every city that has experienced racial disruption since the summer of 1964—abrasive relationships between police and Negroes and other minority groups have been a major source of grievance, tension and, ultimately, disorder. . . . Police misconduct—whether described as brutality, harassment, verbal abuse, or discourtesy— cannot be tolerated even if it is infrequent. It contributes directly to the risk of civil disorder. It is inconsistent with the basic responsibility of a police force in a democracy. Police departments must have rules prohibiting such misconduct and enforce them vigorously. Police commanders must be aware of what takes place in the field, and take firm steps to correct abuses.[1]

The Kerner Commission Report was not the first report to identify police misconduct as a key element of the fragile relationship between police and communities of color. Yet the problem persists in this new century. In the last year alone, two New Jersey state troopers were indicted on attempted-murder and assault charges after shooting three of four Black and Latino men during a traffic stop in 1998. This incident focused national attention on the practice of racial profiling—stopping drivers solely on the basis of their race—by state police, a practice prevalent across the country. The governor of New Jersey has admitted that racial profiling is commonplace.[2] Yet, in September 1999, Governor Gray Davis of California vetoed SB78, a bill that would have mandated collection of racial and ethnic data on all traffic stops.[3]

In Los Angeles, a former member of the Los Angeles Police Department, convicted of stealing eight pounds of cocaine from a police evidence locker, told investigators that in 1996 he and a former partner intentionally shot a gang member at point-blank range, paralyzing him, and then planted a gun to make it appear that the shooting was in self-defense.[4]

Since this case first came to light in September 1999, the growing scandal has implicated much of the LAPD, a force long notorious for abusive and excessive behavior in Black and Latino communities. While no officers have been indicted, forty criminal cases had been overturned by the district attorney's office as of February 2000, and the police concede that at least ninety-nine others have been tainted.[5] The FBI, the United States attorney, and the state attorney general have all begun criminal investigations into police brutality in the LAPD. Lawsuits filed by those wrongly prosecuted are expected to cost Los Angeles in excess of $200 million.

In New York City, where the conduct of the NYPD was the subject of a federal investigation by the U.S. Civil Rights Commission in 1999, settlements in claims and lawsuits alleging police brutality reached a record $40 million that fiscal year alone. The number of complaints increased by 10 percent, to 2,324, the highest figure in a decade.[6]

Yet much of America remains in denial about the magnitude of police brutality, reflecting a historical pattern that continued throughout the twentieth century. Occasionally, as in the Diallo case or the case of Abner Louima, a Haitian American who was beaten and then sodomized with a broken broom handle by a police officer, Justin A. Volpe, in a Brooklyn, New York, police precinct, the sheer violence and horror of the crimes creates a sense of mass outrage and leads to mass activism. Police officers are actually indicted, tried, and possibly convicted. This, alas, rarely occurs.

Such public outrage and judicial action appears to demand a specific set of circumstances. The victims must have a spotless record. They must not be involved in any altercation that might attract the police. Ideally they should not drink or smoke and should be straight and devout. The circumstances of their abuse and demise must be especially heinous. Disturbingly, we seem more able to respond to victims who, while Black, are not African American. Yet even when these circumstances are in place, deaths at the hands of the police will likely go largely unnoticed and unpunished.

The notion of the "Black male predator" is so historically rooted in the American consciousness that we have come to accept the brutalization and murder of citizens by the police as an acceptable method of law enforcement. The assumption is that Black men are the bad guys, the police are the good guys, and if the police killed someone it must have been for good reason. They must have done *something*. This attitude, ingrained since slavery, is nurtured and manipulated by the police, who are quick to release the prior-arrest or medical records of their victims, as if getting a speeding ticket, or jumping a subway turnstile, or being a graffiti artist, or smoking marijuana, or being mentally ill, or serving time in prison for any reason whatsoever, somehow justified being killed by the police.

As a result, the Black community is inured to police violence. Abusive behavior on the part of the police has become commonplace; we are used to the small harassments. According to a 1997 joint report from the Bureau of Justice Statistics and the National Institute of Justice, while men, Whites, and persons in their twenties were most likely to have face-to-face contact with the police, Hispanics and Blacks were about 70 percent more likely to have contacts with the police as Whites were. An estimated 500,000 people were hit, held, pushed, choked, threatened with a flashlight, restrained by a police dog, threatened or sprayed with chemical or pepper spray, threatened with a gun, or subjected to some other form of force. Approximately 400,000 were also handcuffed. Men, minorities, and people under thirty represented a relatively large percentage of those handcuffed. Of those who had face-to-face contact with the police, 1 in 430 alleged that the police threatened or used force.[7]

In short, abuse by the police is common in Black, Latino, and other minority communities, and, as a result, the price of our outrage, the ante, has been insidiously upped. We too need a more perfect or egregious victim to transform our outrage into activism.

As for those who attract police attention because of some sort of aberrant behavior, their brutalization is treated as an appropriate response—the police go unpunished and the incident is quickly forgotten. Kevin Cedeno, shot in the back while holding a machete and running away from the police. Eleanor Bumpurs, an elderly, mentally ill woman, killed by police who broke into her apartment to evict her for rent arrears. Lewis Rivera, a homeless man sitting and eating at a shopping mall, was chased by at least five police officers, sprayed with pepper spray, kicked, thrown to the ground, bound hand and foot, and dragged to a police car; he died less than an hour later in a holding cell.

Anthony Baez, who paid with his life for the crime of accidentally hitting a police car with a football. Or Tyisha Miller, unconscious in her broken-down car at night at a gas station with a gun on her lap, shot twelve times by cops a relative called to help her. Or Gidone Busch, a mentally ill man high on marijuana, talking to himself and allegedly brandishing a hammer, shot by police twelve times. Or Margaret Laverne Mitchell, a fifty-five-year-old mentally ill homeless woman shot by a police officer after she allegedly lunged at him with a screwdriver. Or Daniel Garcia Zarraga, shot and killed after police said he lunged at them with that ubiquitous "shiny object." Or Yong Xin Huang, sixteen, shot at close range behind his left ear after what police allege was a struggle over an air gun. The list of similar victims is extensive. With the exception of Police Officer Francis X. Livoti, Anthony Baez's attacker, who was acquitted of criminally negligent homicide but subsequently convicted of federal civil rights violations and sentenced to seven and a half years in prison, no police officer has been charged with any of these murders.

The majority of cases of police brutality—whether occasioned by Black people driving on an interstate, or laughing with friends on a street corner, or waiting for a subway or bus, or simply being Black and walking to the store—go unpunished. We live in a country in which many Black and brown communities define themselves as under siege, not only by poverty, miseducation, and crime but also by the police. In need of protection, we are instead given an army of occupation.

Meanwhile, White Americans too often remain surprised, at best insisting that what happened to Abner Louima and Amadou Diallo is exceptional. Most Whites believe that Louima and Diallo are exceptions—good Blacks—and that there is in the police department no systemic problem, just a few rotten apples who need to be thrown out.

All Americans pay an enormous price as a result of these divergent and extreme attitudes. Police misconduct toward people of color is a cornerstone of the perpetuation of racism and White privilege. Fear, indifference, paranoia, passivity, rage, alienation, and violence are a few of the by-products of living in a society in which we are victims of, or silent partners in, abusive, brutal, and racist behavior by the police. Such behavior rends the fabric of democracy, not only for the immediate victims of police violence and their families, but for all of our neighborhoods, towns, and cities and for the whole nation.

According to a 1999 report from Amnesty International, *United States of America: Race, Rights and Police Brutality,*

> . . . the organization documented patterns of ill treatment across the USA, including police beatings, unjustified shootings and the use of dangerous restraint techniques to subdue suspects. While only a minority of the many thousands of law enforcement officers in the USA engage in deliberate and wanton brutality, Amnesty

International found that too little was being done to monitor and check persistent abusers, or to ensure that police tactics in certain common situations minimized the risk of unnecessary force and injury. The report also noted that widespread, systemic abuses had been found in some jurisdictions or police precincts. It highlighted evidence that racial and ethnic minorities were disproportionately the victims of police misconduct, including false arrest and harassment as well as verbal and physical abuse.[8]

Given the existence of these intransigent racial and social problems, I felt that I as a writer and a community activist needed to do more than respond to each new incident as it came along. It grew clear to me that the entire issue of police brutality has become a crucible that reflects both the continuing despair and the anger of the community. Indeed, the political ramifications of continued police harassment and violence take us way beyond the initial encounter that may occur in the privacy of one's house, in the street, in a car, or in a police station. Therefore, I felt that by examining the issues in this sort of literary manner, I could make all Americans more aware of these divisive and deeply entrenched problems. After all, recognition is the first step on the long road of transformation.

I specifically sought out a wide range of essayists, drawing voices from the academic community as well as a broader community. My intention all along has been not only to provide an opportunity for Black Americans to speak out but also to present a great diversity of opinions.

Accordingly, each of the essays in *Police Brutality* explores a different aspect of the issue in an effort to understand how America reached this current situation—and how we extricate ourselves from it. Essays examine the roots of the police presence in African American communities from the era of slavery until today, as well as the ways in which race and crime are framed and how the racialization of crime justifies and perpetuates police brutality. A twenty-nine-year veteran of the NYPD offers a view of police misconduct from the inside looking out, while an urban planner and former member of the Black Panther Party details his politicization as a twelve-year-old boy after being kidnapped by the police. A historian places the surveillance of the Nation of Islam and Elijah Muhammad by the FBI and the Chicago police within the framework of police brutality, while an attorney examines the ways in which the legal system codifies and encourages it. A political and constitutional rights activist discusses both recent responses to police brutality and ways in which the police force might be transformed.

Each of the essays in *Police Brutality* brings critically needed light to the subject of the banally abusive and often violent relationship between the Black community and the police and the White community's ignorance of, indifference to, or tacit sanctioning of police misconduct. Each makes clear the price all Americans pay when any are denied their constitutional rights. Each essay suggests, directly or indirectly, possible remedies. As a whole, this collection of essays makes clear that police brutality toward African Americans and other people of color is, like slavery, part of the birth of this nation—real, systemic, and devastating to all of us.

In a booklet entitled *Persecution of Negroes by Roughs and Policemen*, excerpts of which are included in this book, a fifteen-year-old boy named Harry Reed states in his affidavit, one of many given by African Americans victimized by mobs of White citizens and police officers in New York City,

> We five boys were sitting on the seat of an open Eighth Avenue car. When we got at the corner of 37th Street and Eighth Avenue we saw a mob, and the mob called out, "There's some niggers; lynch them!" and they made a rush for the car, and I jumped out. Then I ran up to the corner of 38th Street, where there were four policemen. Of these four policemen three were standing on the corner, and one ran into the street to stop me. When he saw me coming I was running hard, as fast as I could. When I reached this policeman in the street, he hit me over the head with his club. He hit me twice over the head, and I saw the other three policemen coming, and I fell down. I thought if I fell down the others would

not attack me, but they did; they hit me over the legs and on my arm, when I raised it up to protect my head, and they hit me in the back. . . . I wanted to get protection, but instead the cops hit me, as I have told. I did not resist arrest and I did not struggle to get away from the cops. I only wanted to get away from the mob. . . . I did not even try to run away after I had been hit. I was afraid to run, because I knew if I did they would hit me again.[9]

Harry Reed's affidavit is dated August 22, 1900. And little has changed in a century.

The hope is that *Police Brutality* will not suffer the fate of its predecessors, become another report to be read, clucked over, and put aside to gather dust. Rather, it should be read as a challenge to each of us to change the way we think about the issue and an inspiration for each of us to take action.

Now that would be something!

NOTES

1. *Report of the National Advisory Commission on Civil Disorders* (New York: E. P. Dutton, 1968), 299, 305.

2. *New York Times*, September 8, 1999, sec. B, p. 1.

3. Ibid., September 30, 1999, sec. A, p. 20.

4. Ibid., September 26, 1999, sec. 1, p. 32.

5. Ibid., February 24, 2000, sec. A, p. 12.

6. Ibid., October 1, 1999, sec. B, p. 1.

7. Bureau of Justice Statistics and the National Institute of Justice, *Police Use of Force: Collection of National Data* (Washington, D.C., 1997), 4.

8. Amnesty International, *United States of America: Race, Rights and Police Brutality* (New York: Amnesty International USA, 1999), 1.

9. *Persecution of Negroes by Roughs and Policemen, in the City of New York, August, 1900*, 73–74.

Part I

HISTORICAL

PERSPECTIVES

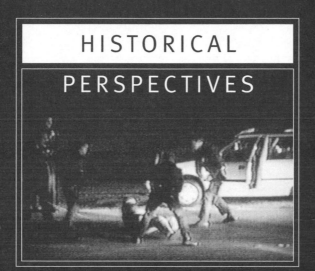

"Slangin' Rocks . . . Palestinian Style"

Dispatches from the Occupied Zones of North America

ROBIN D. G. KELLEY

The only way to police a ghetto is to be oppressive. . . . They represent the force of the white world, and that world's criminal profit and ease, to keep the Black man corralled up here, in his place. The badge, the gun in the holster, and the swinging club make vivid what will happen should his rebellion become overt. . . . He moves through Harlem, therefore, like an occupying soldier in a bitterly hostile country, which is precisely what, and where he is, and is the reason he walks in twos and threes.

—James Baldwin, *Nobody Knows My Name* (1962)

You can't trust a big grip and a smile
And I slang rocks Palestinian style

—The Coup, "The Shipment,"
Steal This Album (Polemic/Dogday 1998)

Memorandum: The Accidental Ethnographer

G reat. *The 9:07 bus hasn't left yet. Three long blocks to go. I break into a sprint, hearing only the sound of my own footsteps, asthmatic wheezing, books and papers knocking around my oversized legal briefcase. The night is cool and quiet and very dark. No crickets or porch dwellers or porch lights, just a big dog chained to a tree, barking out of habit. Two more blocks to go. Suddenly the sound of helicopters interrupts the rhythm of my feet and breath. An invasion so swift it is like a "Surround Sound" demonstration in a high-tech movie theater. Deafening noise. Wind. Lights. My silhouette appears before me, a lengthening shadow extending down the block, almost to my destination. All this is not for me, I thought. Not me.*

"Drop the package and put your hands on top of your head, enclosing your fingers! Don't turn around!" The voice is coming through a loudspeaker, probably a patrol car. But I cannot see. What package? My briefcase is all I have, so I set it down carefully and comply.

"Walk backward and do not turn around! I repeat, do not turn around!" My long shadow is now obscured in a flood of lights. It feels bright and hot like the sun. I walk back, slowly, blind as a bat. Drowning in a sea of light. Step one, two, three, four. . . .

Crack! *A nightstick crashes down on my fingers and head. One blow is all it takes. On the ground, face crushed against the damp pavement still wet from yesterday's rain, arms twisted behind my back, a man's knee to restrain me. I protest.*

"Shut the fuck up!" What did I do? What is my crime.

"I said shut the fuck up or I'll use this nightstick for real."

Moment of silence. I lay still under the heavy weight of this uniformed man, my arms searing with pain. A flashlight shined directly into my eyes. Footsteps, live voices, walkie-talkies, car doors slamming, engines purring. I break my silence. Why did you stop me? What did I do?

"You ran, nigger! Criminals run." I cannot see who said this; I see only lights and shadows and floating red ringlets, most likely produced by the blow to the head and the flashlight pointed directly into my eyes. Besides, I no longer had a reason to run: the last bus from Bellflower to Long Beach left without me.

I ask for badge numbers, but their lips are sealed. Over the din of idling patrol cars and radios, I hear them rifling through my "package" looking for loot. Books and papers yield nothing of interest, no smoking gun, no contraband. So they dump the contents in a shallow pothole half filled with muddy rainwater. My face is wet from the moistened pavement, from sweat forming on my neck and forehead, from uncontrollable tears. No more words. Lights off. Doors slam. Cars drive off in different directions. All I hear now, besides a lone helicopter fading in the distance, is heavy wheezing punctuated by dry coughs. Then voices, some Spanish, some English; some fearful, some angry. Eyewitness to public terror. With kindness, unknown bystanders collect my papers and books, wiping off the mud, putting pieces back together.

I WILL NEVER forget that autumn night in 1981. The Lakewood Sheriff's Department was known for harassing Black and Latino men and leaving the scene without a trace. And in 1981, police departments throughout the Greater Long Beach area were feeling pressure from community activists for the death of Ron Settles, an African American student at Cal State Long Beach and star football player who was found dead in a holding cell. Settles had been arrested the night before while driving through Signal Hill, a tiny town smack dab in the middle of Long Beach. He was stopped by Signal Hill police officers allegedly for a routine traffic violation, but they arrested him for possession of cocaine—a strange charge in light of the fact that he had no prior history of drug use. What happened next really isn't much of a mystery, but the official story presented by the Signal Hill Police Department went something like this: high on drugs and possibly distraught, Settles mysteriously obtained a blunt object, beat himself, and then hanged himself in his cell.

My own efforts to file a complaint with the Lakewood Sheriff failed miserably. I had no badge numbers and was told that the department had no record of the incident. I might as well have been in Johannesburg in the days of apartheid or, for that matter, any ex-colonial metropole where the color line keeps the world's darker people under an omnipotent heel. Whether we are speaking of North Africans in Paris, West Indians in London, indigenous peoples in Sydney, Australia, Black people in Birmingham (Alabama or England), or Palestinians in the West Bank, relations between the police and people of color have been historically rooted in a colonial encounter. Some might balk at the Coup's lyrical analogy between African American youths' confrontations with the police and the street battles of Palestinians against Israeli authority, but in my view it speaks directly to the historical foundations of police brutality in America. The clever pun ("slangin' rocks," for those who may not know, also means to sell crack cocaine) not only provides a broader, international political context for violent confrontations between police and people of color, but raises the specter of transformation, of the powerless turning the weapons of self-destruction into weapons for social change.

The Coup represents a long line of hip-hop groups that draw on metaphors of war to describe inner-city communities and relations between police and residents. For at least a decade and a half, beginning perhaps with Toddy Tee's 1985 street tape "Batteram," to songs such as Ice-T's "The Killing Fields," Public Enemy's "Anti-Nigga Machine," 2 Black, 2 Strong MMG's "War on Drugs" and "Ice Man Cometh," KRS-One's "Who Will Protect Me from You," Ice Cube's "Endangered Species (Tales from the Darkside)," W.C. and the MAAD Circle's "Behind Closed Doors," Compton's Most Wanted's "They Still Gafflin," Cypress Hill's "Pigs," and Kid Frost's "I Got Pulled Over," rappers have been painting vivid portraits of the ghetto as a war zone and the police as an occupying army. These young artists are not alone. The mainstream media have also employed metaphors of war and occupation to describe America's inner cities. The recasting of poor urban Black communities as war zones was brought to us on NBC *Nightly News*, Dan Rather's special report "48 Hours: On Gang Street," Hollywood films like *Colors* and *Boyz N the Hood*, and a massive media blitz that has been indispensable in creating and criminalizing the so-called underclass.[1]

The position of the police as an occupying army in America's inner cities is not a new phenomenon. It is not a recent manifestation of a postindustrial condition in which the disappearance of jobs in urban areas generated lawlessness and disorder, nor is it the result of the federal government having declared war on drugs, though these things have certainly heightened police-community tensions in urban neighborhoods of color. To understand the roots of this relationship, we need to go back . . . way back to the days of slavery and colonial rule.

Dispatches from the Grave: State Violence in the Context of Slavery and Empire

> *Run, nigger, run*
> *De Patteroll get you!*
> *Run, nigger, run,*
> *De Patteroll get you!*
> *Watch, nigger, watch,*
> *De Patteroll trick you!*
> *Watch, nigger watch,*
> *He got a big gun!*
> —"Run, Nigger, Run" (slave song, n.d.)

The policing of Black, Latino, and Native American communities in the United States initially took the form of occupation, surveillance, and pacification. Even before formal police forces were established in cities at the end of the nineteenth century, people in power relied on "legal" and extralegal violence and terrorism to pacify, discipline, and exploit communities of color. We might point to the colonial wars against the indigenous populations from the time of European settlement up to the end of the nineteenth century. These wars of "pacification" resulted in forced marches, land seizures, the containment of whole societies within reservations, genocide, and the occupation and annexation of northern Mexico. In the antebellum South, the work of "policing" was geared almost entirely to the maintenance of slavery. "Patrollers," or individuals employed for the purposes of tracking down fugitive slaves, were the most visible manifestation of an active police force throughout the South, and virtually any adult White male could be conscripted to help put down a slave revolt.

The kind of violent, draconian punishment we now associate with brutality and excess was not only part of the culture but codified in law. For example, a Virginia law of 1705 allowed slaveholders to burn, whip, dismember, or mutilate slaves as punishment for crimes, and a 1723 Maryland law provided for cutting off ears of Africans— slave or free—who struck a White person. When the Constitution was ratified in 1787, it guaranteed, among other things, the use of federal armed forces to put down any slave insurrections, a promise reinforced by the Fugitive Slave Law of 1793.[2]

Once the Civil War brought an end to chattel slavery, most African Americans expected the state to protect them, to provide a safe environment so that they could get on with the work of rebuilding their lives as free citizens. And at times Union troops, whose ranks included Black people, actually defended and protected the newly freed people. But before the momentary rise of Radical Reconstruction, southern Blacks felt the heel of state repression and extralegal violence once President Andrew Johnson was in office, in 1865, and decided to practically hand the South back to the ex-Confederates. In 1866, around the same time the federal government opted to disarm Black militiamen and soldiers, a wave of terror and repression swept the South. The planter class formed terrorist groups such as the Ku Klux Klan and the Knights of the White Camellia, which burned Black homes, businesses, and crops and intimidated, beat, even lynched African Americans who they believed did not know their "place." The ex-Confederate-dominated provisional governments not only looked the other way but contributed directly to the overall atmosphere of terror and subordination by passing "Black codes," a series of laws that sharply restricted landownership, the right to purchase firearms, freedom of movement, and the right to work in independent trades, among other things. Indeed, the codes included various "apprenticeship laws," which bound "unattached" ex-slave children and teenagers to their plantation. "Apprenticeship" was nothing less than a return to slavery; only mass informal adoptions saved many of these young people.[3]

During the era of the Black codes as well as in the period following the end of Reconstruction and the consolidation of White supre-
macy, informal modes of terrorism and violence became the most
pervasive form of policing and disciplining African Americans.
Although several cities and counties established formal police forces
during the late nineteenth century,[4] this was nevertheless the era of
lynch law. Lynching, a practice that also occurred throughout the
colonial world—from Southwest Africa to the Philippines—was as
American as apple pie. Indeed, the United States was busy exporting
Jim Crow to the rest of the world. Often described by its defenders
as a form of popular justice, lynching in the United States was
employed primarily against African Americans. Between 1882 and
1946, there were at least five thousand recorded lynchings in this
country. Much more than a mob-style hanging in which the mob
appoints itself judge, jury, and executioner, lynching was a form of
public torture often involving the severing of limbs and mutilation of
genitalia. Sometimes a lynching might draw a large crowd of White
families (children included), and the victim's body parts might be
sold or distributed to spectators. Lynching was not a substitute for
the day-to-day policing of a subordinate group; rather, it was a public
spectacle intended to terrorize entire communities. A charred, muti-
lated body hanging from a tree served as a visible and potent
reminder of the price of stepping out of line.[5]

Lynching is essential for understanding the history and character
of police violence in the America of the twenty-first century precisely because it reveals the sexual and gendered dimensions of maintaining the color line and disciplining Black bodies.[6] Even though
only about one-fourth of the lynchings from 1880 to 1930 were
prompted by accusations of rape, and though a significant number of
lynch victims were political activists, labor organizers, or Black men
and women deemed "insolent" or "uppity" toward Whites, the most
sensational and highly publicized lynchings involved a Black man
accused of raping a White woman: hence the genital mutilation. (The
sexual undertone of racist violence, rooted in slavery and lynching,

continues to this day—manifest most recently in the brutal beating and rape of Abner Louima by New York City police officers.) More than anything else, lynching was a means of protecting the purity of White womanhood from Black male rapists. This position was so universally held that even Dr. Daniel G. Brinton, considered the first professor of anthropology in the United States and once president of the American Association for the Advancement of Science, implicitly defended lynching as a last resort to protect White women and racial bloodlines. In his *Races and Peoples* (1890), he wrote,

> It cannot be too often repeated, too emphatically urged, that it is to the women alone of the highest race that we must look to preserve the purity of the type, and with it the claims of the race to be the highest. They have no more holier duty, no more sacred mission, than that of transmitting in its integrity the heritage of ethnic endowment gained by the race throughout thousands of generations of struggle. . . . That philanthropy is false, that religion is rotten, which would sanction a white woman enduring the embrace of a colored man.[7]

At the same time, Ida B. Wells and others exposed the myth of the Black rapist. They demonstrated, among other things, that most interracial rape victims were Black women who endured the assaults of White men for which they were never punished, and explained how these myths affected the lives of men and women on both sides of the color line. As the historian Jacquelyn Dowd Hall points out, the myth of the Black rapist allowed southern White males to demand subordination and deference from White women in exchange for their "protection." This is the real meaning of chivalry. A White woman desiring a non-White man was out of the question, so any such encounter was presumed to be rape.[8]

All sexual encounters between White men and Black women, in distinct contrast, were presumed to be not only consensual but even initiated by the woman. The virginal White woman and Black rapist dialectic also produced the myth of the promiscuous Black woman.

Black women in such a world could not be raped, because they were deemed natural-born prostitutes. And as prostitutes, they too had to be policed. The lynch mentality created a situation in which police officers assumed that unescorted Black women were engaged in solicitation. In fact, the New York race riot of 1900 began when a Black woman was falsely arrested for solicitation and a Black man came to her defense; she had merely been waiting for her husband. In Atlanta, the police enforced what was called "a sundown law" directed primarily at Black women. Often it did not matter whether the woman was a known prostitute or not; if she was by herself in a restaurant or a club, she was likely to be arrested.[9]

Although most accounts characterize lynching as "extralegal," because it takes place outside of the criminal justice system, we must acknowledge the complicity of both the police and the law in upholding and facilitating lynching in the South. First, throughout this period, every effort to persuade Congress to pass a federal anti-lynching law failed. Second, not only have police officers and deputies openly participated in lynchings, but it was not uncommon for law enforcement officials to release a Black prisoner into the waiting arms of a lynch mob.[10]

By the turn of the century, it seemed as if the nation was embroiled in a domestic race war—one almost as violent as America's imperialist expeditions in Cuba and the Philippines, which became known as the Spanish-American War of 1898. Indeed, a few Black troops in both theaters noted the similarities between racial violence in the States and the treatment of America's new colonial subjects. One Black soldier in the Philippines expressed his utter contempt for the way Whites "began to apply home treatment for colored peoples: curse them as damned niggers, steal from and ravish them, rob them on the street of their small change . . . kick the poor unfortunate if he complained, desecrate their church property, and after fighting began, looted everything in sight, burning, robbing the graves."[11]

Black communities during this period had to deal not only with a steady stream of lynchings (in February 1893 alone, there was nearly one a day!) but with a constant threat of invasion by armed, murderous White mobs. In the years from 1898 to 1908, "race riots" broke out in Wilmington, North Carolina, Atlanta, New Orleans, New York City, Phoenix, South Carolina, Akron, Ohio, Washington Parish, Louisiana, Birmingham, Alabama, Brownsville, Texas, and Springfield, Illinois, to name but a few. The catalysts for these atrocities varied, ranging from revenge to punishment for a crime for which there were no viable suspects, competition over jobs, suppression of Black voting rights, an assertive gesture by an "insolent" Black person. In most cases, local police officers either stood by as these pogroms unfolded or actively participated on the side of White supremacists.[12]

With the outbreak of World War I, African Americans once again found themselves fighting on two fronts. While 400,000 Black men geared up to defend American democracy in Europe, tens of thousands back home found themselves having to defend their lives, often against the very men hired to protect and serve. The summer of 1917 turned out to be particularly bloody. In East St. Louis, Illinois, police and local militia joined White mobs in their attack on the Black community. Racial tensions were at an all-time high in this river town, exacerbated by the rising number of Black southern migrants, who competed with Whites for jobs. As a result of these tensions, incendiary headlines in the local paper called on readers to "Make East St. Louis a Lily White Town." And try they did. On the night of July 1, 1917, gangs of White men drove through the Black community and began shooting into homes indiscriminately. According to a report by a special congressional committee investigating the riot, the local police "became part of the mob by countenancing the assaulting and shooting down of defenseless negroes and adding to the terrifying scenes of rapine and slaughter." When the smoke cleared, at least 150 Black residents had been shot, burned, hanged, or maimed for life, and about 6,000 were driven from their homes. Thirty-nine Black people lost their lives, including small children whose skulls were crushed or who were tossed into bonfires.[13]

During that same summer, "war" also broke out in Houston, Texas, a city with a reputation for police brutality in a state that led the nation in lynching statistics. Just a year after the gruesome lynching of seventeen-year-old Jesse Washington in Waco, the War Department dispatched the all-Black Third Battalion of the Twenty-fourth Infantry to guard Camp Logan, which was still under construction. The presence of Black military personnel intensified an already tense racial atmosphere. As the historian Herbert Shapiro observed in his book *Black Violence and White Response*, "The hostility of racist Houston to the black servicemen was made clear as soon as the troops arrived in the area. White policemen assaulted and arrested black soldiers for refusing to obey Jim Crow signs. City detectives, early in August, beat two of the new arrivals on a streetcar."[14] Then, on August 23, two Houston police officers beat and arrested a Black soldier, Private Edwards, who had come to the defense of a Black woman they had physically and verbally abused. When Corporal Charles Baltimore approached the officers about the arrest, he too was beaten and shot at before finally being arrested. This was too much for the other members of the Third Battalion to bear. "To hell with going to France," shouted one of the enlisted men, "get to work right here." And they did. Approximately one hundred Black soldiers seized weapons and marched into town to take revenge. A shoot-out erupted between the soldiers, police, and armed civilians; when it was over, sixteen Whites (four policemen) and four Black soldiers lay dead. A lynching was averted, but the U.S. government acted swiftly to punish the men: nineteen were executed and fifty were sentenced to life imprisonment.[15]

Those Black men who did get to Europe to "make the world safe for democracy" returned home to segregation, lynching, race riots, and more police brutality. In what became known as the "Red summer" of 1919, race riots erupted in Chicago, Washington, D.C., Elaine, Arkansas, Longview, Texas, Omaha, Nebraska, and Knoxville, Tennessee. Lynchings took place almost daily. In Georgia alone, twenty-two people were lynched that year, most of whom were returning veterans. The following decade, known to some as the Jazz Age, may be remembered by others less nostalgically as the era of the

Ku Klux Klan. No longer limited to the South, the Klan developed strongholds in the West and the Midwest, notably in the state of Indiana. And in the cities police violence rose steadily; according to one study conducted by the sociologist Arthur Raper, during the 1920s approximately half of all Black people who died at the hands of Whites were murdered by the police.[16]

Toward the end of the 1930s, the problem of police violence became more apparent as lynching began to decline. Despite President Franklin D. Roosevelt's refusal to sign an antilynching bill, several factors contributed to lynching's slow demise. First, organizations such as the Association of Southern Women for the Prevention of Lynching, the NAACP, and the Communist-led International Labor Defense waged campaigns that generated worldwide opposition to lynching. Second, southern elites embarrassed by the negative publicity and interested in attracting northern capital, quietly discouraged lynching. In some cases, southern governors began insisting that local police forces keep Black suspects in their custody rather than release them to a mob. However, the decline in lynching did not mean the abandonment of the sexual color line. Even in northern cities such as New York and Chicago, where interracial couples could exist relatively openly, police officers frequently harassed Black men escorting White women.[17]

Dispatches from the Home Front:
Exchanging White Sheets for Rap Sheets

These new pressures did not make the police any more conscientious. On the contrary, the decline in lynching coincided with the expansion of urban police forces and a rise in reported incidents of police brutality. In Harlem, for example, the accumulation of police abuses over the years eventually exploded into a massive riot in 1935. The incident that touched off the uprising was a rumor that fourteen-year-old Lino Rivera had been killed by police after he was arrested for shoplifting. It turned out that he was very much alive, but it didn't matter. The NYPD had terrorized, harassed, and murdered so many Black Harlem residents that the collective anger over police abuses had reached a boiling point. Indeed, a special commission appointed by Mayor Fiorello La Guardia to investigate the causes of the riot noted that "nothing revealed more strikingly the deep-seated resentments of the citizens of Harlem against exploitation and racial discrimination than their attitude toward the police." Harlemites overwhelmed the commission with testimony of the daily abuses they endured, compelling commissioners to condemn the entire department: "inasmuch as the Police Department makes no effort to discipline policemen guilty of these offenses . . . then the Police Department as a whole must accept the onus of these charges."[18]

The situation grew worse during World War II. Urban police not only had to contend with an increased number of migrants, but African Americans—especially the youth—adopted a more defiant posture than usual. First, many African Americans were initially reluctant to support the war because they could not forget the unfulfilled promises generated by World War I. This time around, they would fight on two fronts: home and abroad. Amid antifascist rhetoric, daily confrontations with the police, segregation laws, or intolerant Whites took on political significance. As African Americans became increasingly politicized by the war, "Double V," victory at home and abroad, became the cry heard from Black communities. The National Association for the Advancement of Colored People (NAACP), for example, enjoyed a tenfold increase in membership, while groups like the Nation of Islam (whose members resisted the draft) suddenly became a force to be reckoned with. The period also saw the creation of new organizations, such as the Congress on Racial Equality (CORE), which came into being during the war.[19]

Not surprisingly, police repression became a major issue for African Americans. In Birmingham beginning in 1941, a wave of police homicides and beatings reignited resistance to police brutality. In one incident, O'Dee Henderson, who was arrested and jailed for merely arguing with a White man, was found the next morning in his jail cell handcuffed and fatally shot. A few weeks later, John Jackson, a Black metal worker in his early twenties, was shot to death as he lay in the back seat of a police car. Jackson made the fatal mistake of arguing with the arresting officers in front of a crowd of Blacks lined up outside a movie theater.[20] Reminiscent of those of the First World War, confrontations between Black residents and White policemen occasionally sparked full-scale riots. During the "Red summer" of 1943, when race riots erupted in almost a dozen cities, in New York, Detroit, and Los Angeles police violence was the match that lit the fuse. The Harlem riot of 1943 was almost a repeat of what had happened eight years earlier, and yet like the 1900 riot it began when a Black man, army private Robert Bandy, came to the defense of a Black woman, Marjorie Polite. The police had been staking out Harlem's Hotel Braddock for illegal activities, including solicitation, when a policeman named James Collins arrested Polite after an argument with hotel employees. When Bandy stepped in to protest the officer's actions, a scuffle ensued and Collins shot him. When word of the shooting hit the streets, Harlem roared like a bonfire. It looked as if the war had come home: 6 people lay dead, 550 had been arrested, and 1,450 stores had been damaged or burned to the ground.[21]

In Harlem, Mayor La Guardia called on the police to exercise restraint, and compared with the police in the 1935 conflagration, they seemed much more compliant. In Detroit, however, the police behaved like partisans in a race war. They had already shown their colors one year earlier, when policemen joined White mobs in preventing Black tenants from moving into the Sojourner Truth Housing Project. During the riots, White mobs moved through Black communities relatively unmolested, while African Americans were being arrested and shot at left and right. All seventeen people killed by police were Black. The police refused to use force to stop White assailants, and at one point they besieged an apartment building in an African American community in search of a suspect who had shot a police officer. The officers surrounded the building, fired indiscriminately into the windows, and tossed in several tear gas canisters. They then ransacked individual apartments and, according to some residents, stole money and personal property. Thurgood Marshall, the NAACP counsel who reported on police abuses during the riot, said the apartment building "resembled part of a battlefield." In an editorial about the Detroit riots, the *Pittsburgh Courier* columnist P. L. Prattis spoke for many Black observers when he wrote,

> What were the police doing when Negroes were being beaten in the Negro district? Arresting Negroes. What were the police doing when streetcars were stopped by the mob and Negroes mobbed and beaten? They were arresting Negroes. What were the police doing when automobiles bearing Negroes were stopped, turned over and demolished and their occupants beaten? They were arresting Negroes. It is crystal clear that in no American community is the police power going to be used against the majority from which the mob comes to protect the minority from which the victims come.[22]

In Los Angeles during that fateful summer of 1943, young Chicano males became primary targets of racial violence and police repression. These "zoot suit riots" revealed underlying tensions between a growing number of young "pachucos," on the one hand, and White servicemen and police officers in the city, on the other. These young people exhibited a cool, measured indifference to the war, as well as an increasingly defiant posture toward Whites in general. Tensions between the zoot suiters and servicemen came to a head in June 1943, during which White soldiers engaged in what amounted to a ritualized stripping of the zoot. The police chose sides carefully; although the zoot suiters were victims of white racial violence, when it was over six hundred Chicanos ended up in jail and the assailants essentially got a slap on the wrists. The police excused their behavior, explaining that they were "letting off steam." But these so-called riots were just the beginning. More violence followed in the wake of the Sleepy Lagoon case, in which police arrested some three hundred Chicano youths after José Díaz was found dead near the Sleepy Lagoon, a water reservoir in East Los Angeles. Twenty-two of the youths went to trial, and seventeen were convicted of crimes ranging from first-degree murder to assault, despite the lack of evidence. There were no eyewitnesses and no evidence that Díaz had, in fact, been murdered. What evidence did exist suggests that he had gotten drunk, fallen asleep on the road, and been hit by a car. Nevertheless, amid mass anti-Mexican sentiment and pressure to dismantle street gangs, these young men were sent to San Quentin. Two years later, however, the U.S. District Court of Appeals overturned their convictions, acknowledging that they had been railroaded.[23]

In both the Sleepy Lagoon trials and the zoot suit riots, the media contributed to the demonization of Chicano youth by portraying them as bloodthirsty, violent thugs. While large numbers of White gangs roamed the streets of Los Angeles at the time, the press treated the gang issue as strictly a Mexican and a Black problem. After the war, police repression against Chicanos only intensified, especially once the High Court overturned the Sleepy Lagoon convictions. On Christmas day in 1951, for example, a group of police officers removed seven young Chicanos from the Lincoln Heights jail and beat them ruthlessly. Two years later, two LA sheriffs severely beat fifteen-year-old David Hidalgo while other deputies looked on. As the officers thrashed him within an inch of his life, all he could do was beg for mercy.[24]

Dispatches from the Killing Fields of North America: Notes on Urban Insurrection and Right-Wing Reaction

"Law and order" became a coded battle cry as the police were transformed into an army defending white power and the status quo.

—Frank Donner, *Protectors of Privilege* (1990)

It is astounding that, at least at the outset, the modern Civil Rights movement did not take up police brutality as one of its top priorities. A study conducted by the Department of Justice found that in the eighteen-month period from January 1958 to June 1960, some 34 percent of all reported victims of police brutality were Black.[25] And given the general fear of police retaliation, especially in the South, it is likely that the percentage was actually much higher. Not that Civil Rights activists ignored police brutality cases: the files of the NAACP are overflowing with complaints about police abuses that date back to the organization's founding. However, despite hours of dramatic footage of southern cops beating down Civil Rights marchers and a long and public history of police repression in cities such as Memphis, Birmingham, Atlanta, and Columbia (Tennessee and South Carolina), the movement focused most of its energies on the desegregation of public facilities and on voter registration.[26]

Class and ideology may partly explain why police brutality took a back seat to desegregation. Although middle-class African Americans were never immune from police abuse, incidents of brutality and harassment disproportionately affected the urban poor and working class. Indeed, in the 1950s Birmingham's Black middle class often expressed greater concern over the high crime rate than over the police use of excessive force. But this posture did not last long. By the early to mid-1960s, as police violence and rioting escalated in America's urban centers, the problem of racist policing could no longer be sidestepped. Soon after the 1963 confrontation with Bull Connor, Birmingham's Civil Rights leaders began placing the issue of police brutality at the top of their agenda. They had no choice: in the fourteen months between January 1966 and March 1967, ten Black men, the majority of whom were teenagers or young adults, were killed by police. During this same period, there were no White victims or Black female victims of police homicides. The Reverend Fred Shuttlesworth not only threatened to build alliances with Black militant organizations, but his group distributed a flier proclaiming in no uncertain terms, "Negroes are TIRED of Police Brutality and Killing Our People. Negroes are tired of 'One Man Ruling' of 'Justifiable

Homicide' every time a NEGRO IS KILLED!" During the early 1970s, a number of poor and working-class African Americans joined grassroots organizations that investigated and fought police misconduct, such as the Committee against Police Brutality and the Alabama Economic Action Committee (which investigated at least twenty-seven separate incidents in 1972).[27]

These last two movements, which received very little support from the Black elite, reflected a fundamental ideological shift in thinking about police repression. Radical organizations such as the Black Panther Party for Self-Defense, Community Alert Patrol, the Republic of New Afrika, the Brown Berets, and the American Indian Movement, to name but a few, began to argue more explicitly that urban communities of color constituted "occupied zones" or that they functioned as "internal colonies" vis-à-vis the U.S. nation-state. Many of these organizations focused their activity on armed self-defense and monitoring police activity in their neighborhoods. Because the police were the most direct manifestations of the colonial state, struggles against the police often resembled an anticolonial war. One of the earliest organizations to frame the Black freedom struggle as an anticolonial war was the Revolutionary Action Movement (RAM), whose members went on to help found groups such as the Black Panthers and the Republic of New Afrika. Founded in 1962, RAM issued a twelve-point program calling for the development of freedom schools, national Black student organizations, rifle clubs, a guerrilla army made up of youth and unemployed, and Black farmer cooperatives—not just for economic development but to keep "community and guerrilla forces going for a while." They also pledged support for national liberation movements in Africa, Asia, and Latin America as well as the adoption of socialism to replace capitalism across the globe.[28]

RAM had been greatly influenced by Robert Williams, ex-Marine and former NAACP leader in Monroe, North Carolina, who believed that armed self-defense was more effective for dealing with White terrorists than nonviolent resistance. With the help of the National

Rifle Association, Williams in 1957 created a rifle club within his NAACP branch and began talking of the need to "meet lynching with lynching." Within two years, Williams was being attacked and disowned by the national NAACP and hounded as a fugitive by local and national law enforcement agencies. In 1961, he fled the country altogether, finding political asylum first in Cuba and later in China. His call for armed self-defense, physical retaliation, and the recognition of "violence as the only language that White America knows and respects" resonated powerfully with RAM militants who believed that Black people were capable of launching a war against the U.S. state. From exile, Williams anticipated Black urban uprisings in a spring 1964 edition of his magazine, *The Crusader*. In an article entitled "USA: The Potential of a Minority Revolution," Williams announced, "This year, 1964 is going to be a violent one, the storm will reach hurricane proportions by 1965 and the eye of the hurricane will hover over America by 1966. America is a house on fire— FREEDOM NOW!—or let it burn, let it burn. Praise the Lord and pass the ammunition!!"[29]

He was not alone in this assessment. A year earlier, the writer James Baldwin had predicted that in the coming years race riots would "spread to every metropolitan center in the nation which has a significant Negro population." The next six years proved them right. Nineteen sixty-four was indeed a "violent" year, with riots erupting in the Black communities of Harlem, Rochester, New York, Jersey City, and Philadelphia. By 1965, these urban revolts had in fact reached "hurricane proportions." The eye of the storm landed on the West Coast in the Black Los Angeles community of Watts. Sparked by residents witnessing yet another Black driver being harassed by White police officers, the Watts rebellion turned out to be the worst urban disturbance in nearly twenty years. By the time the smoke cleared, thirty-four people had died, and more than $35 million in property had been destroyed or damaged. The remainder of the decade witnessed the spread of this hurricane across America: violence erupted in some three hundred cities, including Chicago, Washington, D.C.,

Cambridge, Maryland, Providence, Rhode Island, Hartford, Connecticut, San Francisco, and Phoenix. Altogether, the urban uprisings involved close to half a million African Americans, resulted in millions of dollars in property damage, and left 250 people (mostly African Americans) dead, 10,000 seriously injured, and countless Black people homeless. Police and the National Guard turned Black neighborhoods into war zones, arresting nationwide at least 60,000 people and employing tanks, machine guns, and tear gas to pacify the collective community. In Detroit in 1967, for instance, 43 people were killed, 2,000 were wounded, and 5,000 watched their homes be destroyed by flames that engulfed fourteen square miles of the inner city.[30]

Elected officials, from the mayor's office to the Oval Office, must have seen these uprisings as a war of sorts since they responded to the crisis militarily, followed by a battery of social science investigators, community programs, and short-lived economic development projects. Just as the American military advisers in Southeast Asia could not understand why so many North Vietnamese supported the Communists, liberal social scientists wanted to find out why African Americans rioted. To the surprise of several research teams, those who rioted tended to be better educated and more politically aware than those who did not. One survey of Detroit Black residents after the 1967 riot revealed that 86 percent of the respondents identified discrimination and deprivation as the main reasons behind the uprising. Hostility to police brutality was also near the top of the list.[31]

The wave of urban insurrections had consequences for politics and police practices: in Watts and elsewhere, freeway exits were widened partly to facilitate the movement of military personnel. Numbers were painted on the roofs of houses in South Central Los Angeles so that aerial and ground forces could be better coordinated. In 1968, the conservative Republican Richard M. Nixon won the White House largely on a law-and-order ticket. One of Nixon's campaign promises was to get rid of "trouble makers," especially militant Black nationalist organizations like the Republic of New Afrika, the

National Committee to Combat Fascism, the Black Liberation Front, and the Black Panther Party—which FBI Director J. Edgar Hoover once called "the greatest threat to the internal security of this country." Under Hoover's Counter-Intelligence Program (COINTEL-PRO), FBI agents on numerous occasions used fake press releases to spread false rumors about movement leaders, hired undercover agents to provoke violence and/or commit crimes in the name of militant organizations, violently attacked competing organizations, and created an atmosphere of tension, confusion, and division within the organizations under surveillance. In addition to covert action, police squads across the country launched a bloody military offensive. In 1969 alone, 27 Black Panthers were killed by police and at least 749 arrested. When it came to protecting the rights of militant or radical organizations, virtually all civil liberties were suspended. The police raided offices and seized documents, sometimes without a warrant. They beat and arrested organizers on trumped-up charges, and even resorted to political assassination, the most notable example being the murder of the Chicago Panther leaders Mark Clark and Fred Hampton in 1969, both of whom were killed in their sleep during a raid coordinated by local police and the FBI.[32]

The police targeted Chicano activists as well. One of the best-known victims was Rubén Salazar, a popular journalist known for his penetrating investigative reporting on police repression and the Chicano community in Los Angeles. Because of his writing, he had received several death threats from police officers. Immediately following the Chicano Moratorium demonstration of August 29, 1970 (organized by the Brown Berets), where police teargassed and shot at unarmed, largely peaceful demonstrators, police surrounded a bar where Salazar and his co-workers had stopped. Claiming they were searching for an unidentified gunman, they filled the bar with tear gas. One of the canisters struck Salazar and knocked him unconscious. Everyone escaped except Salazar. When his co-workers attempted to retrieve him, the police kept anyone from entering the bar, including medical personnel. Two hours later, Salazar was dead.[33]

Faced with urban insurrections and the proliferation of community-based militant organizations, most urban police departments viewed ghettos as war zones. By drawing on methods of surveillance and antiguerrilla tactics developed in Vietnam, the police widened the chasm between themselves and urban communities of color as well as liberal politicians. Indeed, when city officials tried to respond to civilian complaints about police abuses, they often faced a mutiny. In the late 1960s in New York City, for example, conservative, openly racist elements came to dominate the police force, mobilizing in large part in opposition to the liberal mayor John Lindsay, who supported a civilian review board to adjudicate the growing number of complaints of police abuses. The Patrolmen's Benevolent Association became so powerful and contentious that in August 1968 its president, John J. Cassese, told his 29,000-member constituency to disregard orders by their superiors to use restraint when dealing with rioters and protesters. That same year, off-duty cops participated in a mob attack on Black Panther Party members and their supporters in front of a Brooklyn courthouse. They were there to attend a hearing in the case of three Panthers accused of assaulting a police officer. The strengthening of racist elements in urban police departments was not limited to New York. In cities like Chicago, Los Angeles, Philadelphia, and Oakland, groups such as the John Birch Society and the Ku Klux Klan were having success recruiting police officers.[34]

Cops were not the only ones moving farther right. With the exception of Jimmy Carter's fleeting term in the White House, this period marked the beginning of two and a half decades of Republican rule, an anti-Black and anti-immigrant backlash, and a general dismantling of radical organizations fighting for communities of color. As a result of intense police repression, incarceration, internal squabbling (caused in part by paid agents provocateurs), and a national right-wing drift among the populace, most of these movements went down in flames. Fearing that ghetto rebellions would spill into White suburbs, and that their taxes were being used to support lazy colored folks on welfare, White Americans increasingly came to believe that "minorities," particularly African Americans, needed to stop complaining. Black people, they rationalized, no longer had any excuses since the Civil Rights movement had succeeded in abolishing racism once and for all.[35]

Most African Americans, however, knew another reality altogether. The next two decades were characterized by deindustrialization, permanent unemployment, White flight, disinvestment in urban areas, the shrinking of city services, the elimination of state and federal youth and job programs, a rollback of affirmative action programs, cutbacks in housing, urban development, and education, and a scaling back of agencies that investigate and enforce civil rights laws, to name but a few disastrous consequences of the rightward turn. During Reagan's two terms in office, military spending increased by 46 percent, while funding for housing was slashed by 77 percent and education by 70 percent. The number of families eligible for Aid to Families with Dependent Children was cut back substantially. While pushing for tax breaks for the very rich in hopes of stimulating the economy, the Reagan administration reduced the Federal Food Stamp program by $2 billion and cut back federal child nutrition programs by $1.7 billion.[36]

Racist violence was also resurgent during this period. The number of racially motivated assaults rose dramatically, many of them occurring on college campuses across the country. Between 1982 and 1989, the number of hate crimes reported annually in the United States grew threefold. In 1981, police officers in Florida and Mississippi generated an atmosphere of terror by circulating a mock hunting flyer announcing "open season" for shooting "Porch Monkeys. Regionally known as Negro, Nigger, Saucer Lips, Yard Apes, Jungle Bunnies, Spear Chuckers, Burr Heads, Spooks, and the Pittsburgh Pirates." Other signs pointing to a resurgence of racism in the 1980s include the proliferation of White supremacist organizations such as the Ku Klux Klan. By the late 1970s, the Klan had tripled its membership and even gained some influence in electoral politics. In 1980, Tom Metzger, the "Grand Dragon" of the Ku Klux Klan, garnered enough votes to win the Democratic primary in Southern California's Forty-third Congressional District. Similarly, David Duke, former Klansman and founder of the National Association for the Advancement of White People, was elected to the Louisiana House of Representatives. Despite such electoral affirmation, the Klan did not trade in their white sheets or their guns. In 1978–79, Klansmen initiated a reign of terror against Black people, which included the firebombing of homes, churches, and schools in over one hundred towns and rural areas, and drive-by shootings into the homes of southern NAACP leaders.[37] Very few of these incidents led to convictions, in part because in some instances local police were complicit. Perhaps the worst incident occurred on November 3, 1979, in Greensboro, North Carolina, where five members of the Communist Workers Party were murdered by Klansmen and Nazis during an anti-Klan demonstration. Not only did the Greensboro police know of the Klan's plan to attack the demonstration but, just minutes before the confrontation, nearly all on-duty officers were called to the other side of town for a "lunch" break. When the shooting stopped, there was not a cop in sight. Although the entire episode was caught on videotape, the all-White jury concluded that there was insufficient evidence to convict anyone.[38]

Emboldened by the changed mood in America, police violence seemed to escalate beginning around the mid- to late-1970s. Throughout the country, African Americans had become the most likely victims of police violence. According to one study, African Americans constituted 46 percent of the people killed by police in 1975. Out West, the better-known victims of police homicides include Chicanos such as Danny Trevino, murdered by San Jose police in 1976; Jose Barlow Benavidez, fatally shot by Oakland police officers; and Juan Zepeda, blackjacked to death by San Antonio police. Civilians filed so many complaints against the Los Angeles Police Department that when Chicano community activists demanded an investigation and greater accountability, LAPD officials destroyed their files to cover up an obvious pattern of violence against Latinos and Blacks. One incident they could not bury was the 1979 killing of Eula Mae Love. Love, a thirty-nine-year-old woman who stood about five feet four inches tall, was shot a dozen times by two LAPD officers who were called to the scene after she tried to stop a gas maintenance man from turning off her gas. When they arrived, she was armed with a kitchen knife, but the only thing she stabbed was a tree in her yard. Three years later, at least fifteen deaths were caused by chokeholds administered by Los Angeles police officers attempting to subdue suspects. Police Chief Darryl Gates noted, "We may be finding that in some blacks when [the chokehold] is applied the veins or arteries do not open up as fast as they do on normal people."[39]

Residents of these communities did not accept police abuse without a fight. The radical movement against police repression was a mere shell of its former self, but as long as the police acted like an occupying army, war was still on. In a predominantly Black community outside of Miami, yet another unjustified police homicide sparked one of the worst urban insurrections in over a decade. It began back in December 1979, when Arthur McDuffie, a thirty-three-year-old Black insurance executive, was beaten to death by police officers in Dade County, Florida. The police said he was driving recklessly and had resisted arrest, but eyewitnesses believed it was a clear cut case of brutality. However, in May 1980, to widespread shock and dismay, an all-White jury returned a not-guilty verdict for all of the officers involved. Local activists quickly took to the streets of Miami and organized a silent protest march of 5,000 to the police department and courthouse in downtown Miami. Not everyone was silent, though; several participants began chanting, "We want justice!" That night, the predominantly Black and poor communities of Liberty City, Brownsville, Overton, and Coconut Grove exploded in anger— turning over cars, setting fire to buildings, looting, throwing rocks and bottles at police and National Guardsmen. When the smoke cleared, Miami's gross fiscal losses exceeded $250 million; at least 400 people were injured and several were killed; over 1,250 were arrested; and a fifty-two-square-mile area of Dade County was placed under curfew from 8 P.M. to 6 A.M.[40]

On closer inspection, the Miami rebellion was not just a spontaneous response to an unfair verdict. For the residents of Liberty City and other poor Black communities, McDuffie's death was one of a string of incidents of police brutality and racial harassment that had gone unchecked during the 1970s. The riot was a product of Black frustrations caused by joblessness, economic deprivation, and immigration policies that clearly favored White Cubans over Black Haitians. It also marked the most dramatic example of the growing feeling of political powerlessness among poor and working-class African Americans. In an age when the number of Black elected officials had increased dramatically and Civil Rights leaders had achieved tremendous influence in national policy making, Miami's Black rebels viewed their "leaders" with a mixture of distrust and apprehension.[41]

The Miami uprising and the failure of Black leadership were but forebodings of more ominous times yet to come. By the end of the 1970s, police killings and nonlethal acts of brutality emerged as a central political issue among African Americans. Between 1979 and 1982, protests were organized throughout the country around specific cases of police violence, some of the more highly publicized incidents occurring in Philadelphia, New Orleans, Memphis, Miami, Washington, D.C., Birmingham, Oakland, and Detroit (where the police department was notorious for sexually harassing Black female arrestees). In Philadelphia, for example, police-civilian tensions escalated into one of the most brutal episodes of violence in at least a decade. After Wilson Goode was elected the first Black mayor in Philadelphia's history in 1983, he immediately found himself caught between a White constituency that wanted a law-and-order mayor and a police force with a legacy of corruption and brutality. In fact, in 1986 a federal grand jury indicted seven Philadelphia police officers who had worked in the narcotics division for racketeering and extorting at least $400,000 plus quantities of cocaine from drug dealers.[42]

But the key event was Goode's decision to allow the police to bomb the headquarters of a Black nationalist organization called MOVE in May of 1985. Situated in the Philadelphia neighborhood of Powelton Village, MOVE had attempted to create a rural, communal environment in the middle of the city. As a result of complaints from neighbors and MOVE members' hostile attitude toward police, Mayor Frank Rizzo tried to root the group out in 1978. This culminated in a shoot-out that left one officer dead and several injured on both sides. In a similar standoff seven years later, Goode authorized the dropping of an aerial bomb, which killed 11 people, including 5 children, destroyed sixty-one homes, and left 250 people homeless. The MOVE bombing marred Goode's administration and his relations with Philadelphia's Black community until he left office in 1991. Perhaps the biggest blow to Goode's administration was that the commission appointed to investigate the bombing concluded that racism strongly influenced the actions of the Philadelphia police force. This was absolutely clear from the first words spoken by Philadelphia Police Commissioner Gregore J. Sambor, who announced over the bullhorn at the beginning of the assault, "Attention MOVE! This is America!"[43]

Dispatches from Lala Land:
On Seeing the Future in the Present

It's been happening to us for years. It's just we didn't have a camcorder every time it happened.
> —Ice Cube on the Rodney King beating
> (*MTV News* interview, May 3, 1992)

While civil rights activists and civil liberties advocates from across the country condemned the bombing, the Goode administration, surprisingly, seemed to get less criticism from African Americans for the bombing of MOVE than one might have expected. Of course, being a Black mayor may have had something to do with it, but that's not all. Goode had his share of defenders in Philadelphia's Black community, some of whom regarded MOVE activists as nuisances or, worse, common thugs. More significantly, legitimate concern for crime in the 1980s—often referred to as the "age of crack," when street violence intensified as various gangs battled for control over drug markets—contributed to a kind of uneasy tolerance for the police. The fact that poor inner-city residents are twenty-five times more likely to be a victim of street crime than someone living in a wealthy suburb speaks profoundly to the complex, often ambivalent relationship urban Blacks have toward the police. Unfortunately, the government-declared "war on drugs" did more to promote unbridled police repression than to make the streets safer.[44]

The "model community" for the war on drugs was South Central Los Angeles, where high-powered police helicopters, patrolmen in riot gear, and even small tanks armed with battering rams became part of the urban landscape in the early 1980s. Housing projects resembled minimum-security prisons equipped with fortified fencing and mini police stations; many residents were required to carry identity cards and visitors were routinely searched. In 1988, LA Police Chief Gates implemented Operation HAMMER, resulting in the arrest of some 1,500 Black youths in South Central for merely "looking suspicious." Although most were charged with minor offenses like curfew and traffic violations, some were not charged at all but simply had their names and addresses logged in the LAPD anti-gang task force database.[45]

Ironically, new technologies have in some ways made matters worse for poor, inner-city residents. The use of computer databases has had a profoundly negative impact on justice. First, street access databases generally do not indicate the disposition of the case (whether or not the accused was convicted or acquitted), nor are they error free. Yet, the new technology is used as if it were value free and error free, thus enabling some officers to act as both judge and jury in the street. If your name appears, you are guilty unless proven innocent. And given the backlog of cases and racial prejudice among police, juries, and judges, public defenders tend to plea-bargain for Blacks and Latinos even when a client appears innocent, because it *reduces* jail time and speeds the process. In the long run, however, it means that a young person just beginning his or her adult life now has a conviction, whether or not he or she has ever, in fact, been convicted. And when one is convicted, one is practically unemployable, and it is difficult to rent an apartment or obtain insurance. Second, the proliferation of new high-tech patrol cars, helicopters equipped with sophisticated infrared cameras and 30-million-candlepower spotlights, radios, radar, telemonitors, and phone taps has widened the chasm between the police and those being policed. Few urban cops can boast of the kind of intimate, local knowledge that earlier generations of officers assigned to, say, urban White ethnic communities might have had. Finally, one of the worst manifestations of the new technology has been the rapid increase in "home incarceration." To deal with the problem of overcrowding in jails and prisons, some offenders are allowed to stay home but must wear an electronic monitoring device. While this may seem more humane on the surface, it actually shifts the burden of "state support" for prisoners to the family. The entire household becomes incarcerated, and the neighborhood where the offender lives falls under heavier surveillance.[46]

That the war on drugs could result in more police abuses, greater repression, and a suspension of civil liberties for all inner-city residents should not be surprising, given the long history of policing communities of color. The colonial relationship that originally structured the police presence remains virtually unchanged. As occupying armies with almost no organic connection to the neighborhoods to which they are assigned, these big-city police forces operate no differently from the imperial forces of yesterday: every colonial subject is suspect. It is a rare cop, even among Blacks and Latinos, who sees his or her primary task as working *for*, or being employed *by*, poor urban communities of color. Instead, the police work for the state or the city, and their job is to keep an entire criminalized population in check, to contain the chaos of the ghetto within its walls, and to make sure the most unruly subjects stay in line. They operate in a permanent state of war.

It just so happened that the "model community" for the war on drugs was the site for one of the most recent and most devastating insurrections in the long, brutal history of urban America's colonial wars. Not surprisingly, the catalyst for the Los Angeles rebellion of 1992 was a police brutality trial that ended in the acquittal of four officers who had viciously beaten Rodney King thirteen months earlier. Unlike most incidents of police brutality, this one was captured on videotape. The entire nation watched King writhe in pain as he absorbed fifty-six blows in a span of eighty-one seconds. In addition to punching, kicking, and whacking him with a wooden baton, police shocked him twice with a high-voltage stun gun. When it was all over, King was left with a broken cheekbone, nine skull fractures, a shattered eye socket, a broken ankle, and the need for twenty stitches in his face.

For most viewers, irrespective of race, the video tape proved irrefutably that the officers involved in the beating used excessive force. Thus, when the all-White jury handed down a not-guilty verdict on April 29, 1992, the city exploded with rage. Buildings burned from West Los Angeles and Watts to Koreatown, Long Beach, and Santa Monica. Of the first 5,000 people arrested, 52 percent were Latino and only 39 percent were African American. By the time the rioting came to a halt on May 2, at least 58 people had been killed (26 African Americans, 18 Latinos, 10 Whites, 2 Asians, 2 unknown) and thousands were injured. The fires left more than 5,000 buildings destroyed or badly damaged. The estimated property damage totaled a staggering $785 million. The riots had a ripple effect beyond Los Angeles, as smaller and less volatile protests erupted in San Francisco, Atlanta, Las Vegas, New York City, Seattle, Tampa, and Washington, D.C. More than any other event, the LA rebellion dramatized to the rest of the world the tragic plight of urban America and the racist and classist character of policing. And because it occurred during a presidential election year, there was enormous pressure on President George Bush to offer a prompt response. Bush proposed Operation Weed and Seed, an urban policy that would provide big tax breaks to entrepreneurs willing to invest in inner cities, some limited programs for disadvantaged children, and, most important, a massive buildup of the police and criminal justice system. Indeed, the real emphasis was on the "weed" component rather than the "seed" component;

nearly 80 percent of the proposed $500 million allocation was earmarked for policing.[47]

Every farmer knows by now that all the "weeding" and "seeding" in the world are meaningless if the structure of the garden is flawed. What needs to change is the role of the police and their relationship to urban communities of color. The colonial mentality, rooted in slavery and imperialism, that has structured the entire history of policing in urban America needs to be overturned.

Indeed, I would go so far as to propose the complete dismantling of police departments (and consequently the entire criminal justice system) as we know it. Perhaps we might return to the long-standing radical proposal for community-based policing. Imagine institutions for public safety structured along nonmilitary lines and run by elected community boards! I am not simply proposing that community members be employed to do the work of policing; rather, I am suggesting that the very job itself be reinvented. New institutions of public safety would require radically new modes of training. Employees and volunteers would have to attend intensive workshops on race, gender, sexuality, domestic abuse, rape, violence, and inequality, among other things, and the institutions of public safety would have to reflect the racial and ethnic makeup of the communities they serve and to maintain an equal gender balance in all areas of work. They would be required to reside in the neighborhood in which they work and to conduct a thorough study of that neighborhood in all of its historical, social, economic, and psychological dimensions—a little like writing an honors thesis before graduating from the "academy of public safety."

Pipe dreams, perhaps. Of course, I am all too cognizant of the very real problem of crime and violence in the inner cities, and I know that the kind of public safety institutions I'm imagining will require significant ideological and cultural changes before anything like this can happen. Still I'm left wondering: what would we really lose by dismantling the police and reconstructing new ways of ensuring our collective safety? After all, how many big-city precincts have become havens for corruption, crime rings, drug dealing, prostitution, and the like? How many lives have been lost or people maimed because racist police officers feel free, if not obligated, to terrorize communities of color? When do we begin to break the cycle of state terror?

Memorandum: Why We Can't Wait

Eleanor Bumpurs. Michael Stewart. Anthony Baez. Michael Wayne Clark. Yong Xin Huang. Benjamin Nunez. Kuthurima Mwaria. Julio Nunez. Maria Rivas. Mohammed Assassa. Leonard Lawton. Diogenes Paolina. Aswan "Keshawn" Watson. Nathaniel Gains. Dion Hawthorne. Lori Leitner. Donald Fleming. Kenneth Arnold. Paul Mills. Stanley "Rock" Scott. Donnell "Bo" Lucas. Tommy Yates. Darryl Edwards. Gilberto Cruz. Kenny Johnson. Jorge Guillen. Eric Smith. Angel Castro Jr. Bilal Ashraf. Maneia By. Anthony Starks. Jonny E. Gammage. Malice Green. Gary Glenn. Jose Itturalde. James Johnson. Darlene Tiller. Crystal Lujan. Bobby Mitchell. Vickey Finklea. Roy Hoskins. Donnie Alexander. Mark Anthony Longo. Osiris E. Galan. Torrey Donovan Jacobs. Yvon Guerrier. Alvin Barroso. Marcillus Miller. Brenda Forester. Michael Wayne Johnson. David Ortiz. Arturo Jimenez. Miguel Ruiz. Josie Gay. Damian Garcia. Manuel Hernandez. Eliberto Saldana. Elzie Coleman. Tracy Mayberry. De Andre Harrison. John Daniels Jr. Michael Bryant. Jose Manuel Sanchez. Justice Hasan Netherly. Sonji Taylor. Fernando Herrera Jr. Dwight Stiggons. Hue Truong. Salomon Hernandez. Raphael and Luke Grinnage. Baraka Hall. Carolyn Adams. Dannette Daniels. Andre Jones. Tama T. Ava. Leon Fisher. James Quarles. Kuan Chung Kao. Brandon Auger. Amadu Diallo. Tyisha Miller. Devon Nelson. LaTanya Haggerty. Robert Russ. Michael Zinzun. Brother Akenshahn. Mumia Abu Jamal. You. Me. Our children. . . .

NOTES

1. Robin D. G. Kelley, *Race Rebels: Culture, Politics, and the Black Working Class* (New York: Free Press, 1994), 202–5; idem, "Straight from Underground," *The Nation* 254, no. 22 (June 8, 1992): 793–96.

2. Rodolfo Acuna, *Occupied America: A History of Chicanos*, 3rd ed. (New York: Harper Collins, 1988), 1–33; Patricia Nelson Limerick, *The Legacy of Conquest: The Unbroken Past of the American West* (New York: Norton, 1987); Dee Brown, *Bury My Heart at Wounded Knee: An Indian History of the American West* (New York: Holt, Rinehart, 1971); A. Leon Higginbotham Jr., *In the Matter of Color: Race and the American Legal Process* (New York: Oxford University Press, 1978); Mary Frances Berry, *Black Resistance/White Law: A History of Constitutional Racism* (New York: Appleton-Century-Crofts, 1971).

3. W. E. B. Du Bois, *Black Reconstruction in America, 1860–1880: An Essay toward a History of the Part Which Black Folk Played in the Attempt to Reconstruct Democracy in America, 1860–1880* (reprint, New York: Atheneum, 1962); Eric Foner, *Reconstruction: America's Unfinished Revolution, 1863–1877* (New York: Harper & Row, 1988); Leon Litwack, *"Been in the Storm So Long": The Aftermath of Slavery* (New York: Knopf, 1979); Dan T. Carter, *When the War Was Over: The Failure of Self-Reconstruction in the South, 1865–1867* (Baton Rouge: Louisiana State University Press, 1985); Allen W. Trelease, *White Terror: The Ku Klux Klan Conspiracy and Southern Reconstruction* (New York: Harper & Row, 1971); George C. Rable, *But There Was No Peace: The Role of Violence in the Politics of Reconstruction* (Athens: University of Georgia Press, 1984); Ira Berlin, Barbara Fields, Leslie Rowland, and Joseph Reidy, *Slaves No More: Three Essays on Emancipation and the Civil War* (New York: Cambridge University Press, 1992); Peggy Cooper Davis, *Neglected Stories: The Constitution of Family Values* (New York: Hill and Wang, 1997), 147–49, 153–54.

4. Sidney L. Harring, *Policing a Class Society: The Experience of American Cities, 1865–1915* (New Brunswick, N.J.: Rutgers University Press, 1983).

5. Arthur Franklin Raper, *The Tragedy of Lynching, 1899–* (Chapel Hill: University of North Carolina Press, 1933); Walter White, *Rope & Faggot: A Biography of Judge Lynch* (New York: Knopf, 1929); Ida B. Wells-Barnett, *On Lynchings: Southern Horrors, A Red Record, Mob Rule in New Orleans, 1862–1931* (New York: Arno Press, 1969); Stewart Emory Tolnay, *A Festival of Violence: An Analysis of Southern Lynchings, 1882–1930* (Urbana: University of Illinois Press, 1995); W. Fitzhugh Brundage, *Lynching in the New South: Georgia and Virginia, 1880–1930* (Urbana: University of Illinois Press, 1993); idem, ed., *Under Sentence of Death: Lynching in the South* (Chapel Hill: University of North Carolina Press, 1997); Leon F. Litwack, *Trouble in Mind: Black Southerners in the Age of Jim Crow* (New York: Knopf, 1998), 280–325; Herbert Shapiro, *White Violence and Black Response: From Reconstruction to Montgomery* (Amherst: University of Massachusetts Press, 1988), 30–144, passim. Shapiro does an excellent job of placing lynching in the context of empire.

6. My formulation owes a great deal to Joy James, *Resisting State Violence: Radicalism, Gender, and Race in U.S. Culture* (Minneapolis: University of Minnesota Press, 1996), 28–33.

7. Daniel G. Brinton, *Races and Peoples: Lectures on the Science of Ethnography* (New York: Hodges, 1890), 287, quoted in Lee D. Baker, *From Savage to Negro: Anthropology and the Construction of Race, 1896–1954* (Berkeley: University of California Press, 1998), 36.

8. Jacquelyn Dowd Hall, *Revolt against Chivalry: Jessie Daniel Ames and the Women's Campaign against Lynching*, rev. ed. (New York: Columbia University Press, 1993), 129–57; idem, "'The Mind That Burns in Each Body': Women, Rape, and Racial Violence," in *Powers of Desire: The Politics of Sexuality*, ed. Ann Snitow, Christine Stansell, and Sharon Thompson (New York: Monthly Review Press, 1983), 328–49.

9. Clifford M. Kuhn, Harlon E. Joye, and E. Bernard West, *Living Atlanta: An Oral History of the City, 1914–1948* (Athens: University of Georgia Press, 1990), 190; Kelley, *Race Rebels*, 49.

10. Robert L. Zangrando, *The NAACP Crusade against Lynching, 1909–1950* (Philadelphia: Temple University Press, 1980); U.S. Congress, Committee on the Judiciary, *Crime of lynching: Hearings before a Subcommittee of the Committee on the Judiciary, United States Senate, Eightieth Congress, Second Session, on S. 42 [and Other] Bills to Assure to Persons within the Jurisdiction of Every State Due Process of Law and Equal Protection of Laws, and to Prevent the Crime of Lynching, and for Other Purposes* (Washington, D.C.: U.S. GPO, 1948). There are numerous examples of police officers releasing suspects into the hands of lynch mobs in Ralph Ginzburg, ed., *100 Years of Lynching* (Baltimore: Black Classics Press, 1996); see also, Litwack, *Trouble in Mind*, 263–65, 424–25; Shapiro, *White Violence and Black Response*, 30–249, passim.

11. Willard B. Gatewood Jr., *"Smoked Yankees" and the Struggle for Empire: Letters from Negro Soldiers* (Urbana: University of Illinois Press, 1971), 32, 35–36.

12. Shapiro, *White Violence and Black Response*, 93–201, passim; Robert V. Haynes, *A Night of Violence: The Houston Riot of 1917* (Baton Rouge: Louisiana State University Press, 1976); Charles Crowe, "Racial Violence and Social Reform—Origins of the Atlanta Riot of 1906," *Journal of Negro History* 53 (July 1968): 234–56; William Ivy Hair, *Carnival of Fury: Robert Charles and the New Orleans Race Riot of 1900* (Baton Rouge: Louisiana State University Press, 1976); Anne J. Lane, *The Brownsville Affair: National Crisis and Black Reaction* (Port Washington, N.Y.: Kennikat Press, 1971); John D. Weaver, *The Brownsville Raid* (New York: Norton, 1970); John Dittmer, *Black Georgia in the Progressive*

Era, 1900–1920 (Urbana: University of Illinois Press, 1977), 138–39; Howard N. Rabinowitz, "The Conflict between Blacks and the Police in the Urban South, 1865–1900," *Historian* 39 (November 1976): 62–76.

13. Elliot Rudwick, *Race Riot at East St. Louis* (Urbana: University of Illinois Press, 1964); "Report on the Special Committee Authorized by Congress to Investigate the East St. Louis Riots," in *The Politics of Riot Commissions, 1917–1970*, ed. Anthony Platt (New York: Macmillan, 1971), 68; Shapiro, *White Violence and Black Response*, 115–17.

14. Shapiro, *White Violence and Black Response*, 107.

15. Ibid., 108; Haynes, *A Night of Violence*.

16. Shapiro, *White Violence and Black Response*, 145–57; Mary Frances Berry and John Blassingame, *Long Memory: The Black Experience in America* (New York: Oxford University Press, 1982), 242.

17. Hall, *Revolt against Chivalry*; Robin D. G. Kelley, *Hammer and Hoe: Alabama Communists during the Great Depression* (Chapel Hill: University of North Carolina Press, 1990), 78–91; Gail Williams O'Brien, *The Color of Law: Race, Violence and Justice in the Post-World War II South* (Chapel Hill: University of North Carolina Press, 1999).

18. City of New York, *The Complete Report of Mayor LaGuardia's Commission on the Harlem Riot of March 19, 1935* (reprint, New York: Arno Press, 1969), 113, 114; Cheryl Greenberg, *Or Does It Explode: Black Harlem in the Great Depression* (New York: Oxford University Press, 1991), 193–94, 211.

19. Pete Daniel, "Going among Strangers: Southern Reactions to World War II," *Journal of American History* 77 (December 1990). 886–911; Roi Ottley, *"New World A-Coming": Inside Black America* (Boston: Houghton Mifflin, 1943); Richard Dalfiume, *Fighting on Two Fronts: Desegregation of the Armed Forces, 1939–1953* (Columbia: University of Missouri Press, 1969); Herbert Garfinkel, *When Negroes March: The March on Washington Movement in the Organizational Policies for FEPC* (Glencoe, Ill.: Free Press, 1959); Peter J. Kellogg, "Civil Rights Consciousness in the 1940's," *Historian* 42 (November 1979): 18–41; Neil A. Wynn, *The Afro-American and the Second World War* (New York: Holmes and Meier, 1975); Harvard Sitkoff, *A New Deal for Blacks: The Emergence of Civil Rights as a National Issue* (New York: Oxford University Press, 1978), 298–325, Philip Foner, *Organized Labor and the Black Worker, 1619–1981* (New York: International Publishers, 1981), 239, 243; George Lipsitz, *Class and Culture in Cold War America: "A Rainbow at Midnight"* (New York: Praeger, 1981), 14–28; Gerald R. Gill, "Dissent, Discontent and Disinterest: Afro-American Opposition to the United States Wars of the Twentieth Century" (unpublished book manuscript, 1988).

20. Kelley, *Hammer and Hoe*, 216–17.

21. James A. Burran, "Urban Racial Violence in the South during World War II: A Comparative Overview," in Walter J. Fraser Jr. and Winfred B. Moore Jr., eds., *From the Old South to the New: Essays on the Transitional South* (Westport, Conn.: Greenwood, 1981), 167–77; Dominic J. Capeci Jr., *Race Relations in Wartime Detroit: The Sojourner Truth Housing Controversy of 1942* (Philadelphia: Temple University Press, 1984); idem, *The Harlem Riot of 1943* (Philadelphia: Temple University Press, 1977).

22. Capeci Jr., *Race Relations in Wartime Detroit*; quotations from Shapiro, *White Violence and Black Response*, 319, 327.

23. Mauricio Mazon, *The Zoot-Suit Riots: The Psychology of Symbolic Annihilation* (Austin: University of Texas Press, 1984); Acuna, *Occupied America*, 254–58; S. Guy Endore, *The Sleepy Lagoon Mystery* (San Francisco: A and E Research Associates, 1972); Alice Greenfield, *The Sleepy Lagoon Case: A Pageant of Prejudice* (Los Angeles: Citizen's Committee for the Defense of Mexican-American Youth, 1942); Carey McWilliams, "Second Thoughts," *The Nation* 228 (April 7, 1979): 358; James S. Dimitroff, "The 1942 Sleepy Lagoon Murder, Catalyst for Mexican-American Militancy in Los Angeles" (B.A. honors thesis, UCLA, 1968).

24. Acuna, *Occupied America*, 292–93.

25. Berry and Blassingame, *Long Memory*, 242.

26. The best examination of police repression in the postwar urban South is Gail Williams O'Brien's stunning *The Color of Law*. As she demonstrates, immediately after World War II, legal and extralegal violence was a key issue facing the Black community in Columbia, Tennessee.

27. Kelley, *Race Rebels*, 92–99.

28. Maxwell C. Stanford, "Revolutionary Action Movement: A Case Study of an Urban Revolutionary Movement in Western Capitalist Society" (M.A. thesis, Atlanta University, 1986), 205–6; Donald Freeman, "The Cleveland Story," *Liberator* 3, no. 6 (June 1963): 7, 18; Rolland Snellings (Askia Muhammad Toure), "Afro American Youth and the Bandung World," *Liberator* 5, no. 2 (February 1965): 4–7; RAM, *The World Black Revolution* (pamphlet, 1966).

29. *The Crusader* 5, no. 4 (May–June 1964). On Williams, see Timothy B. Tyson, *Radio Free Dixie: Robert Williams and the Roots of Black Power* (Chapel Hill: University of North Carolina Press, 1999); Marcellus C. Barksdale, "Robert Williams and the Indigenous Civil Rights Movement in Monroe, North Carolina, 1961," *Journal of Negro History* 69 (Spring 1984): 73–89; as well as Williams's own writings, particularly *Negroes with Guns* (New York: Marzani and Munsell, 1962) and *Listen, Brother* (New York: World View Publishers, 1968).

30. James Baldwin, *Nobody Knows My Name: More Notes of a Native Son*

(New York: Dial Press, 1961), 192; Herbert J. Gans, "The Ghetto Rebellions and Urban Class Conflict," in *Urban Riots: Violence and Social Change*, ed. Robert H. Connery (New York: Vintage, 1969), 45–54; Manning Marable, *Race, Reform and Rebellion: The Second Reconstruction in Black America, 1945–1990*, 2nd ed. (Jackson: University Press of Mississippi, 1991), 92–93.

31. Tracy Tullis, "A Vietnam at Home: Policing the Ghetto in the Era of Counterinsurgency" (Ph.D. diss., New York University, 1998); Harlan Hahn, "Ghetto Sentiments on Violence," *Science and Society* 33 (Spring 1969): 197–208; Gerald Horne, *The Fire This Time: The Watts Uprising and the 1960s* (Charlottesville: University Press of Virginia, 1995); *Report of the National Advisory Commission on Civil Disorders* (New York: Bantam Books, 1968).

32. Kenneth O'Reilly, *Racial Matters: The FBI's Secret File on Black America, 1960–1972* (New York: Free Press, 1989), 229–324; Donner, *Protectors of Privilege*, 98, 105–6.

33. Edward Escobar, "The Dialectics of Repression: The Los Angeles Police Department and the Chicano Movement, 1968–1971," *Journal of American History* 74, (March 1993), 1483–504; Acuna, *Occupied America*, 345–50.

34. On the Cassese statement, see Donner, *Protectors of Privilege*, 194–95, 241–43, 246, 253. On the rising racism and its impact on urban policing, see John C. Cooper, *The Police and the Ghetto* (Port Washington, N.Y.: Kennikat Press, 1980); idem, *You Can Hear Them Knocking: A Study in the Policing of America* (Port Washington, N.Y.: Kennikat Press, 1981); A. L. Kobler, "Figures (and Perhaps Some Facts) on Police Killing of Civilians in the United States, 1965–1969," *Journal of Social Issues* 31 (1975), 163–91; Bruce Pierce, "Blacks and Law Enforcement: Towards Police Brutality Reduction," *Black Scholar* 17 (1986): 49–54; D. M. Rafky, "Racial Discrimination in Urban Police Departments," *Crime and Delinquency* 21, no. 3 (1975): 233–42.

35. George Lipsitz, *The Possessive Investment in Whiteness: How White People Profit from Identity Politics* (Philadelphia: Temple University Press, 1998), esp. 1–46; Michael Goldfield, *The Color of Politics: Race and the Mainsprings of American Politics* (New York: New Press, 1997), 310–14; Jill Quandango, *The Color of Welfare: How Racism Undermined the War on Poverty* (New York: Oxford University Press, 1994); Stephen Steinberg, *Turning Back: The Retreat from Racial Justice in American Thought and Policy* (Boston: Beacon Press, 1995); Thomas Byrne Edsall and Mary D. Edsall, *Chain Reaction: The Impact of Race, Rights, and Taxes on American Politics* (New York: Norton, 1991); Peter N. Carroll, *It Seemed Like Nothing Happened: The Tragedy and Promise of America in the 1970s* (New York: Holt, Rinehart and Winston, 1982).

36. Marable, *Race, Reform and Rebellion*, 180–83.

37. Ibid., 174–78; flier quoted in Manning Marable, *How Capitalism Underdeveloped Black America* (Boston: South End Press, 1983), 239; Kelley, *Into the Fire*, 73.

38. Elizabeth Wheaton, *Codename Greenkil: The 1979 Greensboro Killings* (Athens: University of Georgia Press, 1987).

39. Mike Davis, *City of Quartz: Excavating the Future in Los Angeles* (London: Verso, 1990), 267–92; M. W. Meyer, "Police Shootings at Minorities: The Case of Los Angeles," *Annals* 452 (1980): 98–110; *Report of the Independent Commission on the Los Angeles Police Department* (Los Angeles, 1991); Charles P. Wallace, "Blacks More Susceptible to Chokeholds?" *Los Angeles Times*, May 8, 1982; Kofi Buenor Hadjor, *Another America: The Politics of Race and Blame* (Boston: South End Press, 1995), 105–6.

40. Manning Marable, *Blackwater: Historical Studies in Race, Class Consciousness and Revolution* (Dayton, Ohio: Black Praxis Press, 1981), 129–32.

41. Ibid., 133–43.

42. Frank Donner, *Protectors of Privilege: Red Squads and Police Repression in Urban America* (Berkeley: University of California Press, 1990), 243.

43. Ibid., 244–45; Margot Henry, *"Attention, MOVE!: This Is America!"* (Chicago: Banner Press, 1987), 55–72, 105–26; Michael Boyette and Randi Boyette, *"Let It Burn": The Philadelphia Tragedy* (Chicago and New York: Contemporary Books, 1989), 14–24, 126–30, 134, 139, 144–50, 233–35; Hizkias Assefa and Paul Wahrhaftig, *The Move Crisis in Philadelphia* (Pittsburgh University Press, 1990); John Anderson and Hilary Hevenor, *Burning Down the House: Move and the Tragedy of Philadelphia* (New York: Norton, 1987), 86–87, 93–99, 104, 108–37, 249–50.

44. Mike Davis, *City of Quartz*, 267–322; David Cole, *No Equal Justice: Race and Class in the American Criminal Justice System* (New York: New Press, 1999), 16–55; Clarence Lusane, *Pipe Dream Blues: Racism and the War on Drugs* (Boston: South End Press, 1991); Marc Mauer, *Race to Incarcerate: The Sentencing Project* (New York: New Press, 1999), 142–61; Jimmie L. Reeves and Richard Campbell, *Cracked Coverage: Television News, The Anti-cocaine Crusade, and the Reagan Legacy* (Durham, N.C.: Duke University Press, 1994).

45. Davis, *City of Quartz*, 268.

46. Diana R. Gordon, *The Justice Juggernaut: Fighting Street Crime, Controlling Citizens* (New Brunswick, N.J.: Rutgers University Press, 1990). A recent, excellent critique of contemporary urban policing is Christian Parenti, *Lockdown America: Police and Prisons in the Age of Crisis* (London: Verso, 1999).

47. Much has been written on the Rodney King beating and the subsequent rebellion in Los Angeles. My synopsis draws primarily on the following sources:

Mike Davis, "In L.A., Burning All Illusions," *Nation* 254, no. 21 (June 1, 1992): 743–46; L.A. Weekly, 14, no. 23 (May 8–14, 1992); Los Angeles Times, *Understanding the Riots: Los Angeles before and after the Rodney King Case* (Los Angeles: Los Angeles Times, 1992); Robert Gooding-Williams, ed., *Reading Rodney King, Reading Urban Uprising* (New York: Routledge, 1993); Haki R. Madhubuti, ed., *Why L.A. Happened: Implications of the '92 Los Angeles Rebellion* (Chicago: Third World Press, 1993); Hadjor, *Another America*, 99–117; Urban Strategies Group, *A Call to Reject the Federal Weed and Seed Program in Los Angeles* (Los Angeles: Labor/Community Strategy Center, 1992); Labor/Community Strategy Center, *Reconstructing Los Angeles from the Bottom Up* (Los Angeles: Labor/Community Strategy Center, 1993).

2

PERSECUTION OF NEGROES

BY

Roughs and Policemen, in the City

of New York, August, 1900

STATEMENT AND PROOFS WRITTEN AND COMPILED BY FRANK MOSS AND
ISSUED BY THE CITIZENS' PROTECTIVE LEAGUE

I t might seem strange to some to include a document from a hundred years ago in a contemporary anthology on police brutality. Yet the words from these Black citizens brutalized by White mobs and police in New York City in August 1900 have a powerful and chilling resonance today. In some ways, the testimony may at first appear overwhelming, but it is precisely this repetition of incidents and observations that gives these voices a stunning authority.

What follows here are selections from some of the affidavits collected from law-abiding and innocent men and women, both Black and White. These eyewitness accounts of police brutality, official indifference, and the holding of what is essentially a people's tribunal eerily echo the responses to police brutality today. Many of those whose words are included here were illiterate; their affidavits are signed with an X. It is reasonable to assume that many were also former slaves who had moved North to search for opportunity and to escape the terrors of both slavery and the vigilante tactics of the post-Reconstruction South.

One must appreciate the landscape of both the country and New York City at the time of this violence. According to the U.S. census, there were almost nine million African Americans living in the United States as the nineteenth century became the twentieth, or 11.6 percent of the entire population. Nearly 90 percent of Blacks still lived in the South, and slightly more than one-fourth in urban areas of the South and the North. In 1900, Booker T. Washington published Up from Slavery, while in London, W. E. B. Du Bois was elected vice president of the first Pan-African Congress. There were 115 recorded lynchings in the United States that year, yet the first bill to make lynching a federal crime, introduced by Representative George H. White of North Carolina, the last African American elected during Reconstruction, never got out of congressional committee.

The writing had been on the wall for the three preceding decades. In fact, nothing underscored the loss of rights more than the case of Plessy v. Ferguson, in 1896, in which the U.S. Supreme Court decided that the practice of "separate but equal" was a "reasonable" solution to prevent the mingling of the races. But the Supreme Court decision was merely the latest in a series of laws that had effectively created a climate where lynchings were not only condoned but encouraged in the last thirty-five years of the nineteenth century. Although key events are too numerous to list here, one might briefly mention the creation of the Ku Klux Klan in 1865, the dissolution by Congress of the Freedmen's Bureau in 1872, which had been established to assure fair treatment of African Americans after the Civil War, and the brokered presidential election of Rutherford B. Hayes in 1876, which resulted in renewed southern control of state governments without federal interference, as well as the end of Reconstruction. By 1898, it was hardly surprising that the Supreme Court would rule in Williams v. Mississippi that the poll tax did not violate the Fourteenth Amendment.

That the riots described in this chapter occurred in New York reflects the fact that conditions were different in the North but hardly better. What we know of the cause of the riot is the following: on August 12, 1900, Arthur Harris and his wife were at Forty-first Street and Eighth Avenue, when Harris left his wife to buy a cigar. While she was standing *alone and waiting for her husband to return, a plainclothes police officer named Robert J. Thorpe attempted to arrest Mrs. Harris for "solicitation." Harris saw a man in civilian clothing taking his wife away and attempted to rescue her. Thorpe struck Harris with a club, and Harris responded by stabbing Thorpe with a penknife and fled the scene. Thorpe died of his wounds, and the riots, led by police officers and mobs of White citizens, began on August 15, the day of Thorpe's funeral.*

One month later, on September 12, some 3,500 people convened at Carnegie Hall to protest police brutality and the failure of the city government to act on behalf of all of its citizens. Out of this meeting came the formal collection of eighty pages of sworn affidavits, some of which are excerpted here. They stand as a record of the events that occurred in New York City on August 15 and 16, 1900.

City and County of New York, ss.:

John Hains, being duly sworn, deposes and says:

I reside at No. 341 West 36th Street. I am a laborer, and am at present employed as a longshoreman at Pier 16, North River. On the evening of August 15, 1900, I went to bed as usual at 9:30 o'clock. About two o'clock in the morning I was awakened by somebody beating me on the back with a club. When I awoke, I found six policemen in the room; they had broken in the door. They asked me for the revolver with which they said I had been shooting out of the window. I told them I did not have a revolver. One of the officers said that he had seen me shoot out of the window. Three officers then began to club me, while the other three were searching the house. They found an old toy revolver, which was broken and not loaded, and could not shoot if it had been loaded, and said that that was the pistol I had used. I denied that, which was the truth. They dragged me out of the house, and proceeded to take me to the station house. I was only in my undershirt, being asleep at the time they broke into the house, and begged them to allow me to put on my trousers and my shoes. They only sneered at this, and one of the officers said, "You'll be d—d lucky if you get there alive." Here another of the officers pulled out a revolver and said, "Let's shoot the d—d nigger," to which a third officer replied, "We can take the black son of a b— to the station house as he is." When I got to the station house, I was bleeding from my head and other parts of my body, as a result of these clubbings. There were only two other persons in our apartments that evening—William Seymour, from whom I rent my apartments, and Walter Gregory. When they saw the officers running into the house, acting as they did, they ran out of the house, leaving me asleep. They did not shoot out of the window, and we never kept any weapons in the house. Mrs. Lucy Jones, who lives next door to us, saw the officers beat me. She was in the house during all this time, and saw no firing from our windows. Her affidavit is hereto annexed. When I arrived at the station house, after the entry had been made on the blotter, I was placed in a cell. Before this I was struck by one of the officers in the station house in front of the sergeant's desk, and in his presence, without any interference on his part. After I was placed in the cell somebody (I believe the police surgeon) bandaged my head. The next morning the police loaned me a pair of old trousers, so that I could be taken to the Police Court. Officer Ohm, one of the officers who struck me and abused me, as aforesaid, made the charge against me; he charged me with firing a pistol through the window. I was brought before the magistrate, and he asked me if this was so. I told him it was not, and endeavored to explain matters to him, but he would not listen to me and sent me to the Penitentiary for six months. There were a great many similar cases before him that day, and he was very impatient. I did not have a lawyer to represent me, and I was given no opportunity to deny the false charges of the officer. While I was being taken to the station house, one of the officers said to another officer who was clubbing me, "Club as hard as you can; this is a d—d hard head." Another said, "I will teach you d—d niggers to club white people. We will kill half of you." I have the sheet which was on the bed on the night in question. It is full of blood stains. I had six stitches put into my head by a surgeon at the building in which the Magistrates' Court is located on 54th Street. This was before I was taken to Blackwell's Island. After I had been there ten days, I was released, I do not know the reason why. Sentenced August 16, released August 25, about eight A.M. The only one of the officers I could recognize is Officer Ohm, who made the formal complaint in the Magistrates' Court. I was almost beaten into insensibility that night, and all of the officers were in uniform. Last summer I was employed for the season as a butler by General O. O. Howard, at his summer home in Burlington, Vermont, and I have a recommendation from him. I am not a drinking man, and never was arrested before in my life.

JOHN HAINS.

Sworn to before me this 28th day of August, 1900.
GEO. P. HAMMOND JR., Notary Public (164), N.Y. County.

City and County of New York, ss.:
Chester Smith, being duly sworn, deposes and says:
I reside at No. 320 West 37th Street. I am employed in Flannery's drug store, at No. 103 West 42nd Street, and have been so employed for the last ten months. On August 15, 1900, at about ten o'clock P.M., while going to my home, walking on the west side of Eighth Avenue between 38th and 39th Streets, I saw a crowd of people, composed mostly of police officers and children. Some one in the crowd said, "There is a nigger!" pointing at me. One of the policemen ran towards me, and seeing that I was in physical danger I ran away from the place, going north to 39th Street on Eighth Avenue. Somebody threw a brick at me, which struck me in the back, and then one of the policemen came up to me and struck me in the left eye with his club. My eye and my forehead are still lacerated and discolored. I then ran into the saloon at the southeast corner of 39th Street and Eighth Avenue. One of the policemen ran in after me, and told me to go outside and run towards Broadway; that the mob had dispersed. I started toward the door, and as I reached it I saw that they were still waiting outside. I said to the officer as I started back into the saloon, "No, sir, I can't go out there; they'll kill me." The policeman then lifted me from the ground and threw me through the swinging door into the street. The glass in the door was broken, and I fell on my hands and knees. The policemen and the mob then began beating

me, the policemen beating me with their clubs. They did not disperse the crowd or protect me from it. I then started to run towards Broadway; another policeman ran after me and struck me in the back with his club. I staggered, made one or two jumps, and fell in front of No. 236 West 39th Street. The lady of the house, a white woman, came out, and I was taken into the house by someone, I don't know whom. Two or three days after she told me that the officers soon left the house, but that the mob tried to break in, and that she told them that if they would not leave she would kill them. The lady rang for a messenger boy and sent word to my employer to call. He came and brought some bandages, etc., and bandaged my head. He then called two police officers and asked them to take me to the station house. They refused. He insisted, and they finally yielded and took me to the station house. I was treated there by a police surgeon. My employer remained with me until three o'clock the next morning. I did not work for three days after this. I saw one man treated very harshly at the station house, being clubbed by police officers, and I believe he would have been treated still worse if it had not been for the presence of reporters. I did nothing whatever to justify this brutal treatment on the part of the police officers. I believe that had it not been for the presence of my employer I would have been beaten still more. There were over twenty-five policemen in the crowd. I was unconscious part of the time. I have never been arrested in my life.

CHESTER SMITH

Sworn to before me this 5th day of September, 1900.

GEO. P. HAMMOND JR., Notary Public (164), N.Y. County.

City and County of New York, ss.:

Charles Bennett, being duly sworn, deposes and says:

I reside at No. 309 West 37th Street. On August 15, 1900, I was working for a man named Mr. O'Connor, who keeps a saloon at Coney Island. I quit work at one o'clock A.M. the next day (August 16), and started for home with a man named Wilson. We boarded an Eighth Avenue car at Warren Street and Broadway, which was going north; just before we reached the street whereon I reside, the conductor of the car upon which we were riding told us that there had been a riot, that it was because of the death of the police officer, and that they were attacking every colored man that they caught. I then said that we had better get off; the conductor then said that it was "pretty quiet" when he came down. We got off the car at Eighth Avenue and 37th Street, and at 3:30 A.M. had almost reached the front door of my home when several police officers from among a group of about a dozen called to me asking me where I was going. I told them, "Home here." I was then in front of my door, and immediately after making my reply an officer hit me with his club, knocking me down. I struggled to my feet and endeavored to run towards 8th Avenue, but was pursued by the officers and knocked down again at the corner of Eighth Avenue and 36th Street. It was raining very hard at the time, and they threw me into the gutter, which was full of rain water; they kept my head in the water until I strangled, when they let up, jumped on me, and pushed me back again into the gutter. After a while they called a patrol wagon, into which they threw me, and beat me all the way to the station house in 37th Street. Upon my arrival there my head had been cut open; I was covered with blood and bruises from the beating and clubbing I had received. While in the station house I told Captain Cooney that I had been clubbed by policemen. I remained in the station house for about half an hour, and while there I heard a man who was dressed in citizen's clothes say to the officers present, "Club every d—d nigger you see; kill them; shoot them; be brave, the same as I was." The man answered, "All right; will you stick to us?" He answered, "Yes, I'll stand by you." I heard this man called Thompson by some of the officers. He went among the colored men who were present and who were in almost as bad condition as I was, asking their names, where they had lived, and what they had been doing. After receiving their answers, he said to each of them, "Get ter h—l home out of here; they'd ought ter have killed yer!" When he came to me he said, "What's your name?" I told him; then he said, "What were you doing?" I said, "I just come from work at Coney Island." He exclaimed, "Coney Island, eh! That's a d—d nice place to be working. Where do you live?" I told him, when he said, "Another nice place right in my district, the worst block in the whole district." He did not tell me to get out, but I was shortly after taken to Roosevelt Hospital and from there to Bellevue Hospital, where I remained a week, when I was taken to 54th Street Court, where I had a hearing and was discharged on August 28, 1900. While I was being clubbed in the street, one of the officers said, "Search him," whereupon they stopped the clubbing long enough to search my pockets and take fourteen dollars in bills from me, which I had in my hip pocket of my trousers. I have never had the said money returned to me. While I was in the station house, Captain Cooney was there, but not in uniform, and the aforesaid man whom they called Thompson was giving orders to the men, in the presence of Captain Cooney. At the time that I had reached my home on the said night there was no disturbance in the neighborhood, and there was but one man in sight, and he was chased away by the officers. Everything was quiet in the neighborhood, and on the way uptown on the car I saw no signs of a disturbance, and would not have known anything about there having been anything of the kind if I had not been informed by the car conductor. I can identify two of the officers who took part in the clubbing, one of whom was dressed in citizen's clothes, and who, I think, was one of the wardmen attached to that precinct. (The witness subsequently identified Officer Herman Ohm.) Deponent further states that he has resided in the City of New York for the past fifteen years, and has never been arrested before in his life, and has always been a quiet, law-abiding citizen.

his

CHARLES x BENNETT.

mark

Sworn to before me this 31st day of August, 1900.

GEO. P. HAMMOND JR., Notary Public (164), N.Y. County.

City and County of New York, ss.:

Statement of Paul Leitenberger and Alfred E. Borman (white), of 105 East 22nd Street:

On August 15 we were on 28th Street, and were going home, walking up Seventh Avenue, and at 29th Street a crowd was coming down about ten P.M. We followed the crowd up 35th Street, and it went into the Dorê (a dive), and yelled, "Give us a coon and we'll lynch him!" They then went to Corbett's on Broadway. He has a colored man working for him. Then the police came with their clubs and dispersed the crowd, which went up Broadway. A cable car was coming downtown, and someone cried, "There's a nigger; lynch him!" and several white men jumped on the car. A colored man was standing in the car, and with a cane or umbrella warded off the blows. The car went on with him; the gripman would not stop it, though they called on him to stop. Some of the men were thrown off of the car and nearly run over. There was a Negro on the second car behind that, and the crowd pulled him off, and the man escaped by running into the Marlborough Hotel, where he was sheltered. There were no policemen present at these times, but some policemen appeared and the mob moved up Broadway to about 41st Street, and tried to get into the Vendome Hotel. Some got in, and one cried out, "Give us the coon!" The police coming up, they moved on and went up as far as the Hotel Cadillac at 43rd Street, and went in to get the colored hall man, and an officer came up and clubbed right and left. Other officers came and the crowd scattered. We waited a half hour, and the police kept the people moving. We walked through 42nd Street to Eighth Avenue, and saw more of the rioters, and several policemen would not allow them to make any disturbance, and the rioters spread, breaking up. The whole aim of the rioters was to catch Negroes. We saw Devery the first night. We didn't see him the second night. He was in command. We observed the first night that the police generally made no effort to disperse the crowds, but ran along with them. The only places where they attacked the crowds were at Corbett's and the Cadillac. The disturbing element were young fellows, such as frequent "Hell's Kitchen." We talked with a ringleader at the northeast corner of 28th Street and Eighth Avenue, a few nights after. He said he had been a leader in the riots and would do it again—that the "niggers" must be treated the same as down South.

At the Cadillac there was an officer who did splendid work in dispersing the crowd. For a while he was alone, and he clubbed the crowd indiscriminately; in a little while two other officers came and helped him, and those three men ejected the mob from the hotel, and when they were in the street other officers appeared and effectually dispersed the crowd. This showed what could be done when they wanted to. They protected the hotel in good shape, also Corbett's, when the mob tried to get in.

PAUL LEITENBERGER.
ALFRED E. BORMAN.

Sworn to before me this 13th day of September, 1900.
FRANK MOSS, Notary Public, N.Y. County.

City and County of New York, ss.:
Solomon Russell Wright, being duly sworn, deposes and says:
I reside at No. 129 West 27th Street; on Thursday, August 16, 1900, about 6:30 P.M., I left the house and walked to the corner of Seventh Avenue and 28th Street, where I met a friend of mine, with whom I stood and chatted for about three-quarters of an hour, when I left and returned down Seventh Avenue towards 27th Street, and had got within about one hundred feet of 27th Street, when I was struck by a missile thrown by an Italian boy. I naturally turned around and asked him what he had done that for. I passed on, however, and had got about fifty feet east of Seventh Avenue, on 27th Street, when a police officer ran after me, and seizing me commenced feeling around my clothes as if in search of something. I had an ordinary pocket knife in the change pocket of my coat, and the officer finding it said, "What are you doing with this?" I answered, "Do you see me doing anything with it?" He then took me to the 30th Street station house (19th Precinct), and while going up the steps of the station house I stumbled, and the officer then hit me on the back of the neck with his club. I was arraigned before the sergeant, who took my pedigree, and at the close of that proceeding the officer who had me in charge, and whose name is Kennedy, said to the sergeant, "What will we do with this feller?" The sergeant

replied, "Kill the black son of a b—!" The said officer then brought me back, and when we reached a flight of stairs leading down to the cells he shoved me down the whole flight; when I reached the bottom some other officers who were down there grabbed me and punched and beat me with their fists. I was arraigned the next day and charged with carrying a knife, and I was committed for ninety days. I served part of the time, when I was released on bail. I was not intoxicated, and had never been arrested before in my life. I never have and do not stand around the corners of the neighborhood; and further, I am employed by the Standard Oil Company as a porter.

SOLOMON R. WRIGHT.

Sworn to before me this 22nd day of September, 1900.

GEO. P. HAMMOND JR., Notary Public (164), N.Y. County.

City and County of New York, ss.:

Robert Myrick, being duly sworn, deposes and says that he resides at 414 West 39th Street, and is employed by Bernard Brennan, saloon keeper at 49th Street and Broadway; that on Thursday evening, August 16, at about eight P.M., he left his work at the said saloon and walked to Eighth Avenue between 47th and 48th Streets; that he entered a restaurant on that block, and after eating a meal he asked the proprietor whether there was any trouble downtown tonight. He replied, "No, it is kind of quiet tonight, but I guess you had better take a car and ride down, it will be safer." He replied, "I guess that will be the best way," and then walked out onto the avenue and boarded a car bound downtown, and had gone as far as 42nd Street when a mob of about one hundred boys, none of whom apparently were over nineteen years of age, began to throw stones at the car and yell, "There's a nigger in the car; let's kill him!" Some woman on the car said, "Come over here, mister; don't stand there and get killed." I went along the footboard from the rear of the car, where I had been, and got under the seat, where the mob could not see me; but the mob continued following the car and stoned it until I reached 39th Street, where I wanted to get off, but was advised there by three men (who were the only passengers that had remained on the car) not to get off. I continued on until the car reached 38th Street, when the car stopped and the mob caught up with it. I then got off the east side of the car, and ran over to the southeast corner of Eighth Avenue, to where I saw five men standing, and going up to one I said, "Officer, will you please see me home?" He said, "Where do you live?" I told him. He then said, "What are you doing on the street at this time of night?" I answered, "Going home from work." He then asked me where I worked. I told him. He then said, "Have you got a gun or a razor?" I said, "I have neither." He then proceeded to search me, when I remembered having a razor in a case in my out-side coat pocket, and I told the officer and showed him where it was. He then took the razor out of my pocket, and, striking me across the back of the neck with his club, said, "You black son of a b—!" and then struck me several times on the head. I said to him, "I come over to you for protection, and this is what I get." He then said, "Shut up!" I was then taken to the 37th Street station house, and while there I was kicked by the officers in the section room, and by the doorman, and when I protested I was told to shut up. I was locked in cell No. 13, and in the morning I was brought to the 54th Street police court, where the judge turned me loose. While in my cell I got into conver-sation with a colored man who is a porter for the N.Y.C.&H.R.R., and he said that he was dragged from a streetcar and clubbed by police officers. Deponent further states that he had the aforementioned razor in his pocket by reason of the fact that it needed repairing, and he had taken it to a barber to see if he could fix it, and finding that he could not fix it he was taking it to his home to lay it away in its place. Deponent says further that the time of the clubbing was about 8:30 P.M.

ROBERT MYRICK.

Sworn to before me this 1st day of September, 1900.

GEO. P. HAMMOND JR., Notary Public (164), N.Y. County.

City and County of New York, ss.:

Adolphus Cooks, being duly sworn, deposes and says:

I reside at No. 243 West 32nd Street, and work for the Anchor

Steamship Company, foot of West 24th Street, as a longshoreman. On Tuesday morning, August 14, 1900, I went to work for the said company, worked all that day, all that night, and until Wednesday night at 10:30 P.M.—39½ consecutive hours. At the said hour I left the pier at the foot of West 24th Street, and walked east on 24th Street, and when I reached the northwest corner of Eighth Avenue and 24th Street a white gentleman advised me not to go up Eighth Avenue, as there was a riot up there and they were fighting "like he did not know what." I continued east on 24th Street until I reached the northwest corner of Seventh Avenue and 24th Street, when I met another white man, who advised me not to go up Seventh Avenue, as there was a riot in progress, and that they were fighting at that time in the neighborhood of 41st Street and 37th Street, but, thinking that I could get home in 32nd Street before the riot could get down to that street, I started uptown on the west side of Seventh Avenue, and had reached the northwest corner of Seventh Avenue and 28th Street, when I saw three officers coming down Seventh Avenue. In the meantime three other colored men, whom I did not know, had caught up with me, and were walking behind me. I had gone about one hundred feet north of the aforesaid corner when I saw the three officers break into a run in our direction. I was grabbed by one of them, while the other two chased the three men who had come behind us and overtook them and clubbed them; the officer who had me immediately, without saying a word, struck me on the body with his club; then between the blows he said, "Get out of here, you black son of a b—!" One of the blows he aimed at my head, but I threw up my arm and received the blow on it. It was such a severe blow that I was lame in it for quite some days. I escaped from him as soon as I could, and ran to 28th Street, and down 28th Street to No. 211. I ran into the hallway and out into the back yard, where I stayed all night in fear of my life. The officer followed me, and when I ran into the hallway he clubbed the colored people who were on the front stoop, and drove them into the house. During the heavy rainstorm Wednesday night and early Thursday morning I took refuge in a small place that led into the cellar of the said house. Thursday morning about six o'clock I ventured out and went towards the dock at the foot of West 24th Street, where I intended to go to work again, and had reached Eighth Avenue between 25th and 26th Streets, when I saw two police officers on the opposite side of the street, one of whom started to run towards me, but his companion stopped him, and drew him back. Deponent states further that if he had not been interfered with and clubbed by the police officer he could have reached his home in safety, and that he saw no signs of a disturbance, such as a large crowd of people, as far as he could see up the avenue; that deponent was watching for such signs by reason of his having been warned twice. Deponent also declares that he can identify the officer who clubbed him; that he knows him by sight, and that, about a month before the said clubbing, the same officer had come to him at his home, where he lived at that time, in West 28th Street, and had told him that the roundsman had got him, and that he had given him as an excuse that he was at the house where deponent then lived and was quelling a disturbance there, and asked deponent to verify that statement if the roundsman asked him. Deponent promised so to do, notwithstanding the fact that nothing of the kind had occurred there, and promised to do so simply to get the officer out of trouble. That the officer's first name is "Joe," and that he is attached to the 20th Precinct. Deponent further declares that he was perfectly sober, and that the assault by the officer was unwarranted and an outrage upon a peaceable citizen.

his

ADOLPHUS x COOKS.

mark

Sworn to before me this 4th day of September, 1900.
GEO. P. HAMMOND JR., Notary Public (164), N.Y. County.

City and County of New York, ss.:
P. A. Johnson, M.D., being duly sworn, deposes and says:
I reside at 203 West 33rd Street, and am engaged in the active practice of my profession at that address. On Thursday morning,

August 16, 1900, about ten A.M., I heard a noise in the street, and going to the window I saw a colored man trying to get into one of the flats on the opposite side of the street. He failed, and went east to the corner saloon, kept by a man Gallagher, and entered. After he went in, I noticed three policemen in the saloon. Almost immediately a mob came down Seventh Avenue. At the saloon they commenced to shout, "Bring him out, we'll lynch him!" Several of the rioters went into the saloon, and in a few minutes they came out again and formed in a semicircle, evidently waiting for something. The police officers appeared with the colored man, clubbing him unmercifully. They then shoved him into the mob. He managed to get through them and ran down the street, and I heard him shortly shouting for mercy, saying, "For God's sake don't kill me, I have a wife and children." Deponent has been informed that two of the officers ran down the street after him and knocked him senseless.

P. A. JOHNSON.

Sworn to before me this 10th day of September, 1900.

GEO. P. HAMMOND JR., Notary Public (164), N.Y. County.

City and County of New York, ss.:

Stephen Small, being duly sworn, deposes and says:

I reside at the northwest corner of Seventh Avenue and 34th Street. On Wednesday evening, August 15, 1900, I went to the home of a sick brother on Lexington Avenue, and started then to go to my lodge on 29th Street near Seventh Avenue, and had reached Eighth Avenue and 41st Street, opposite Driggs' saloon, when two officers jumped on the car. One hit me on the head with his club, and the other struck me in the eye with his club. A white man interfered, and the police desisted. I stayed on the car, and when we had gone a little further the mob boarded it and attacked me. The car had quite a number of women in it, who began to scream, and some of them told me to get under the seat, which I did, and it proceeded down the avenue. I reached the neighborhood of Hudson Street House of Relief, where the white gentleman who interfered in the first instance took me, and where I had my head bandaged. I could not get home that evening, and I remained in a cellar in 30th Street between Sixth and Seventh Avenues. The next morning I started to get home, and had reached the corner of 32nd Street and Seventh Avenue, when I was stopped by an officer who wanted to know where I was going, and what weapon I had on me. I told him I had nothing on me. He said, "You look as if you had been in the scrap. They ought to have killed you; get out of here." As he said this he struck me across the back with his club, and I yet am unable to lay flat on my back without suffering extreme pain. Deponent further states that he was perfectly sober and was not creating any disturbance, and that the assault by the police officers was entirely unjustified and an outrage.

his

STEPHEN x SMALL.

mark

Sworn to before me this 11th day of September, 1900.

GEO. P. HAMMOND JR., Notary Public (164), N.Y. County.

City and County of New York, ss.:

William Hamer, of No. 494 Seventh Avenue, being duly sworn, deposes and says:

I am a musician. I am employed at "The Fair," kept by Mr. Samuels, on 14th Street between Third and Fourth Avenues. My wife is employed there also. On August 15 I finished my work about 11:30 P.M. I took the crosstown 14th Street car and changed to the Seventh Avenue horse cars. I had not heard anything of the riot. The car stopped between 36th and 37th Streets, and my wife and I were dragged from the car by a crowd of men and lads armed with sticks and stones. I ran into a stable at 37th Street and Seventh Avenue, and they beat me in there and left me for dead. A stone or something hit me in the stomach, and I fell into a water trough. My wife and I were separated, and she did not find me. I crawled out of the stable into a lumber yard and lay there in my blood until three A.M. I have been in the doctor's care ever since, and am out today for the first time. My doctor is Dr. Yarnell, of Park Avenue near 84th Street. When I was pulled out of the car, I noticed a colored man lying unconscious on the ground. There were at least a dozen policemen standing around. They did nothing, and made no effort to protect me.

WILLIAM HAMER.

Sworn to before me this 31st day of August, 1900.
FRANK MOSS, Notary Public, N.Y. County.

City and County of New York, ss.:

Mrs. Annie Hamer, being duly sworn, deposes and says that she resides at 494 Seventh Avenue; that she is employed as a musician at "The Fair," in East 14th Street; that on Wednesday, August 15, 1900, about midnight thereof, she in company with her husband arrived at Seventh Avenue between 36th and 37th Streets on a Seventh Avenue car; that when she alighted from the car she found herself surrounded by a mob, and almost instantly was struck in the mouth with a brick, thrown by someone whom she does not know. She became separated from her husband, and did not know what became of him until three A.M. the next morning, when he came home all covered with blood. Deponent states further that she has read the affidavit of her husband, hereto attached, and knows of her own knowledge that the facts therein stated are true. Deponent further states that she has been informed by her mother that the "captain" stationed officers at the door of her residence, and told them to "not let anyone in or out, and if anyone attempted it to shoot them."

ANNIE HAMER.

Sworn to before me this 6th day of September, 1900.
GEO. P. HAMMOND JR., Notary Public (164), N.Y. County.

City and County of New York, ss.:

Walter W. Coulter (white), 481 Seventh Avenue, being duly sworn, deposes and says that on Wednesday evening, August 15, 1900, there was quite a disturbance around his place of business, and at about 11:30 P.M. he saw a number of officers and men in citizen's clothes go into the houses 481 and 483, and he, thinking they were part of the crowd of roughs, stepped up to a police officer, who was quite tall and stout and of reddish complexion, and said to him,

"Why do you allow those rowdies to go up into that house? There is no one except a lot of respectable women and children in there, and possibly one man." The police officer replied as follows: "You go on and mind your own respectability, and you will have enough to do; they just shied a brick at us." Deponent further states that no brick had been thrown; that, in fact, they could not get a brick, as he was looking for one a short while before that to do some repairing with, and could not find one; that the only apparent reason for their going into the house was the fact that a large, tall man, whom he can identify if he sees him again, came along Seventh Avenue, and seeing this colored man in the window called out, "There's a big nigger; get him!" and immediately there was a rush made for the house. Deponent states further that the police knew there were none but respectable people in that house, as deponent had gone to a great deal of trouble to get rid of a lot of dissolute people who were in the house about a year ago, and in his endeavors to get rid of them had called upon the police to aid him, so that they were perfectly cognizant of the facts in the case.

WALTER W. COULTER.

Sworn to before me this 31st day of August, 1900.

GEO. P. HAMMOND JR., Notary Public (164), N.Y. County.

City and County of New York, ss.:

Mrs. Elizabeth Mitchell, being duly sworn, deposes and says that she resides at 481 Seventh Avenue; that on Wednesday evening, August 15, 1900, about 11:30 P.M., two police officers in citizen's clothes and one in citizen's dress broke in the door of her apartments claiming to be looking for "the man that threw the bottle." She answered and said that "no bottle was thrown," and that it was a shame for them to break in the door of respectable people; that her sister, Mrs. Kate Jackson, became frightened at the uproar, and thinking that the life of her children and herself was in danger, jumped out of the window with her three-year-old child in her arms, thereby endangering the life of herself and child, and in consequence is now confined to her bed with shock, fright, and bruises. That at six A.M.

the next morning she saw a colored man and woman assaulted on the corner of 36th Street and Seventh Avenue. Also at 52nd Street and Seventh Avenue, between eleven and twelve A.M., she saw a colored man assaulted by a white man, and when the officer attempted to interfere and arrest the white man the motormen around the stables refused to allow him to arrest him. She states further that one of the officers' first name was "Jim," as she heard him so addressed by the man in citizen's clothes.

MRS. ELIZABETH MITCHELL.

Sworn to before me this 31st day of August, 1900.

GEO. P. HAMMOND JR., Notary Public (164), N.Y. County.

City and County of New York, ss.:

Mrs. Margaret Taylor, being duly sworn, deposes and says:

I reside at 339 West 36th Street. On Thursday, August 16, 1900, about two A.M., while lying on a lounge in the front room of my house, I was aroused by hearing a shot fired, followed by several others. I went to the window, when someone in the street shouted with a curse, "Get your head in there or I'll shoot it off." I withdrew my head, and then realized that some of the shots had entered my windows. One imbedded itself in the ceiling, and another passed through a glass door leading into an inner room, and occupied by a lodger named Floyd Wallace. I awoke the said Wallace, and told him that someone was firing into the windows. Shortly after I heard sounds as of a number of people coming down the stairs from the roof, past my door, and stopping on the floor below me. In a very short while they returned, and without asking to be let in broke open my door, and then I saw that they were police officers in full uniform, six in number. They asked me if I knew who fired the shots. I said I did not know. They then told me I lied. Then they asked me if there were any guns in the house, and I answered no; whereupon I was again told that I lied. I then said, "All right, go ahead and search for them," which they proceeded to do. They went from room to room, and broke into a closet in the front room, which contained my husband's and my own clothes; they then opened a small satchel in which was my pocketbook. In the said pocketbook I had six dollars in bills and one dollar and seventy-five cents in silver. While part of the men were making the search, the others seized the aforesaid Wallace and took him out into the hallway, where deponent has been told they clubbed the said Wallace on the wrist and face. When he came in, after the officers left, deponent saw that his face and cheek were bruised and his wrist swollen. Deponent declares it to be her belief that the bullets which were shot into her room (one of which she has) could not have been fired from the street, but must have come from the houses opposite. Further, that when the officers left she remembered having left her pocketbook in the aforesaid satchel, and immediately ran into the front room to see if it was safe; she found that the six dollars in bills was gone, and declares it to be her belief that the same was taken by the three officers who were in the room making the search. Deponent further states that when her husband returned on the following Saturday she told him of the visit of the police officers. He then searched in the closet for some money, amounting to about sixty dollars, which he stated to have left there without my knowledge, and could not find it. Deponent declares it to be her belief that this money was also taken by the police officers aforementioned. Deponent further declares that there were no shots fired from her apartments, and that no one therein had a firearm of any sort.

MAGGIE TAYLOR.

Sworn to before me this 7th day of September, 1900.

GEO. P. HAMMOND JR., Notary Public (164), N.Y. County.

City and County of New York, ss.:

John L. Newman, being duly sworn, deposes and says:

I reside at No. 351 West 37th Street, in the rear house. On August 15, 1900, I went to the restaurant which is in the front building for supper. This was about 10:30 P.M. After I had been there a few minutes some one told me that the mob was coming. I had seen them beat colored people during the morning without any cause, so I walked out of the restaurant into my apartments, which are in the rear, only a few steps away; I live in the basement floor. I did this so as to avoid any trouble. As I reached the front door and walked in, I closed it and proceeded to go into my apartments. Four officers immediately came, and one of them said, "Stop!" and kicked open the door. Then one of them grabbed me and said, "Here is a d——d nigger; kill him!" The four officers then beat me with their clubs until I became unconscious. They then carried me to the station house. I was unconscious during all this time, but my friends tell me that the police were beating me all the way to the station house. It is located one block west from where I live. At the station house I recovered my consciousness. I was arraigned before the sergeant, and the officer who struck me first made the complaint against me. At the sergeant's desk I felt very weak, bleeding from my head and eye, and I held on to the railing for support. One of the officers struck me in the ribs with a night stick, and said, "God d——n you, stand up there!" I fell forward on the sergeant's desk, and I said, "For God's sake, take a gun and blow out my brains! If you have got to take a life, take mine, and don't murder me this way!" The sergeant then said very gruffly to the officer, "Take him away!" While all this was going on, Chief of Police Devery was in the station house standing about ten feet away, talking to somebody whom I did not know. He saw all this, but did not interfere, conversing with the man all the time, as if nothing unusual was going on. I have known Chief Devery for three or four years, and have spoken with him in a friendly way many times. When I was brought into the muster room, in the rear of the station house, I saw several colored people being treated for their wounds. I was bleeding from my head and eye, and could not see well, and I sat down in the wrong chair. Two policemen then came over to me, pulled me out of the chair, and were raising their clubs to strike me when someone said, "Don't hit this man any more," and they obeyed. My wounds were then dressed, and I was taken to a cell. About twelve o'clock, when the officer who was making the prison rounds came to my cell, I asked him for permission to see the sergeant. He asked why, and I told him that my house was unlocked, and that I wished he would send an officer to lock it. He said he would speak to the sergeant about it. In a few minutes he returned and said, "The sergeant said, 'D—n him,' and that 'he had no business with the house'" and he did not send anyone to lock it and protect my property. While I was in the station house I saw a colored man, John Haines, struck by several officers with their clubs. He was naked, only wearing a little under-shirt. The officers were striking all the colored men in the station house, and without any interference. In court, the next morning, I was arraigned before Judge Cornell. The officer swore that I was causing a riot in the street. I denied this. I did not have any witnesses in court, because I did not have any opportunity to produce them. The Judge did not ask me whether I wanted an examination or not, and expressed his doubts as to my guilt, and said the case was "very curious." But the officers were persistent in their false statements, aforesaid, and the magistrate put me under $100 bonds to keep the peace. Not being able to furnish this, I was sent to the Penitentiary, where I was for thirty days. I was treated at the Penitentiary by Dr. Thomas Higgins, who told me that my head would never be right as long as I lived. I have been sick ever since. Dr. Higgins told me that he would testify for me in any proceeding which I might institute. I am employed by the Metropolitan Street Railway Company as a rockman, but am unable to work at present. I have lived in New York City for over forty-three years, and have never been arrested before in my life. I did not participate in the riots, was not on the street, and did nothing whatever to justify this conduct on the part of the police. I can recognize the officer who made the charge against me; he was the first to strike me.

JOHN L. NEWMAN.

Sworn to before me this 19th day of September, 1900.
JOHN F. MACCOLGAN, Notary Public (4), N.Y. County.
(The officer in the case was Holland.)

City and County of New York, ss.:

Lucy A. Jones, being duly sworn, deposes and says:

I reside at 341 West 36th Street, on the fourth floor front, west side. John Hains resides on the same floor on the east side. I have read his affidavit, which is hereto annexed, and so far as it relates to the occurrences at said address on the evening of August 15 it is true. I had only returned to the city at six o'clock that evening, having been in the country for two months. I had been in the house, looking out of the window occasionally. I saw shooting in the street, but this was all done by white people. There were no colored people on the street. This shooting was done mostly by white people living at 342 West 36th Street, which is a tenement, and is occupied by a very low class of rowdies, who have constantly abused and insulted the colored residents of the block. The police officers constantly go in and out of this house. On the night in question I saw a great many police officers enter this house and talk with its occupants. They were shouting and using abusive language, and saying, "Kill every d—d one of the niggers!" "Set the house afire!" etc., etc. About two o'clock in the morning I heard somebody at the door of Mr. Seymour's flat next door, saying, "G— d— you; open this door, or I'll kill every d—d nigger in the house." Mr. Hains, who was the only one in the house just then, was asleep, and he did not open the door. They broke the door open, and I saw them club Hains and accuse him of firing a pistol out of the window. He denied this. Then three of the officers beat him, while the other three were searching the house. They did not find any pistol there, so they came into my apartments, and one of them said to me, "You G— d— black son of a b—, you know a lot about this d—d shooting, and if you don't tell me I'll blow the brains out of you." I told them that they could look through my flat, which they did, but did not find anything. Then they went back to the Seymour flat, and I heard one of the officers say, "I've got the revolver; let's kill the G— d— son of a b—," and began to club him in the head and other parts of his body unmercifully. He begged them to allow him to put on his clothes, but the one who had the revolver said, "Shoot the d—d nigger," and he was led to the station house only in his undershirt. Another officer said, "You will be glad if you get there alive." At one time during this fracas I attempted to look into the Seymour flat to see what was going on, but one of the officers said to me, "You G— d— black b—, get back where you belong, or I'll club the brains out of you." After they left I went into the room, and I found the pillows and sheet on the bed full of blood stains. The people in 342 inspired the policemen, telling them to "Burn the house!" "Lynch the d—d niggers!" etc., etc. I am a widow. My daughter, who is about twenty-one years of age, saw this clubbing, and heard the police use this vile and abusive language. After they had arrested Hains I looked out of my window to see how he was being led by the officers. One of the rowdies in 342 said, "Look at the d—d nigger wench looking out of the window. Shoot her! Shoot her!"

LUCY A. JONES.

Sworn to before me this 28th day of August, 1900.
STEPHEN B. BRAGUE, Notary Public (125), N.Y. County.

City and County of New York, ss.:
Mrs. Florence Randolph, being duly sworn, deposes and says:
I reside at 117 West 134th Street. On Wednesday, August 15, 1900, I resided at 433 West 36th Street. On the said 15 of August I was ill in bed, and while I lay in bed I heard at different intervals during the night, and until about three or half past three the next morning, the screams and shouts as of persons in agony, and cries of "Why are you hitting me? I haven't done anything!" Deponent states that these cries and screams came from the 37th Street station house, the rear of which abuts on the rear of the house in which deponent then resided. Deponent states further that her husband was unable to reach his home for four nights on account of the disorder in that neighborhood. Further, that her husband works at 43rd Street and Fifth Avenue.

FLORENCE RANDOLPH.

Sworn to before me this 12th day of September, 1900.
GEO. P. HAMMOND JR., Notary Public (164), N.Y. County.

City and County of New York, ss.:
Susie White, being duly sworn, deposes and says:
I reside at 444 Seventh Avenue, New York City. On Sunday morn-

ing, August 12, 1900, about six A.M., two officers in full uniform came upstairs and, pushing the door of my room open, said, "Did not a man come up here just now?" I answered, "Yes." The officer then said, "Where is he? Bring him out." I then started to call the man, but before I got to the room the officer had preceded me, and he called the man out (his name is Joe Netherland) and took hold of him, and rubbing his hand over his head said, "Got a scar?" Netherland said, "No. Who are you looking for—the man that cut the officer?" The officer said, "Yes. We're going to make it hot for you niggers!" After making a further examination they found two more men, and after making a close examination of them they found that they were not the men they wanted. After threatening to do up all the "niggers" for killing Officer Thorpe they left.

SUSIE WHITE.

Sworn to before me this 10th day of September, 1900.

GEO. P. HAMMOND JR., Notary Public (164), N.Y. County.

City and County of New York, ss.:

Miss Alice Lee, being duly sworn, deposes and says:

I reside at 433 West 36th Street (in the rear of the 37th Street station house). On the night of Wednesday, August 15, 1900, also Thursday, the 16, I heard people screaming and groaning, and shouts of people pleading not to be clubbed any more. I saw one man lying on the station house floor, apparently almost helpless. One man who was pleading seemed to be between the main building and the out building where the cells are located. An officer who was on one of the upper floors leaned out of the window and threw a bottle down at the said man, saying, "Kill the black son of a b—!" Deponent further declared that it was impossible to sleep during both of the aforesaid nights on account of the heartrending shrieks and groans coming from the station house; and further, that she saw a number of colored men lying up in a corner of the station house.

ALICE LEE.

Sworn to before me this 20th day of September, 1900.

GEO. P. HAMMOND JR., Notary Public (164), N.Y. County.

City and County of New York, ss.:

Cynthia Randolph, being duly sworn, deposes and says:

I reside at 433 West 36th Street, New York City, Manhattan Borough. My home is directly in the rear of the 37th Street station house. On the evening of Wednesday, August 15, 1900, and the evening of August 16, 1900, I heard cries and shrieks of people being beaten, coming from the 37th Street station house—such groans as, "O Lord! O Lord! don't hit me! don't hit me!" spoken in pleading tones. This continued all of Wednesday night, with such frequency, and was so heartrending, as to make it impossible to sleep. It was not quite so bad Thursday evening. Deponent states further that it is a common thing to hear coming from the 37th Street station house cries of people, as if they were being beaten, except since last Labor Day; since which day it has been exceptionally quiet.

CYNTHIA RANDOLPH.

Sworn to before me this 15th day of September, 1900.

GEO. P. HAMMOND JR., Notary Public (164), N.Y. County.

City and County of New York, ss.:

Headly Johnson, being duly sworn, deposes and says:

I reside at 330 West 53rd Street. I am employed as a Pullman car porter, on the cars running out of the West Shore depot, Weehawken, N.J. I arrived on my train at the said depot on Thursday, August 16, 1900, at 2:35 P.M. I arrived in New York about 5:30 P.M. the same day, and, having heard of the riots, I had prepared to protect myself from the mob by carrying home with me a revolver. I boarded a car at the West Shore ferry at the foot of West 42nd Street and transferred to an Eighth Avenue car at 34th Street, and had proceeded as far as 40th Street, when the car was assailed by a mob shouting, "There's another nigger! Kill him! Lynch him!" I stood up and was ready to defend myself, when a passenger on the car asked me to sit down, saying that if the mob got on the car he would help me defend myself. I sat down as requested, and happening to look over my shoulder I saw three police officers in uniform running after the car. They boarded the car, and, seizing me, one of the officers put his hand in my pocket and took the revolver from me, then pulled me off the car, saying, "Come off of here, you black son of a b—!" When they had pulled me off the car, they immediately commenced clubbing me, and continued to do so all the way to the station house. While in the station house I saw several colored men beaten by police officers. The sergeant at the desk, when I was sent to a cell, shouted to the police officers, "Don't hit this man!" repeating the same several times. I was taken to the police court the next day, where I was discharged. Deponent states further that the officer who arrested him and appeared against him in the police court is the one who did the most of the clubbing; in fact, all of it except one blow. Deponent declares further that he was proceeding quietly to his home, where he was determined to go, and was not molesting anyone, and that when the officers signified their intention to arrest him he made no show of resistance, and that therefore the clubbing was unjustifiable and an outrage.

HEADLY JOHNSON.

Sworn to before me this 8th day of September, 1900.

GEO. P. HAMMOND JR., Notary Public (164), N.Y. County.

City and County of New York, ss.:

Maria Williams, of No. 206 West 27th Street, and Carrie Wells, of No. 239 West 29th Street, in the Borough of Manhattan, being severally duly sworn, depose and say:

On Wednesday, August 15, 1900, we were sitting on the stoop of No. 239 West 29th Street, talking; we had been sitting there since 9:30 P.M. We had there learned of the assaults on the Negroes in this section, and heard the noise of the crowds and the stopping of the cars on Eighth Avenue. There was no crowd in the street at this time. There were white and colored folks sitting on nearly all the stoops, the same as occurs on any ordinary warm night. About 11:30 several officers came through the street from Eighth Avenue and walked towards Seventh Avenue, three on the north side and four on the south side. No one in the street had been molested by anyone. These officers walked up the stoops, and without any warning ordered us into our houses, at the same time striking at us. Mrs. Wells, the mother of deponent Carrie Wells, was on the stoop one step from the bottom with three of her children, aged respectively fourteen, thirteen, and twelve years. An officer who is called "Joe," and whom we know, stepped up to Mrs. Wells, and said, "Get in there, you black son of a b—," and struck her viciously across the right hip, when she ran in with her children, the officers still following, striking at her until he reached the top step, looked around, and threatened to strike us if we came out again, and he then went away. Deponent Williams looked out of her window and saw these officers go through the same procedure wherever colored folks were sitting. Nothing was said or done to any white people. We see this officer every day. At about 2:15 in the morning some officers came through the block and clubbed colored people wherever they saw them, men as well as women. Deponent Wells lives at home with her mother and helps her keep house; deponent Williams keeps house for herself and husband. Deponent Wells is a member of the Church of the Transfiguration, at 29th Street and Fifth Avenue, where I have attended for years. Mr. and Mrs. Miller, of West 29th Street, know of us; Mrs. McGurk, of No. 225 West 29th Street, Mrs. Kloze, of 223 West 29th Street, all can vouch for our character.

CARRIE WELLS.

her

MARIA x WILLIAMS.

mark

Sworn to before me this 4th day of September, 1900.
SAMUEL MARCUS, Notary Public, N.Y. County.

3

Police Brutality

Portent of Disaster and Discomforting Divergence

DERRICK BELL

*I could not but feel, in those sorrowful years, that this human indif-
ference, concerning which I knew so much already, would be my portion on the day that the United States decided to murder Negroes
systematically instead of little by little and catch-as-catch can. I was,
of course, authoritatively assured that what had happened to the
Jews in Germany could not happen to the Negroes in America, but I
thought bleakly, that the German Jews had probably believed similar counselors.*

—James Baldwin, *The Fire Next Time* (1963)

Remarkably, the steady stream of reported instances of police
harassment of Blacks from James Baldwin's time to the present
serves as both a portent of a Black holocaust in America and a divergence of that too awful fate:

- As to the portent, the pattern of incidents clearly reflecting policies unspoken, but no less authorized, conveys the message that
  Black people are now, as they have been throughout the history of
  this country, expendable. No matter their status, income, or
  accomplishments, we are at risk of harassment, arrest, injury, or
  death by those hired to protect the public peace.

- As to the divergence, the reported instances of police brutality against Blacks are often so blatantly cruel that we who are the potential victims are so diverted by our outrage and fear that we fail to consider that Baldwin's concern expressed almost forty years ago remains potently authentic. For while much that is positive has occurred since Baldwin's time, a great many of this country's White citizens continue to view Blacks as the source of their fears, the cause of their sense of danger, the ultimate scapegoat in times of economic anxiety.

Professor Patricia Williams senses that notwithstanding all our accomplishments and contributions to this country, "White America wishes that Blacks would just go away and shut up and stop taking up so much time and food and air and then the world would return to its Norman Rockwell loveliness and America could be employed and happy once more."[1]

Politicians from the presidents on down get this message and translate it into policies that give priority to Whites most of the time, and only work for Black people in the short run as a way of working for Whites in the long run. The police are not stupid. They understand their unspoken mission and that it conforms to the fears and prejudices regarding Black people many of them have harbored since childhood. Of course, what my mother said about Whites—namely, that unless there were some good White folks, all the Black folks would be dead—applies as well to the police. It is a tough, stressful job that in many places offers only modest monetary compensation. No one can deny the dangers of carrying a weapon and enforcing the law in crime-ridden neighborhoods. The wearing of bulletproof vests is not a fashion statement. It has saved an estimated 1,500 officers since the early 1970s. Police must work all hours of the night, a stressful matter for family life, and in most cities their starting salary averages $30,000.[2]

Acknowledging that police officers have a stressful job, the National Criminal Justice Commission maintained that "no level of stress can justify the mistreatment of citizens or the use of excessive force when making an arrest."[3] There are many methods of increasing police efficiency, such as community policing and reducing the inherent fear of Blacks by hiring more persons of color who are familiar with the communities in which they work. These worthwhile measures, even if adopted, would not reduce the ultimate danger about which Baldwin warns. And our understandable focus on incidents of police brutality serves to divert us from this greater danger, one that history shows White Americans are quite capable of both performing and then excusing.

We live, though, in the present. And prophecies of future disaster are diluted by our daily experience. When we are stopped by the police, the casual can easily become the catastrophic. We know that innocence offers no insulation against abuse, and even graphic evidence of police wrongdoing is no guarantee that their misconduct will be punished rather than condoned. By virtue of color alone, Blacks are suspect, and when stopped, the "wrong" move or the "wrong" response on their part can be fatal. These are the conclusions rather easily drawn from cases that gain media attention. Given the reluctance of most Blacks to file complaints after experiencing racial discrimination when looking for a home, searching for a job, or even gaining equal service in a restaurant or other public facility, it is not surprising that, fearing further harassment or worse, a great many victims of police harassment do not report incidents of racially motivated police misconduct. Getting beyond the traumatic event and mending the possible physical and certain emotional damage to self and others involved serves as sufficient challenge. The mind simply cannot bear thoughts of more widespread terror than has already been experienced at first hand.

Consider one of my top students at the Harvard Law School, who was also getting her medical degree at the same time. White and a woman, she wrote to me about a highway stop that happened a dozen years ago. I have never forgotten the incident and am sure she and the man involved have not forgotten it either. Let me recall what she said in her own words:

It was about seven on a weeknight. It was summer, so it was still light. We were driving on a four-lane road in Westport, an affluent, suburban community in southeastern Connecticut. John was driving. He is a Black man. Westport is a very White town. I was sitting in the front seat. No one else was in the car. We were driving a 1965 Ford in immaculate condition; not one spot of rust. We owned the car. It was properly registered. It was running perfectly. We were not speeding. Neither of us had consumed any drugs or alcohol. We had pulled over about five minutes prior to the incident I describe to ask an "officer of the law" for directions to the interstate highway. He gave John the directions.

A police car came up behind us, seemingly out of nowhere. Its flashers and siren were on. It was June 1985. Fear, disgust, anger, and then that learned pervasive calm affected each of us in sequence. We did not need any words. We both knew the routine far better than we wished we did. But there was a twist this time. Neither of us was surprised when the cop approached the car. Neither of us was surprised when, instead of saying, "May I see your license and registration, sir," the cop reached in the window, unlocked the door and pulled John from the car. Neither of us was surprised when he threw John against the car and ordered him to spread his legs, sprinkling the sentence with various and assorted profanities and comments about "niggers" and "nigger lovin' White sluts." Neither of us was surprised by the body search. We were not even surprised when the cop removed his gun from his holster, having uncovered no weapon from John's person. We knew better than to speak or ask questions. As far as we were concerned, these were not fellow human beings.

But we were surprised when the cop placed the gun not by his side, or against John's back or abdomen, but against his right temple. Now all the cop wanted was an excuse, any excuse, to pull the trigger. Neither John nor I dared even move our eyes. I sat stone still. He did not flinch. I knew that if I sneezed or burped, they would blow my man away.

Now that they had a gun to John's head, they wanted to talk. Where were we from, where were we going, whose car was it, did I have any identification, did I know this man, for how long, why were we in Westport, etc., etc.? The gun never moved. When they asked me for my license (they had already discovered John's during the body search), I asked if I could reach down to get it or if they would prefer to get it themselves. I told them I was afraid to reach down. "Why is that, ma'am?" the "officer" responded. The other cop came around and retrieved my purse. He pulled out the wallet. He did not search the bag. The partner returned to the patrol car. The other cop's gun remained ready to fire into John's right temple. And the boy in blue just smiled on. Clearly, we had made his day.

About five minutes later, the partner returned. "They do own the car," he mumbled. The gun was placed back in the holster. Then, I received the requisite apology. After all, I was the White woman with the registration and had a medical school ID. The trespass had not been the gun at John's temple, but the ten-minute delay I suffered as a result of "a police computer error." Clearly, John was still a "nigger," but I was apparently no longer a "nigger lovin' slut."

The couple did not file a complaint. More fearful than angry, they saw little value in perpetuating a painful experience. Countless other victims of police abuse must reach a similar conclusion. Under those conditions, pragmatism prevails over courage. Principle is sacrificed to survival. This is America. There is a long history of de facto authorization for police to keep Blacks generally and Black men most specifically in the subordinate place that society approves and the law condones.

Racial rhetoric? Hardly. From the earliest period in our history, a primary role of law enforcement was to keep Blacks under control, quite literally during the slavery era. To curb runaways and prevent the formation of insurrectionary plots, slaveholders developed elaborate systems of patrols made up of conscripted local Whites who traveled the roads and checked plantation quarters. Slaves caught without passes were summarily punished with twenty lashes, but the brutality of the patrols resulted in complaints from slaves and masters alike.[4]

The end of slavery in 1863 increased the danger of the now free Blacks, who posed a greater threat to Whites determined to keep the former chattels in their subordinate place. As a child in Durham, North Carolina, during the second decade of the twentieth century, Pauli Murray viewed the local police "as heavily armed, invariably mountainous red-faced [men] who to me seemed more a signal of calamity than of protection."[5] Albon Holsey, growing up in Georgia at the turn of the century, recalled having lived in "mortal fear" of the police, "for they were arch-tormenters and persecutors of Negroes."[6]

The North was no better. Richard R. Wright Jr. remembered, "I was convinced early that policemen were my enemies. I never approached a policeman with a question until I had been in Chicago for nearly a year."[7] Leon Litwack has written that during the Jim Crow era, the subject of the police often dominated conversations among young Blacks. The stories revolved around chases, harassment, clubbings, illegal arrests, and coerced confessions.[8]

Far worse than what the police did to Blacks is what they *failed* to do. From 1859 through the early 1960s, at least five thousand Blacks lost their lives by lynching.[9] There are few reports that police or other law enforcement officials posed a serious barrier to lynch mobs. And, of course, few, if any, of the perpetrators were ever brought to justice. According to a scholar of the period, lynchers had "little to fear from those who administered the southern legal system," and prosecutors often dismissed lynchings as "an expression of the will of the people."[10]

In 1900, for example, there were at least 105 reported lynchings. In New Orleans during that year, White mobs assaulted Blacks for three days, burning and robbing their homes and stores. Mass murder was not sufficient to save the first of several antilynching measures, this one introduced by G. H. White, a Black congressman from North Carolina, from dying in committee.[11] Despite earnest campaigns by the NAACP, which was founded a decade later, and other groups, the Congress never passed any of the antilynching bills placed before it.

Beyond documented lynchings by vigilante mobs, it is simply impossible to estimate the number of Blacks murdered by individual Whites in cases where the motive was racial antagonism. Only a small number of those who committed these crimes were tried for them. Few were convicted, and almost none were executed. These killings continue. By contrast, in those instances where Blacks kill Whites, the response by law enforcement agencies and the public is swift and often deadly.

Baldwin's suggestion that genocide could be the future fate of Black Americans has an even more fearsome historical support in the literally hundreds of race riots that have marked and marred this country's racial landscape. The motivations for these riots, which invariably became Black massacres, were many, but the patterns were quite similar. Mobs of Whites rampaged through Black communities, burning houses and killing every Black person they could find, usually with a government response that was inadequate or nonexistent.

The patterns were set almost immediately after the Civil War. In Memphis, Tennessee, in 1866, for example, a failed attempt by police to halt alleged disorderly conduct by Black soldiers prompted Whites to begin a general massacre, during which forty-six Blacks and two Whites supporting the Blacks were killed, about seventy-five were wounded, and ninety homes, twelve schools, and four Black churches were burned.[12] E. L. Godkin, cofounder of *The Nation* and its editor at the time, wrote that the killing was "inconceivably brutal, but . . . its most novel and most striking incident was, that the *police* headed the butchery, and roved round the town either in company with the White mob or singly, and occupied themselves in shooting down every colored person, of whatever sex, of whom they got a glimpse."[13]

The period during and after the First World War was a racially turbulent time. Between 1915 and 1919, there were some eighteen major interracial disturbances. In July 1917, serious racial violence occurred in Chester, Pennsylvania, Philadelphia, and Houston. The 1917 riots in East St. Louis were particularly vicious. At least thirty-nine Blacks and nine Whites were killed. Although President Woodrow Wilson's secretary told the press that the details of the riot were so sickening that he found it difficult to read about them, Wilson himself took no action and, despite media criticism, remained silent.[14]

Congress did appoint an investigative committee. This committee reported that racial tensions were brought to the boiling point by mills, factories, and railroads that imported 10,000 to 12,000 Blacks from the Deep South, promising good jobs. Blacks were hired in place of Whites to counteract organizing efforts by labor unions, but many found no work and had no decent places to live. Crowded into East St. Louis and swelling the already large Black population, the newly arrived Blacks found themselves in a center of lawlessness.

When an unidentified car drove through the colored section and its occupants fired indiscriminately into homes, armed Blacks were alerted by a prearranged signal: the ringing of a church bell. They flocked into the streets and attacked a police car that had come to investigate the disturbance. The crowd fired volleys of shots into the car, killing two officers. The next day, mobs of Blacks killed other Whites. On learning of these attacks, Whites began to retaliate by attacking every Black in sight. The committee reported,

> All fared alike, young and old, women and children; none was spared. The crowd soon grew to riotous proportions, and for hours the manhunt continued, stabbing, clubbing, and shooting, not the guilty but unoffending negroes. One was hanged from a telephone pole, and another had a rope tied around his neck and was dragged through the streets, the maddened crowd kicking him and beating him as he lay prostrate and helpless.
>
> The negroes were pursued into their homes, and the torch completed the work of destruction. As they fled from the flames they were shot down, although many of them came out with uplifted hands, pleading to be spared.
>
> It was a day and night given over to arson and murder. Scenes of horror that would have shocked a savage were viewed with placid unconcern by hundreds whose hearts knew no pity, and who seemed to revel in the feast of blood and cruelty.[15]

As for the police, the committee reported that police failed to halt the violence and often participated in it. When soldiers of the state militia took White rioters to jail, the police released them by the hundreds without bond and without having tried to identify them.

When a White mob held several policemen against a wall while other rioters were assaulting Blacks, the police made no effort to free themselves, deeming the situation highly humorous. At one point, the committee reported, "the police shot into a crowd of negroes who were huddled together, making no resistance. It was a particularly cowardly exhibition of savagery." The report found that many of the soldiers joined the rioters, later boasting of how many Blacks they had killed.

There are equally grim reports of subsequent riots: New York City in 1935, Detroit in 1943, Los Angeles in 1965, and again following the acquittal of the police who beat Rodney King in 1992. The patterns of cause, casualties, and subsequent investigating committees were predictably similar. Race riots, whether sparked by Black or by White violence, always resulted in Blacks' suffering a disproportionate number of deaths, injuries, and loss of property. And, once the fighting began, law enforcement forces could not be relied on for protection and often gave aid and support to White rioters.

In the last few decades, the "war on drugs" has become the major vehicle for police harassment of Blacks and Hispanic persons of color. In fact, the arrest, conviction, and lengthy imprisonment of Blacks and Hispanics seems the primary goal of the antidrug campaign, which, despite the expenditure of billions of dollars, has had little effect on either the importation or the use of drugs. Far more drugs are used by Whites living in the middle- and upper-class suburbs and on college campuses, but law enforcement has focused its efforts on communities of color.

For example, one study revealed that, in 1989, drug arrest rates for African Americans were five times higher than arrest rates for Whites, even though Whites and Blacks were using drugs at the same rate. Blacks make up 12 percent of the U.S. population and 13 percent of all monthly drug users, but they constitute 35 percent of those arrested, 55 percent of those convicted, and 74 percent of those sentenced to prison for drug possession.[16] The result: today almost three out of four prison admissions and 90 percent of those imprisoned for drug offenses are Black or Hispanic.[17] Experts predict that, if current trends of imprisonment continue, by 2020 almost two out of every three young Black men nationwide between the ages of eighteen and thirty-four will be in prison.[18]

Even the most serious instances of police harassment pale when compared with the pattern of Black imprisonment that is sparked by politicians more than willing to stand on law-and-order platforms, encouraged by the billion-dollar prison industry and sanctioned by a general sense, which even some Blacks share, that "if you do the crime, you do the time." Unthinking slogans ignore the labor market increasingly closed to African Americans, particularly to those presumed unskilled and deemed by many employers less desirable as employees than recent immigrants.

Dionne Brand, the Black Canadian feminist, writes, "North America does not need Black people anymore . . . for the cheap and degraded labour we've represented across the centuries of our lives here." She asks, "Why empower a Black person in America to demand better wages and better working conditions, when you can ship the work off to a less-enfranchised Colombian or Sri Lankan?"[19]

In a world where technology makes possible the exporting of work and where politics permits the exclusion of those traditionally last hired and first fired, the Baldwin warning becomes chilling prophecy. Black people who have worked the longest and hardest in this nation are increasingly obsolete. What will be our fate? We know that at an earlier time, when the nation lusted for the lands held by the true natives of America, it resorted to phony treaties, open warfare, and finally genocide. What might be the fate of the descendants of Africans brought here to work when the need for their work has ended?

We need not rely on prophecy in dealing with such questions. We can see the answer to them in the policies that ignore the predictable effects that occur "when work disappears," as the title of a recent book by William Julius Wilson puts it. The result will be massive unemployment and not the lack of family values that has devastated our inner cities and placed one-third of our young men—denied even menial jobs when they lacked education and skills—in prison or in the jaws of the criminal court system, most of them for nonviolent drug offenses. Even those of us who escaped the ghetto and acquired education, skills, and perhaps professional status have not been able to gain insulation through success. Nor do the emblems of American success—the fine car, beautiful home, stylish clothes, fancy vacation—enable us to break free of myriad manifestations of racial subordination, some of which are documented by Ellis Cose in his book *The Rage of a Privileged Class.*

Our careers, our very lives, are threatened because of our color. Whatever our status, we are feared because we might be one of "them." And there are few of us who do not have family, former schoolmates, or neighbors who are "them." Success, then, neither insulates us from misidentification by wary Whites nor eases our pain when we consider the plight of our less fortunate brethren who struggle for existence in what some social scientists call the underclass.

There is more, however. I fear that those "fortunate few" Blacks, like this writer, are unintentional, but no less critical, components in the structure of racial subordination. For the charade that people of color are complicit in their conquered condition is made more believable because there are those Blacks who, through enterprise, good fortune, and, yes, sometimes the support of White progressives, have achieved a success that many in the society believe all Blacks could attain—if they just worked hard or were lucky, or both. "You made it despite being Black and subject to discrimination," the question goes, "so why can't the rest of 'them' do the same?" For those who pose it, the question "Why can't the rest of 'them' make it?" carries its own conclusion. It is a conclusion that justifies affirmation of the racial status quo, and opposition to affirmative action and, for that matter, all civil rights protections offering remedies that might disadvantage or inconvenience any White less guilty of overt racism than Bull Connor or the head of the Ku Klux Klan.

Despite the undisputed upward mobility of some Blacks, serious disparities in education, income, quality of housing and health care remain for most of them, with the gap growing both between Whites and Blacks and between poorer Blacks and more successful Blacks.

Efforts by community groups and churches to address these conditions are praiseworthy and sometimes impressive; overall, though, the status of far too many Black people remains on the vulnerable fringe of a society that values wealth and Whiteness.

Given this awesome array of racially related barriers to a full life for Black people, how should we explain the priority concern we give to police brutality? It is, obviously, a serious problem, but it is also dramatic in a media-drenched era in which the drama trumps substance. As I write this, in July of 1999, the nation has ended a full week of media-led mourning over the deaths of John Kennedy Jr., his wife, and his sister-in-law in an airplane crash. During the same seven-day period, perhaps 800 people died of the 40,000 expected to lose their lives in auto accidents this year. Unless the crash is spectacular or ties up traffic for long periods, fatal auto accidents seldom make headlines and may not be reported at all.

Blacks, like all people, allow the dramatic incident to shield the more unnerving reality. We identify with the victim of police violence, but in that very identification we unconsciously embrace a discomfiting divergence. Our citizenship is far more shaky than we wish to acknowledge. And out-of-control police officers, with all the risk they pose, are far from the top of the lengthy list of dangers that threaten us both individually and as a people.

This deconstruction of the danger racist police pose for Black people is not reassuring and is not intended to be so. It is one among many contradictions in the state of Black people in America who, while never wanted, have managed to survive all the racial handicaps intended to obstruct their lives. The human debris of racial restrictions are all around us, and yet, somehow, Black people manage, not as I would have them or as by any objective standards they should function, but they do. As a character in one of my stories, "Redemption Deferred: Back to the Space Traders," puts it as he urges Black people not to accept the offer of aliens from another world to join them,

It's true. Life in America was hard for African Americans, as we all know. But as we all also know, my friends, America, whether

Whites liked it or not, is our land, too. For better or worse, it is our home. Our roots are there. Our work is there. There we have lived our lives, and there we have engaged in the struggle for our dignity, a struggle that—win or lose—is our true destiny. The humanity which so attracts the Space Traders is not a gift that came with our color. It is the hard-earned result of our efforts to survive in a culture everlastingly hostile to our color. It is the quest for freedom and equality that has been our salvation. We must continue that quest or betray the hopes and prayers of those who brought us this far along the way.

Notes

1. Patricia J. Williams, "The Executioners Automat," *The Nation* 262 (July 10, 1995): 59, 63.

2. *The Real War on Crime: The Report of the National Criminal Justice Commission*, ed. Steven R. Donziger (New York: Harper Perennial, 1996), 161.

3. Ibid., 168.

4. Eugene D. Genovese, *Roll, Jordan, Roll: The World the Slaves Made* (New York: Pantheon Books, 1974) 617–18.

5. Leon F. Litwack, *Trouble in Mind: Black Southerners in the Age of Jim Crow* (New York: Knopf, 1998), 15.

6. Ibid.

7. Ibid.

8. Ibid.

9. The names of the victims, along with the place and date of their lynching, are listed in Ralph Ginzburg, ed., *One Hundred Years of Lynchings* (1962; reprint, Baltimore: Black Classic Press, 1988), 253–70.

10. Michael R. Belknap, *Federal Law and Southern Order: Racial Violence and Constitutional Conflict in the Post-Brown South* (Athens: University of Georgia Press, 1987), 8–9.

11. Peter M. Bergman, *The Chronological History of the Negro in America* (New York: Harper & Row, 1969), 330.

12. Ibid.

13. E. L. Godkin, "The Moral of the Memphis Riots," in *Uncivil War: Race, Civil Rights and The Nation: 1865–1995*, ed. Peter Rothberg (New York: The Nation Press, 1995), 3.

14. Elliott Rudwick, "Race Riot at East St. Louis, July 2, 1917," in *The Politics of Riot Commissions*, ed. Anthony Platt (New York: Collier Books, 1971), 83.

15. Ibid., 63.

16. *The Report of the National Criminal Justice Commission*, 115.

17. Ibid., 103.

18. Ibid., 106.

19. Dionne Brand, *Bread out of Stone* (Toronto: Coach House Press, 1994), 116–17.

4

Nation under Siege

Elijah Muhammad, the FBI,
and Police-State Culture in Chicago

CLAUDE A. CLEGG III

In a variety of disturbing ways, the illegal wiretapping and surveillance of Elijah Muhammad and the Nation of Islam constitutes one of the most egregious denials of constitutional rights and police brutality in the twentieth century.

Perhaps to the majority of Americans, the Nation of Islam seemed sinister enough when it first attracted national media attention in 1959. Most disturbing to some was that the Muslims had quietly developed in strength and popularity over three decades, only to suddenly burst onto the historical scene when racial tensions were surging well ahead of the floundering Civil Rights movement.[1] The separatist, millenarian ideology of the quasi-Islamic group was certainly shocking to the sensibilities of those who had previously been unaware of its existence, not to mention its fiercely articulated racial chauvinism and apocalyptic visions. Consequently, to hear it for the first time, especially after having been conditioned by Civil Rights leaders to believe that African American grievances could be nonviolently channeled toward Christian, democratic, and integrationist objectives, unnerved many listeners, regardless of background.

Primarily, the American public found the theology of the Nation of Islam startling and foreboding because of its eschatology and its characterization of the racial status quo and the divinely ordained endgame. Though as intricate and nuanced as any religious system, the broad contours of the Muslims' beliefs can be summarized. According to their leader Elijah Muhammad, the Black "Original People," or the Nation of Islam, had righteously ruled the earth for trillions of years before their sovereignty was interrupted by White people, a "race of devils" created by a Black scientist six millennia ago. According to prophecy, the White man would be naturally evil and deceitful and would brutally rule over the Black Nation until World War I, when his regime would end. Sometime in the late twentieth century, Judgment Day would arrive, during which the "Mother Plane," a huge, circular spaceship piloted by Black scientists, would attack America with bombs. In the wake of the destruction, Allah, the most current of a succession of Black anthropomorphic gods who have ruled since the creation, would appear and initiate a meltdown of the earth's atmosphere. The resulting conflagration would make the United States uninhabitable for a thousand years, sweeping away the devilish White race and its iniquitous civilization. Sheltered from the destruction and spared this horrific fate, the Nation of Islam, more vibrant and sacred than before, would once again rule the planet under a glorious theocracy led by Allah himself.[2]

It was both an incredible and a disquieting message, depending on whom one asked. However, for tens of thousands of people, it was (and is) nothing short of rock-solid religious truth, which endowed everything, from numerals to the celestial bodies, with spiritual meaning. Elijah Muhammad, a Georgia-born sharecropper who moved to Detroit in the 1920s, preached and elaborated on this theology for over forty years, until his death in 1975. During this time, he and his Nation of Islam attracted an abundance of attention, not the least of which was in the form of government scrutiny and persecution. The surveillance and censure of Muhammad's movement in Chicago, the Nation of Islam's headquarters by 1935, provide an interesting example of how investigative and policing agencies responded over time to a group perceived as subversive, extremist, and un-American. In particular, the interactive ways in which the Federal Bureau of

Investigation (FBI), the Chicago Police Department (CPD), and other state agencies attempted to jointly deal with the Nation of Islam once it became nationally known in 1959 reveal much about the historical role of the government in suppressing black dissent.[3]

Of course, there is an interior angle just as interesting. How did the Nation of Islam adapt to, cope with, and evolve in the constant presence of state power and intimidation? More specifically, how did Muhammad's encounter with federal and local authorities within the anti-Communist, antisubversive culture of the 1960s and 1970s shape his leadership style and even his ideology? This essay argues that Muhammad's response to the state over time was saliently marked by the early and ongoing government surveillance of the Nation of Islam, as was his management of the movement. Additionally, the state itself, primarily represented by the FBI, CPD, and Richard Daley's administration in Chicago, was in turn constantly adjusting itself to both the maneuvering of the Chicago Muslims and their leader and the political tenor of the times. By his death in 1975, Muhammad understood the pressure points and moving parts of the government's repressive machinery well enough to establish a relatively generous amount of social terrain for his movement in Chicago. Similarly, the state by then had begun to understand the historical trajectory of the Nation of Islam within a broad enough temporal context to determine that the world it had created was not generally antithetical to national security. In short, this is an examination of two forces often colliding and in conflict but, at the same time, often moving in similar directions. In certain ways, the Muslim experience with police and investigative agencies may be applicable to a number of American social movements that have evolved alongside the twentieth-century American state.

THE FBI'S INTEREST in the Nation of Islam can be traced back to the inception of the movement in the early 1930s when W. Fard Muhammad, Elijah Muhammad's spiritual mentor and the man he later claimed to be Allah in person, organized the first temple in Detroit. The Bureau, though in a downsizing mode because of the budgetary constraints occasioned by the Depression, maintained casual surveillance of the organization, but left day-to-day observation and repression of the movement in the able hands of local law enforcement agencies. By the mid-1930s, the Nation of Islam had nearly collapsed in the wake of infighting triggered by the utter disappearance of Fard Muhammad and Elijah Muhammad's ascension to power as the "Messenger of Allah." But by the time the United States entered World War II, in December 1941, the Nation of Islam had started to recoup its former strength. Not surprisingly, its leaders' criticism of the draft and their complimentary remarks regarding Japan as a champion of people of color illuminated the government's antisubversive radar to the extent that dozens of Muslims were apprehended by the FBI for sedition and refusing Selective Service orders. Claiming allegiance only to Allah, Muhammad, who was arrested first in Washington, D.C., and again after fleeing to Chicago, was incarcerated in July 1943 in the Federal Correctional Institution at Milan, Michigan, where he remained until August 1946.[4]

While Elijah Muhammad and his followers sorted out the pieces of their shattered Nation, the FBI expanded in both structure and function. J. Edgar Hoover, its director since 1924, enjoyed a budgetary largesse unprecedented in earlier times, once he was able to convince his superiors, and many of the American people, that Communism and subversion were threats just as much at home as abroad. Illustratively, the Bureau's treasury, just $6.3 million in 1939, soared to an appropriation of $35.9 million in 1947. Commensurately, it employed over 7,000 agents in 1952, compared with a mere 326 in 1932. Cold War paranoia, the resulting McCarthy hysteria, postwar economic revival, and the popular image of the FBI as a highly trained, professionally managed law-and-order agency were all responsible for the Bureau's gains in wealth and manpower. Under Hoover, these assets would be utilized in multifarious ways, and not always in keeping with the Bureau's official mission.[5]

By the 1950s, the FBI had become much more sophisticated and effective as an investigative organization, not only because of its greater resources and technological advances but also because of its increasingly widespread role in the hunt for subversives. In the context of the Cold War, even the old methods of collecting evidence and pursuing suspected offenders took on new meaning. For example, the assembling of dossiers on criminals, radicals, labor unions, and others by means of secret informants, police intelligence, and occasional raids was a tactic as old as the Bureau itself. However, the political symbolism of these files had changed during the postwar period. Now the very existence of an FBI file on a particular individual or group was an accusation in and of itself, damning the accused to further surveillance and censure. Even worse, one could be found guilty by association, having a file created on one's activities simply because one had been seen with or in some way connected to a party already under surveillance, no matter how fleeting or superficial the contact. The politics of file collecting was fueled by popular images of Communism and subversion as grave ills of the body politic, and thus treatable only through persistent vigilance and eventual eradication. Once tainted, one easily spread the contagion to others, even if one had long ago forsworn any suspect beliefs or had never harbored them in the first place.[6]

Many files on putative subversives were conceived and nourished by the FBI's greater reliance on technological surveillance. Wiretaps and microphone devices, or "bugs," were the primary means of gaining electronic access to targeted parties. Eavesdropping on telephone conversations did not typically force agents to enter residences or other buildings occupied by subjects under surveillance. However, the planting of microphones could require trespassing on private premises, depending on how closely the Bureau wished to follow the activities of an individual or group. Predictably, spying by the FBI spawned complex layers of secrecy, suspicion, and lawlessness. In the case of wiretaps, the Bureau routinely sought the approval of the attorney general. But surveillance techniques that lapsed into criminality, such as breaking and entering, were often used without the approval of Hoover's superiors, as were more egregious violations, such as the purloining of membership rolls, letters, and financial documents from the domiciles of suspected individuals and groups. By the late 1950s, an FBI file on a person or organization might contain a variety of items, from transcripts of recorded telephone conversations and surreptitiously taken photographs to supposedly subversive newspapers and personal correspondence acquired through Bureau-sanctioned burglaries (or "black bag jobs"). Ever conscious of the unlawful nature of these activities, Hoover crafted a tight system of security for illegally acquired records, keeping "June Mail" documents—those made possible by trespassing and microphone surveillance—under lock and key in FBI headquarters.[7]

The FBI never wholly lost sight of the Nation of Islam during its years of decline. Even after it had nearly obliterated the group with raids, mass arrests and detentions, and incessant harassment during the 1940s, the Bureau continued to record the activities of Elijah Muhammad and Muslim officials throughout the country. However, the general public's sudden awareness of the existence of the movement in 1959, inaugurated by high-profile, but rarely favorable, reports on the Nation in the mass media, attracted greater FBI scrutiny. Additionally, the change in the country's political climate, as well as the enhanced membership of the Muslim movement, led to redoubled efforts by the Bureau to comprehend and ultimately diminish the group's appeal and influence.

For the most part, the ideology of the Nation of Islam stayed remarkably stable over time. The core themes of Black superiority, White devilry, and the coming Judgment were now supplemented by a vibrant entrepreneurial drive—the Muslims had been acquiring small businesses and farmland since the mid-1940s—and a largely rhetorical call for a separate Black state. Notwithstanding its doctrinal constancy, Hoover still firmly believed that even the relatively conservative Nation of Islam was as dangerous and Communist friendly as the Civil Rights struggle purportedly was. In keeping with his racial prejudices, he felt that African Americans who challenged the domestic status quo in any fashion were inimical to national security, regardless of their political persuasion or agenda. Thus, the need to escalate surveillance of the Muslims was self-evident to the director, for the group's racialized Islam and Black nationalism were grossly incongruous with his vision of the American future.[8]

FBI reports on the Nation of Islam tended to highlight the potentially violent and seditious nature of the movement. According to intelligence gathered by a Bureau informant in May 1960, the Nation was an "all-Negro organization," which labeled Caucasians "White devils" and preached that "the White race . . . must and will be destroyed in the approaching 'War of Armageddon.'" The informant's synopsis also noted that Elijah Muhammad and his followers denounced any "allegiance to the United States" and employed military drills and martial arts training to prepare for the final race war. Though cloaked in the language of prophecy, this information disturbed Hoover and his operatives enough to take further peremptory actions against the Nation. During the early 1960s, the names of 673 Muslims appeared in the FBI's Security Index, a blacklist that categorized the "degree of dangerousness" of targeted individuals and organizations. Of the 1,497 African Americans in the index, Nation of Islam members made up the largest organizational contingent, followed by 476 Communists, 222 "Black nationalists," and an assortment of others. In existence since 1939, the Security Index was part of the "Bureau War Plans," a veritable blueprint for repression, well into the 1970s.[9]

Even before these incursions against the Nation occurred, FBI surveillance of Muhammad had already become more intimate years earlier. In December 1956, Hoover authorized the wiretapping of the phone lines of Muhammad's Chicago residence and began eavesdropping early the following month. At the Muslim leader's Phoenix, Arizona, residence, which he had purchased as a second home in July 1961, the breach of privacy was even more glaring, for both a wiretap and a microphone surveillance were authorized and installed in September 1961. The microphones, "one in front and one in back of [the] house," actually required entry into the residence to install, and thus were planted either during an FBI break-in or by an informant working within the Nation of Islam. Whatever the case, the FBI office in Phoenix, like that in Chicago, was quite pleased with the "wealth of information concerning the activities of Muhammad" that the surveillance devices had provided. The Bureau clerk C. Barry Pickett, sitting in an air-conditioned room in the Phoenix office, worked eight hours a day, five days a week, for four years listening to Muhammad and others and transcribing whatever he heard that he "would consider of value" from the tapes that he made on a Magnavox recorder.[10]

Muhammad likely suspected that at least some of his conversations were electronically monitored, but had little idea regarding the depth of his vulnerability, especially in his Phoenix home. He certainly knew that the low-intensity warfare between his Nation and the federal government, which had existed since the 1930s, would only become more heated as the Muslim movement attracted more followers and media attention. Muhammad's favorite tactic against government spying was exposing it whenever detected. In a July 1959 speech at St. Nicholas Arena in New York, Muhammad excoriated "the slavemasters' [Uncle] Tom, Boot lickers, and stool pigeons" who had infiltrated the Nation of Islam "to keep the enemies well informed of all we say." He warned that eventually the Muslims would "weed them out from among us as other nations have." In a literary offensive against the FBI, *Muhammad Speaks*, the Muslims' organ, noted in a July 1962 article that discrimination against African Americans and Jews in the FBI was rampant. This assertion was hardly refuted by Hoover's denials, given that his long-standing effort to exclude Blacks, Jews, Hispanics, and, for a time, Catholics from employment was de facto Bureau policy. Finally, in a March 1964 speech, Muhammad, referring to the occasional questioning of Muslims by FBI agents, asked plainly, "Just what are you trying to do?" Offering sardonic reassurance, he added, "We want the FBI to know what we are teaching. . . . We want the government to know we have no secrets." Unfortunately, his last statement rang truer than he probably cared to know.[11]

THE CHICAGO OFFICE of the FBI, under Special Agent-in-Charge Marlin Johnson, was relentless in its surveillance of Elijah Muhammad and the Muslims of Mosque No. 2 in that city. Johnson's periodic reports to Hoover were typically detailed and long, requiring a table of contents and numbered pages. His transmissions became more involved over time, and his dispatches on Muhammad were divided into sections with headings such as "residence," "policy statements," "attendance at meetings," "use of publications," and "Communist Party interest." Information gleaned from the wiretap added to the bulk of the file, as did Johnson's transcribed excerpts from the growing literature by and about the Nation of Islam. The Chicago office faithfully implemented orders from Bureau headquarters and kept Hoover abreast of even small matters relating to the Muslims. Not infrequently, Johnson suggested to his superiors ways in which his office could be more effective still in its pursuit of the "Black Muslims."

Some of Johnson's operations against Elijah Muhammad were simply nuisances, which caused only temporary inconveniences. For example, when the Muslim leader made plans to visit the Middle East and Africa in 1959, the Chicago office was able to have the State Department place a stop on the issuance of passports to Muhammad and a number of his relatives. This artifice was abandoned once it was learned that Muhammad was considering legal action to accelerate the processing of his application. It is unclear whether any of the three hundred or so burglaries reportedly committed by the FBI in Chicago during the 1950s victimized the Muslims. However, Bureau officials in Chicago did regard the Nation of Islam as un-American and subversive, and thus were not necessarily above using a variety of sordid means to expose it as such. Red-baiting the Nation of Islam generally failed, though Johnson reported in April 1961, "Persons associated with Communism are reportedly aware of and interested in ELIJAH MUHAMMAD and the Nation of Islam." In reality, Muhammad himself publicly deplored the atheism inherent in Marxism and was too thoroughly capitalist, bourgeois, and nationalist to justify a Red label. Assailing his politics was a

dead end; there was nothing to talk about except his territorial sepa-
ratism, Islamic heterodoxy, and historical revisionism. Even his racial
chauvinism and determinist theories, which were rarely camouflaged
regardless of his audience, tended to be couched in spiritual and
prophetic terms, not as a political agenda. In the end, little of this
mattered to the FBI. Where it could not successfully persecute the
Nation of Islam on the basis of Muhammad's ideology alone, it
attempted to do so in more circumspect ways.

In continuing attempts "to disrupt and curb [the] growth of the
NOI," the Chicago office embarked upon a campaign to locate W.
Fard Muhammad, Elijah's mentor, hoping "to make MUHAMMAD
appear ridiculous." To its dismay, the founder of the Nation had
never resurfaced after his disappearance in 1934, and tantalizing
leads led nowhere. Stung by an unflattering exposé—planted by the
FBI—that accused Fard Muhammad of various crimes and religious
chicanery, Elijah Muhammad offered one hundred thousand dollars
to whoever could prove that his teacher had been a White ex-con-
vict, as the newspaper articles charged. The FBI, outmaneuvered,
ended its search for Fard Muhammad and looked for new angles
from which to assail the Nation of Islam.[12]

If the failed hunt for Fard Muhammad appeared laughable, other
tactics used by the FBI contained no humor at all. In March 1964,
Malcolm X, the influential minister of New York Mosque No. 7,
departed from the Nation, having fallen out of favor with Muhammad after making intemperate remarks about the assassination of
President John Kennedy. Tensions between Muhammad, Malcolm,
and Muslim officials in Chicago had been building for years, largely
over Malcolm's prominent role in the movement and his more politicized views. Added to the petty jealousies and intrigues that are common in organizations as sprawling as the Nation of Islam, these
pressures created fault lines that would only grow over time.

Even as Malcolm was contemplating leaving the Nation, FBI officials wasted no time in trying to recruit him as an informant. Their
appeals were rebuffed, but their resolve to widen the fissure
between Muhammad and Malcolm stiffened. Hoover was keenly

interested in the escalating mini-war between Malcolm and the Nation, as was Marlin Johnson of the Chicago office. Although the director gave a law-and-order speech in Chicago in November 1964 in which he lamented the moral breakdown of American society, he and his agents nurtured the increasingly destructive feud between Muhammad and his former lieutenant. On February 21, 1965, Malcolm X was killed during a talk in New York. The three men charged with the crime were Muslims, but whether they were renegades or acting under orders from Muhammad remains unclear. The FBI office in Chicago, despite the fact that declassified records obscure its role in the tragedy, had been a major player in the escalation of Muslim infighting. As Johnson would later comment, "Factional disputes have been developed—the most noteable [sic] being MALCOLM X. . . ."[13]

While the FBI spearheaded the surveillance and repression of the Nation of Islam in Chicago, its job was greatly facilitated by the local police department. The FBI worked closely with law enforcement officials in the city to track down putative subversives, routinely sharing intelligence, organizing police raids, and even coordinating extralegal covert activities. Despite this collaboration, the Chicago Police Department did not share the Bureau's popular image as an adept, elite crime-busting agency. A subspecies of Mayor Richard Daley's political machine, which had run Chicago since 1955, the CPD appeared, in many ways, to embody the antithesis of these qualities.

Stained by graft, nepotism, and partisan politics, the department was responsive mostly to the needs and fears of upper-class and sub-urbanized Chicago, protecting the propertied interests of the metropolis as well as the web of political clients that had secured the patronage of City Hall. In depressed areas, such as the Black South Side, the police were largely used for riot control, limited reconnaissance, and some vice work. However, more than a few officers made money by looking the other way as prostitution and narcotics rings flourished, and police brutality, most common in areas that had little political or economic clout, cast a long shadow over it all. In 1957,

Life magazine dubbed the CPD "the worst department of any sizable city," and even the department spokesman Frank Sullivan had to reckon with the "hidden sickness" of corruption a decade later. But as simply a component of a larger bureaucracy, the CPD functioned as Daley wanted it to—that is, without the oversight of a civilian review board, the presence of Blacks in the upper ranks, or many limits on its wide discretion.[14]

Elijah Muhammad understood all of this. In fact, he had apparently made his peace with Daley and the CPD early on, thus sparing the Muslims of Chicago much of the police harassment and repression that their brethren faced regularly in other cities. Like Daley, Muhammad was a master pragmatist, and his doctrinal condemnation of the White world rarely clouded his day-to-day dealings with it. For example, in a 1958 speech in Detroit, he asserted that "God himself is about to remove [the U.S.] government from the planet," but counseled his followers to "[b]e polite, courteous, respectful" to law officers. "By so doing," he told them, "you are teaching the officers that you are probably more intelligent than they, and they will recognize and respect you for your intelligence." To be sure, there were times when Muhammad could not help expressing his disdain for police excesses, such as when an unarmed Muslim named Ronald T. X. Stokes was shot dead during an April 1962 police assault on the Los Angeles mosque. Stokes's death triggered an avalanche of caustic criticism throughout 1962 and 1963, and numerous depictions of White policemen as Klansmen, Nazis, animals, and, of course, devils filled the pages of *Muhammad Speaks*. But even when confronted with atrocities against his followers by law officers, Muhammad advised restraint and legal remedies, not holy war.[15]

By the 1960s, the growing economic empire of the Nation of Islam, and the advancing conservatism of its leadership, required stability and rapprochement with the state and its agencies. The rumor that Muhammad tipped policemen who patrolled the area around his nineteen-room mansion on South Woodlawn Avenue was probably true, as was the assertion by a Daley underling that the mayor had befriended the Muslim leader. In a sense, they were kindred spirits—both were practical bosses of nepotistic machines that they tightly controlled but that were amenable to alliances of convenience. Muhammad's rapport with City Hall and the CPD was amply illustrated in the wake of Malcolm X's assassination, when the Muslim leader's residence, businesses, and other assets were closely guarded against potential avengers of the slain minister. In response to the department's vigilance, Muhammad expressed "great respect for the police," a compliment that reflected his quid pro quo relationship with Daley.[16]

What Muhammad was not familiar with was the underside of the CPD, its antisubversive detail, which was connected as much to federal forces like the FBI as to the Daley administration. Colloquially known as the Red Squad, this organization was a subsidiary of the Intelligence Division, which in turn was a part of the CPD's Bureau of Inspectional Services. Its mission was to track down and curtail the influence of individuals and groups suspected of being involved in seditious or otherwise "un-American" activities. Like the FBI, the Red Squad used a mix of overt and covert methods, the former including raids, monitoring gatherings, writing down license plate numbers, and photographing suspects; the latter involving infiltration of targeted groups, wiretaps, and burglaries. The assembling of a file on an individual or organization was not simply an empirical exercise to gauge the "dangerousness" of a subject. It was a punitive act in itself, stigmatizing the censured party as a political criminal whose rights to assembly, free speech, privacy, and property could now be justifiably abridged. The file allowed the Red Squad to scrape away much of the constitutional skin that protected one's citizenship. By 1960, the CPD, thanks largely to its Intelligence Division, had amassed information on 117,000 Chicagoans and 14,000 organizations, almost certainly including Elijah Muhammad and many of his followers.[17]

Insofar as their missions and methods were intertwined, the Chicago Red Squad had a symbiotic relationship with the FBI and other intelligence agencies. Its personnel shared files with the Chicago FBI office, attended Bureau-sponsored briefings on radicals, used federal funds for surveillance work, and coordinated joint offensives against targeted groups. The relationship was so close that the Red Squad could reportedly have an FBI dossier started on anyone who attended two open gatherings of groups under surveillance, or "whose picture appeared more than four times" in the unit's records. In a particularly devious campaign against Elijah Muhammad, the FBI sought to use CPD intelligence agents to expose adulterous affairs that the Muslim leader had been having with a number of young women in the Nation of Islam.[18]

On July 13, 1962, two of Muhammad's mistresses, protesting his apparent unwillingness to hear their demands, left their two infants at his Chicago residence. Raymond Sharrieff, Muhammad's son-in-law, turned the children over to police custody, which outraged the mothers. F. J. Baumgardner, an FBI operative, wanted to seize this opportunity "to create dissension in the NOI through exposure of Elijah Muhammad's extramarital activity." He proposed having the Security Unit of the CPD publicly investigate the incident, hopefully "causing a bastardy charge to be filed against Muhammad." He assured his superiors in Washington that this could be done "without embarrassment to the Bureau." In the meantime, J. Edgar Hoover instructed the Chicago office to send anonymous letters to Clara Muhammad, Elijah's wife, containing the details of her husband's infidelities. Both tactics produced tangible results, exacerbating tensions in Muhammad's marriage and within the group's leadership. Paternity suits were eventually filed against him in 1964, but were never litigated to their conclusion.[19]

In addition to its FBI connections, the Red Squad also worked with the Central Intelligence Agency (CIA) on countersubversive projects. Though in violation of its charter, the CIA had a significant role in domestic surveillance activities during the 1960s, and in many cases emulated the part the FBI was playing in local spying operations. As early as 1952, CIA documents noted that Muhammad had allegedly advised his male followers to "accelerate efforts to raise an army to assist the Soviet Union in a war against the United States." Moreover, the agency was informed that Muslim officials had described "the Russian and Chinese Communists as the 'Asiatic

Brothers.'" While concerned enough about these sentiments, the CIA did not become deeply involved in repressive measures against the Nation of Islam until the 1960s, though the political conservatism and anti-Communism of the Muslim movement were more discernible during the latter period than when the statements were supposedly first made.[20]

The CIA assault on Stateside dissent was code-named CHAOS and involved the increasingly common mix of illegal methods—such as mail openings, wiretaps, and break-ins—that were being used by the FBI and other intelligence agencies. Over the course of the 1960s and early 1970s, the CIA collected and computerized over 13,000 files, which contained the names of over 300,000 people and organizations. Among these documents were records on the Nation of Islam, which had been monitored along with groups such as the Black Panthers. In the 1970s, when Congress began investigating the exploits of the CIA in the American counterintelligence underworld, it discovered that the agency had an "ongoing relationship" with the Chicago Red Squad, having even recruited a deputy superintendent of the CPD to assist in the surveillance of Black and antiwar organizations. Few of these revelations were wholly shocking in the context of the scandal-ridden Watergate era. However, the breadth of CIA espionage, much of it in violation of numerous laws, made a mockery of the Constitution and democratic procedure.[21]

Given that the Nation of Islam had come into the sights of so many different state agencies by the early 1960s, the discussion of the group and its alleged violent proclivities in the halls of Congress in late 1962 almost seems anticlimactic in retrospect. However, within the culture of political paranoia that characterized that era, this was a very serious matter. Unlike the spying and countersubversive ploys of the FBI, CIA, CPD, and others, a congressional investigation could potentially lead to public rebuke and severe penalties for the Nation and its leadership, on the basis of whatever definitions of subversion and "un-American activities" Congress chose to invoke. The gravity of this scenario was not lost on Elijah Muhammad. As was mentioned earlier, he made it a point to regularly stress the law-abiding nature of the Muslim movement, hoping to avoid a reprise of the dissident roundups of the 1940s.[22]

Regardless of Muhammad's reassurances, in August 1962 Francis E. Walker, chairman of the House Un-American Activities Committee (HUAC), suggested that "a very extensive investigation" of the Nation of Islam might be warranted. The South Carolina Democrat L. Mendel Rivers concurred, charging that the organization was given "to murder, naked violence, hatred, mugging and yoking." Later that month, the House Rules Committee recommended that the HUAC formally investigate the "segregationist cult." A resolution, sponsored by Rivers, which authorized an HUAC vote on the proposal was placed on the calendar. Ultimately, the Muslims escaped, perhaps barely, the abuse that a full-blown HUAC investigation promised. Political interest among congressmen in such a spectacle was not strong enough to initiate the threatened "extensive investigation." Still, the Nation of Islam certainly had enough enemies in Congress and other high places to assure that this was not the last time the group would be mentioned in scornful terms before the national legislature.[23]

Following this congressional episode, representatives of the executive branch joined the chorus of official critics and escalated the government's war against the Muslims. In July 1963, Attorney General Robert F. Kennedy, who had authorized many of J. Edgar Hoover's schemes, asserted before the Senate Commerce Committee that he was cognizant of the Muslims and would pursue them, if they violated the law. Probing further, Senator Strom Thurmond queried, "Would you say the Black Muslim movement is similar to the Nazi party of the United States?" Kennedy replied that it was not—but instead, "closer to the Ku Klux Klan." (Probably unbeknownst to Thurmond, the attorney general's response was based at least in part on a fleeting alliance of convenience between the Nation of Islam and a Georgia KKK faction that the FBI had taken an interest in a year earlier.) President John F. Kennedy, while informing concerned citizens that the Nation of Islam was not violating federal statutes, allowed the FBI and other agencies to step up surveillance of the movement. Most unfortunately, when the chance came to rein in Hoover before his methods thoroughly criminalized and discredited the FBI during the late 1960s, President Lyndon B. Johnson squandered the opportunity altogether. A 1964 executive order allowed Hoover to continue as Bureau director beyond the mandatory retirement age, thus making possible even grosser violations of the civil liberties of Muslims and others.[24]

To Elijah Muhammad, all of the spying, contempt, and criminality that federal and state agencies were inflicting upon his movement were consistent with the inherently wicked and crafty nature of White people. He believed that White racism and hatred of Blacks were too formidable to place "freedom, justice, and equality" within the grasp of African Americans. Despite these sentiments, he personally had maneuvered well within the confines of government surveillance. Actually, Muhammad attempted with some success to lead a relatively unfettered lifestyle, given the array of opposition against him. He traveled when and where he pleased, continually railed against White America in his speeches, lived extravagantly in his well-guarded mansion, and talked freely on his tapped telephones, discussing everything from fund-raising and organizational politics to tax evasion and chastising "hypocrites." In some instances, when discretion would have been the best policy, it was discarded in favor of satiating his appetites, as in the case of his unbridled philandering. Détente with the Daley administration allowed Muhammad a good deal of individual liberty in Chicago, which his followers in other regions usually did not enjoy. Even the Chicago FBI office seemed more intent on exposing Muhammad as a fraud than on ruthlessly eradicating the Nation in a manner reminiscent of its murderous campaign against the Black Panthers during the late 1960s and 1970s.

Nonetheless, state scrutiny and harassment did have a noticeable impact on Muhammad and his movement. The memory of his years in prison during the 1940s was still very much with him, and given that now he had much more to lose in terms of financial ventures and organizational clout, he avoided political engagement and social activism. Age (he turned sixty-eight in October 1965) and affluence mellowed him, and the fear of arousing again the full wrath of the government kept him from offering much more than a black-skinned Islam, petty capitalism, and back-to-Africa dreams to his followers. But his abhorrence of government repression was still acidic and regularly expressed in his talks and writings. Shortly before the proposal of the HUAC investigation in 1962, he sneered in an editorial, "We cannot foresee anything in [White people] but evil." To him, being labeled "un-American" more than substantiated this conclusion.[25]

RATHER ABRUPTLY, electronic surveillance of the residences of Elijah Muhammad was ended in June 1966. Primarily, the fear of disclosure motivated the Justice Department to scale back its wiretaps in general, but diminishing returns were also partly responsible for the discontinuance. Since many of its wiretaps and microphone plantings were illegal, information gathered in this fashion could not typically be used for prosecutorial purposes. Thus, the years of eavesdropping had largely produced intelligence that was valuable only in the subterranean world of countersubversion and political voyeurism, not in a court of law. But this decline in electronic spying was not indicative of a comprehensive reduction of federal surveillance or repressive stratagems. The powers of the FBI and its sister agencies were actually augmented during the late 1960s as a response to ghetto uprisings, antiwar demonstrations, Black Power, and the New Left. Like J. Edgar Hoover, Presidents Johnson and Nixon were absorbed by efforts to forge, even coerce, a broad ideological consensus regarding domestic politics and foreign policy.[26]

On August 25, 1967, the FBI unleashed the most extensive (and felonious) counterintelligence program ever designed to annihilate African American protest and dissent. Code-named COINTELPRO, this operation made past repressive tactics appear polite and tame. Its purpose was candidly spelled out in Hoover's transmittal to the twenty-three participating field offices, including Chicago. The objectives were to keep "militant Black nationalist groups" from coalescing; preclude the emergence of a leader "who could unify, and electrify" such organizations; halt violent activities and growth of these groups; and prevent their "leaders from gaining respectability." In March 1968, eighteen more field offices became involved in the operation to minimize, as Hoover told Congress two months later, the "distinct threat to the internal security of the nation" that Black nationalist groups putatively posed.[27]

In its maneuvers against the Muslims, the FBI continued to try to provoke insurrections in the movement by anonymously alerting followers to the lavish lifestyles of some of their leaders. Conflicts between Muslims and Black Panthers were fomented, sometimes leading to violence. Herbert Muhammad, who the FBI believed might succeed his father as head of the Nation, was targeted for an investigation by the Internal Revenue Service. Additionally, dozens of other "dirty tricks" were employed against the Muslims as part of COINTELPRO, but not always producing the results that the Bureau hoped for. In a January 1969 memorandum to Hoover, Marlin Johnson of the Chicago office lamented that the effort to expose Muhammad "is ineffective" and, even further, "possibly creates interest" in the movement. To the chagrin of both Hoover and his subordinate, the specifics of the electronic surveillance of Muhammad's homes were finally detailed in the media in June 1969.[28]

When it ended in 1971, COINTELPRO had merely sent ripples through the Nation of Islam, not the shock waves that devastated the leftist Black Panthers and other groups. Hoover's belief that Elijah Muhammad was too old to lead a Black nationalist revolt in America had spared the Muslims the brunt of the repression, and his advocacy of Black capitalism and divine remedies simply did not arouse the Bureau like the Marxism of the New Left. But Muhammad did, indeed, feel violated by COINTELPRO and castigated the surveillance as "[b]latant injustice committed by so-called 'Law and Order' agents." In response to Hoover's concerns about subversion, Muhammad proclaimed, "Almighty Allah . . . is the One who is actually destroying the [national] security. . . . It is a threat that God is making against America for freedom, justice and equality for the so-called Negro." None of this exposure lessened the Bureau's counter-intelligence attack on the Nation, but it did shed further light on its shady methods. In fact, Muhammad appears to have genuinely relished pointing out the Bureau's snooping, humorously depicting a short, rotund J. Edgar Hoover, with tape recorder and headphones, in a 1969 *Muhammad Speaks* cartoon.[29]

In Chicago, the law-and-order themes, so frequently mentioned by the FBI director, resonated with Richard Daley. A consummate politician and survivalist, the mayor had always relied upon the police to keep the public peace, but increasingly called on the department to keep the political peace as well. The mayor deplored riots, not only for what they cost in property and human life, but for the damage that they did to his political reputation and the image of the city. Yet he was much more adroit at calling out the CPD and the National Guard to quell Black dissent than at addressing the root causes, such as poverty, police brutality, and unresponsive machine politics, which produced such disturbances. Regarding race, Daley reflexively thought in narrow ethnic terms, a product of a homogeneous Irish-Catholic background. Politically, he mastered Black wards and politicians well into the 1970s, but bitterly opposed court-ordered affirmative action until his death in 1976. When President Richard Nixon visited the city in June 1971, Daley made sure he received a theatrical first-class welcome. Though partisan politics were rancorous in Chicago, the Democratic mayor had no trouble following the political winds rightward, especially when it came to law and order.[30]

By the time COINTELPRO subsided in the early 1970s, police surveillance and corruption in Chicago were coming under greater criticism. There had been some high-profile excesses. For example, an Illinois "mob action" law passed in 1965 gave the mayor wide discretion in handling suspect gatherings, allowing policemen to arrest anyone they believed capable of mayhem. Daley put the law into effect during the summer of 1967, resulting in the arrest of at least two hundred African Americans. Most memorable, however, were the brutal beatings meted out by Chicago policemen to antiwar protesters who had gathered to demonstrate at the Democratic National Convention held in August 1968. The violence appalled many, but was skillfully converted into political capital by Daley, who was intent upon not allowing "the hippies, the Yippies, and the flippies" to overrun Chicago. Stories of police involvement in drug dealing and sex rings were hardly news by this time, and even Daley, according to the CPD spokesman Frank Sullivan, was privy to some of the misconduct. But these instances alone were not enough to trigger what would become a protracted investigation of the CPD. It was the cumulative weight of patterns of law enforcement abuses, in and outside of Chicago, that would bring the police department under fire as never before, along with its staunchest supporter, Richard J. Daley.[31]

Ironically, the walls of secrecy came down just as the CPD was trying to shield itself from a lawsuit. The Alliance to End Repression (AEF), a local community group, threatened to sue the police department in 1974 for what it believed to be unlawful spying. To foil a potentially embarrassing investigation, the Red Squad of the Intelligence Division began purging its files in May, disposing its weekly surveillance reports along with the names of 220 informants. The AEF filed its lawsuit in November, which apparently panicked the Red Squad even more. On January 20, 1975, a mysterious fire began *inside* a filing cabinet of the police headquarters at Eleventh and State Streets and destroyed surveillance documents stored there. Before any further destruction could take place, a federal district judge ordered the CPD to "cease and desist from destroying any records." Unfortunately for the AEF, the injunction had come too late, for the police department, and the mysterious fire, had managed to shred or incinerate dossiers on 105,000 individuals and 1,300 organizations in less than a year's time. Even as a grand jury began investigating the AEF's claims, the Red Squad worked hard to obliterate its long, incriminating paper trail.[32]

By the spring of 1975, the spying scandal was regularly making headlines. Not only was the destruction of the files disclosed, but the covert ties between the Red Squad, the FBI, the CIA, and other agencies were being publicly revealed. Denials by top city officials were expected, but few could feign complete ignorance, since there was enough grand-jury testimony and other evidence to permit a piecing together of at least parts of the story. On March 25, Police Superintendent James Rochford acknowledged the surveillance, but downplayed the extent and criminal nature of it. No more than fifty organizations and one hundred persons, according to Rochford, were subjected to Red Squad file collecting, and this was only because these groups and individuals posed "a danger to the peace of the city." The police chief did admit, "Last year we destroyed tons of out-dated material and reports," but denied that the files had served political purposes.[33]

Even more emphatic than Rochford in his denials, Mayor Daley called the public furor surrounding the scandal "a total political propaganda campaign by certain people." He ardently defended the right of the CPD to participate in surveillance activities, and rather tellingly justified it on the basis of "what is outlined in the FBI manual on police operations." In a less than honest statement, Daley asserted that he had never requested or received intelligence reports; even more incredibly, he denied that he had anything to do with the internal affairs of the CPD. Over the next couple of years, it was discovered that the police did, in fact, spy for political reasons and that Daley had access to their files. However, by then, the public, numb to scandal by Watergate, Hoover's publicized sins, and protracted media coverage of Red Squad abuses, seemed ready to move forward under the leadership of a new mayor, Michael Bilandic.[34]

Despite all the revelations, there were few dismissals and prosecutions of policemen for surveillance-related crimes. Daley's support and influence had a lot to do with the deferring of justice, but even after his death in 1976, the state simply refused to punish police wrongdoing. In June 1977, the Illinois Senate Judiciary Committee, under pressure from the Chicago Democratic lobby, voted down a bill that would have curbed police surveillance of lawful activities. In essence, the committee had concurred with the late mayor, who, in the wake of the file-purging scandal, announced, "I will stand behind whatever the Police Department did."[35]

To Elijah Muhammad and many other Chicagoans under surveillance, the police-spying revelations were not surprising, but the broad media coverage of official lawlessness was new. Who would ever have imagined that the Red Squad would eventually be taken to task by the same judicial, political, and media forces that had been so complacent during its rampage through the 1960s? The Muslim leader, given his tacit understanding with Daley, never publicly criticized the mayor and only alluded to the vices of the CPD on rare occasions. Besides, sporadic infighting in the Nation of Islam and his own illnesses absorbed much of his attention during the early 1970s. In a January 1972 interview, he was kind enough to say that police brutality had not increased in Chicago. Nonetheless, the following year he summarily expelled Muslim policemen from the Nation as a precaution against further state infiltration.[36]

Red Squad surveillance, COINTELPRO, CIA spying, and other forms of state harassment had a chilling effect on Muhammad and on American dissent and democracy in general. The stratagems and political ethos of these agencies injected suspicion, fear, alienation, and, most significantly, fascist tendencies into domestic politics and policing. Despite their claims, J. Edgar Hoover, the CPD, and the CIA were responsible for causing more national insecurity than any of their targets had. In particular, their White "we"/Black "they" frames of reference dichotomized Americans and actually approached the abyss of race war more closely than the beliefs and actions of the Nation of Islam ever did. As was mentioned earlier, Muhammad's Black nationalism and racial prophecies were scarcely affected by the criticisms of others. However, his unwillingness to actively usher in the Armageddon was clearly a result of decades of government surveillance and preemptive actions, including his imprisonment during the 1940s. By the heyday of the Civil Rights movement, he carefully steered the Nation clear of political and legal entanglements. For instance, in the era of Black Power, Muhammad even distanced himself from the militant Black Panthers of Chicago. In the wake of the FBI-assisted assassinations of Fred Hampton and Mark Clark by Chicago policemen in December 1969, he offered only silent sympathy.

Muhammad's accommodation with Richard Daley afforded Chicago Muslims a degree of breathing room in the otherwise stifling atmosphere of federal repression and police license in the city. Although there was no such rapport between the Muslim leader and J. Edgar Hoover, the FBI reserved its most virulent strains of counter-subversion for avowed revolutionaries such as the Black Panthers, the Republic of New Africa, and other nationalist and Marxist groups. In a sense, Muhammad had the best of both worlds; he and his ministers could appear radical in their tirades against White America, but did not have to follow through with armed struggle or other concrete actions, since Allah would do their bidding in his own good time. This aversion to the employment of violence against oppression helped the Nation avoid the worst of COINTELPRO and Red Squad abuses. Yet this stance disenchanted more politically minded Muslims, some of whom wound up in the ranks of the Panthers and other groups. By the 1960s, these sporadic apostacies were bearable, and little organizational credibility was lost because of the social conservatism or capitalist character of the Nation. Most people who joined at this time knew to expect reform and not revolution. They also recognized that the Nation was in the struggle for the long term and that its continuing longevity and growth depended upon an acknowledgment of at least some of the boundaries set by the state.

Only the Daley administration formally embraced Elijah Muhammad once it was abundantly clear that he was not interested in launching an anti-White jihad. But even this public endorsement came in the 1970s, when African Americans constituted nearly 40 percent of the city's population. Toward the end of his fifth term as mayor, Daley openly courted Muhammad, going as far as to proclaim March 29, 1974, "Honorable Elijah Muhammad Day in Chicago." Upon Muhammad's death on February 25, 1975, Daley eulogized the Muslim leader as "an outstanding citizen" and "consistent contributor to the social well-being of our city for more than 40 years." Beyond agreeing to coexist, Muhammad and Daley may actually have liked each other. However, genuine admiration is not a prerequisite for political alliances, and it is just as possible that the two only had a friendship of convenience.[37]

Always the pragmatist, Muhammad was also a survivor, having successfully endured opponents of every stripe, from J. Edgar Hoover (who died in 1972) to a protégé turned nemesis, Malcolm X. The lessons that he had learned from four decades of state surveillance and repression served him well and were put to good practical use. Like so many others, he traded bribes for nonaggression pacts with the CPD, exchanged niceties with Daley's machine, and only verbally protested FBI eavesdropping. When Bureau agents approached him for an interview in November 1974, one could almost guess that he would tell them what they wanted to hear. ("He commented he believed in law and order," the agents reported, "and loved America very much.") Despite the sharp edges of his rhetoric, Muhammad generally lived and dreamed within the system, even when it seemed unfair and corrupt. Ultimately, he carved out inhabitable social space for himself and his followers, having convinced most of his erstwhile critics that his heterodox Islam, capitalist pursuits, and eschewal of politics were essentially conservative, even American, in outlook.[38]

NOTES

1. The word "Muslim" as used in this chapter will refer to Nation of Islam members and their particular brand of Islam.

2. The authoritative text on the theology of the Nation of Islam is Elijah Muhammad, *Message to the Blackman in America* (Chicago: Muhammad Mosque of Islam No. 2, 1965). For other significant discussions, see Claude A. Clegg, *An Original Man: The Life and Times of Elijah Muhammad* (New York: St. Martin's Press, 1997), 41–73; C. Eric Lincoln, *The Black Muslims in America* (Boston: Beacon Press, 1961), 67–134; Richard Brent Turner, *Islam in the African-American Experience* (Bloomington: Indiana University Press, 1997), 147–73; Mattias Gardell, *In the Name of Elijah Muhammad: Louis Farrakhan and the Nation of Islam* (Durham, N.C.: Duke University Press, 1996), 47–118; and Ernest Allen Jr., "Minister Louis Farrakhan and the Continuing Evolution of the Nation of

Islam," in *The Farrakhan Factor*, ed. Amy Alexander (New York: Grove Press, 1998), 52–102.

3. The FBI was simply called the "Bureau of Investigation" when it was established during the Theodore Roosevelt administration. The word "Federal" was added in 1935. Athan G. Theoharis, ed., *From the Secret Files of J. Edgar Hoover* (Chicago: Ivan R. Dee, 1991), 1.

4. Until the early 1960s, the meeting places of the Nation of Islam were known as temples. Athan G. Theoharis and John Stuart Cox, *The Boss: J. Edgar Hoover and the Great American Inquisition* (Philadelphia: Temple University Press, 1988), 6–7; Robert A. Hill, *The FBI's RACON: Racial Conditions in the United States during World War II* (originally compiled by the FBI in 1943; reprinted, Boston: Northeastern University Press, 1995), 544–45; and Clegg, *An Original Man*, 20–40, 80–97.

5. Theoharis and Cox, *The Boss*, 6–7.

6. Frank Donner, *Protectors of Privilege: Red Squads and Police Repression in Urban America* (Berkeley: University of California Press, 1992), 70–71.

7. Ovid Demaris, *J. Edgar Hoover As They Knew Him: An Oral Biography* (New York: Carroll & Graf, 1975), 144; Theoharis and Cox, *The Boss*, 9–15, 259–60.

8. Kenneth O'Reilly, *"Racial Matters": The FBI's Secret File on Black America, 1960–1972* (New York: Free Press, 1989), 39–40; Clegg, *An Original Man*, 97–175 passim.

9. "Nation of Islam," September 18, 1961, sect. 6, pp. 2, 5 (Elijah Muhammad FBI file, 105 24822); O'Reilly, *"Racial Matters,"* 274–75.

10. Muhammad purchased the Phoenix home primarily to avoid Chicago winters, which worsened his bronchial asthma. "Justification . . . ," SAC Chicago to FBI Director, April 29, 1960, "June Mail," p. 4; "Justification . . . ," SAC Chicago to FBI Director, May 28, 1963, "June Mail," pp. 1–4 (E. Muhammad FBI file); Martin Waldron, "Muslim Wiretap Clarified by F.B.I.," *New York Times*, June 6, 1969, p. 24; Martin Waldron, "Wiretaps on Dr. King Made after Johnson Ban," ibid., June 7, 1969, p. 29; and Martin Waldron, "Clay Case Revises Eavesdrop Image," ibid., June 8, 1969, p. 29.

11. Elijah Muhammad, "Mr. Muhammad Speaks: The St. Nicholas Arena," *Pittsburgh Courier*, August 8, 1959, p. 14; "Ex-FBI Agent Says FBI against Negroes," *Muhammad Speaks*, July 1962, p. 21; "The FBI and Civil Rights—J. Edgar Hoover Speaks," *U.S. News & World Report*, November 30, 1964, p. 56; William C. Sullivan, *The Bureau: My Thirty Years in Hoover's FBI* (New York: Norton, 1979), 49; and "Our Day Is Near at Hand," *Muhammad Speaks*, March 13, 1964, p. 4. Interestingly, *Ebony* magazine, a black-owned publication based in

Chicago, featured favorable articles about African Americans in the FBI during the early 1960s. In a September 1962 piece, it called J. Edgar Hoover "a symbol of the robust, physically fit law enforcer with character and tact." Simeon Booker, "J. Edgar Hoover—The Negro in the FBI," *Ebony*, September 1962, p. 30. For the dramatic and laudatory story about Julia Clarice Brown, an African American housewife turned FBI "informant," in the Communist Party and suspected "Communist front groups," see "'I Was A Spy for the FBI': Housewife Bares Communist Plot to Infiltrate Civil Rights Organizations and Negro Churches," *Ebony*, March 1961, pp. 94–98, 100, and 102–3.

12. Around this time, under pressure from the Justice Department to hire an African American agent, Marlin Johnson promoted the office janitor, but employed him primarily as a personal chauffeur. "Nation of Islam," SAC Chicago to FBI Director, May 26, 1959, sect. 3, p. 2 (E. Muhammad FBI file); Bill Grady, "FBI Committed Burglaries Here, Ex-Agent Says," *Chicago Tribune*, February 2, 1979, p. 5; Report—"*Changed*: Elijah Poole," April 7, 1961, sect. 5, p. P* (E. Muhammad FBI file); "Nation of Islam," SAC Chicago to FBI Director, February 19, 1963 (W. D. Fard FBI file); Elijah Muhammad, "Beware of Phony Claims," *Muhammad Speaks*, August 16, 1963, p. 1; Jay R. Nash, *Citizen Hoover: A Critical Study of the Life and Times of J. Edgar Hoover and His FBI* (Chicago: Nelson-Hall, 1972), 151–52; and Clegg, *An Original Man*, 135, 174.

13. Report—"Malcolm K. Little," SAC New York to FBI Director, February 5, 1964, sect. 10 (Malcolm X FBI file), in Clayborne Carson, *Malcolm X: The FBI File* (New York: Carroll & Graf, 1991), 252–53; "FBI Director Hoover Hits Selfish Few," *Chicago Tribune*, November 25, 1964, p. 1; Clegg, *An Original Man*, 180–234; and Memorandum, SAC Chicago to FBI Director, January 22, 1969 (Black Extremists/Black Nationalist-Hate Groups FBI file, 100-448006), reprinted in Ward Churchill and Jim Vander Wall, *The COINTELPRO Papers: Documents from the FBI's Secret Wars against Dissent in the United States* (Boston: South End Press, 1990), 102.

14. Henry Hampton and Steve Fayer, *Voices of Freedom: An Oral History of the Civil Rights Movement from the 1950s through the 1980s* (New York: Bantam Books, 1990), 307, 527–28; Herbert Brean, "A Really Good Police Force," *Life*, September 16, 1957, p. 71; Donner, *Protectors of Privilege*, 90–154; Mike Royko, *Boss: Richard J. Daley* (New York: E. P. Dutton, 1971), 132–45; Milton L. Rakove, *Don't Make No Waves, Don't Back No Losers: An Insider's Analysis of the Daley Machine* (Bloomington: Indiana University Press, 1975), 257–66; Roger Biles, *Richard J. Daley: Politics, Race, and the Governing of Chicago* (DeKalb: Northern Illinois Press, 1995), 64–69, 139–66; and Frank Sullivan, *Legend: The*

Only Inside Story about Mayor Richard J. Daley (Chicago: Bonus Books, 1989), 85, 92, 125.

15. "'Be Polite, Courteous, Respectful': Detroit's Moslems Hear Talk," *Pittsburgh Courier*, January 18, 1958, p. 6; "Bury Slain Muslim in Simple Dignity," *Muhammad Speaks*, July 1962, p. 7; "Muhammad Calls for United Black Front," ibid., June 1962, p. 3; Hakim A. Jamal, *From the Dead Level: Malcolm X and Me* (New York: Random House, 1972), 220–24; and Benjamin Karim, *Remembering Malcolm* (New York: Carroll & Graf, 1992), 135–38.

16. Leon Forrest, *Relocations of the Spirit* (Wakefield, R.I.: Asphodel Press, 1994), 79; Sullivan, *Legend*, 205; "Police Guarding Muhammad's Home Here," *Chicago Tribune*, February 22, 1965, p. 2; Austin C. Wehrwein, "Muhammad Says Muslims Played No Part in Slaying," *New York Times*, February 23, 1965, p. 1; and Austin C. Wehrwein, "Muhammad Says Muslims Must 'Protect' Themselves," ibid., February 27, 1965, p. 10.

17. "The Secret Police in Chicago," *Chicago Journalism Review* 2, no. 2 (February 1969): 1, 7; Donner, *Protectors of Privilege*, 106.

18. Donner, *Protectors of Privilege*, 143–44; O'Reilly, "*Racial Matters*," 250; and "The Secret Police in Chicago," 7.

19. Memo—"Elijah Muhammad," May 20, 1960, sect. 5; F. J. Baumgardner to W. C. Sullivan, July 14, 1962, sect. 7; and "Nation of Islam," FBI Director to SAC Chicago, July 31, 1962, sect. 7 (E. Muhammad FBI file).

20. "Organizational Study" (1958?), p. 7 (Elijah Muhammad CIA file).

21. Donner, *Protectors of Privilege*, 143; Harry Kelly, "CIA's Illegal Spying Bared," *Chicago Tribune*, June 11, 1975, pp. 1, 5; Leonard Sykes Jr., "Link Cop, CIA Spying," *Chicago Defender*, May 10, 1978, p. 3.

22. "Committee Told Bias, Br[u]tality of L.A. Police," *Muhammad Speaks*, October 15, 1962, p. 3.

23. The congressional scrutiny of the Nation of Islam was motivated at least in part by a recent prison uprising in Washington, D.C., in which Muslim inmates were accused of being the instigators. "May Probe Muslims," *Chicago Defender*, August 4–10, 1962, p. 1; "House Rules Group Urges Inquiry on Black Muslims," *New York Times*, August 15, 1962, p. 29; "Black Muslim Inquiry Urged," ibid., August 29, 1962, p. 8.

24. "Attorney General Alert to Black Muslim Moves," *New York Times*, July 3, 1963, p. 10; Lee C. White (Assistant Special Counsel to the President) to Mildred Hull Ahlen, August 1, 1963, White House Name File, box 223, "Black M" folder, John Fitzgerald Kennedy Library, Boston. Hoover turned seventy on January 1, 1965. Theoharis, ed., *From the Secret Files*, 8n.

25. E. Muhammad, *Message to the Blackman*, 177–86.

26. "Immediately Discontinue . . . ," FBI Director to SAC Chicago, June 23, 1966, "June Mail" (E. Muhammad FBI file); Waldron, "Muslim Wiretap Clarified by F.B.I.," 24.

27. "Counterintelligence Program," FBI Director to SAC Albany, March 4, 1968, sect. 1, pp. 3–4 (Black Extremists/BNHG FBI file); "Hoover Finds Peril in New Left Action," *New York Times*, May 19, 1968, p. 1; and Churchill and Wall, *The COINTELPRO Papers*, 105–12.

28. "Counterintelligence Program," SAC New York to FBI Director, February 27, 1968, sect. 1, pp. 4–5; "Nation of Islam," SAC Chicago to FBI Director, April 22, 1968, sect. 2, pp. 2–7; "Counterintelligence Program," SAC Richmond to FBI Director, November 13, 1970, sect. 22, pp. 1–2 (Black Extremists/BNHG FBI file); "Two Blacks Come to Blows, a Melee Flares in Atlanta," *New York Times*, February 16, 1971, p. 37; "Report FBI OKd 2,300 'Dirty Tricks,'" *Chicago Tribune*, May 5, 1976, p. 10; Memo, SAC Chicago to FBI Director, January 22, 1969 (Black Extremists/BNHG FBI file), reprinted in Churchill and Wall, *The COINTELPRO Papers*, 102; Waldron, "Muslim Wiretap Clarified by F.B.I.," 24; and Waldron, "Clay Case Revises Eavesdrop Image," 29.

29. "FBI Wiretappers on Muhammad's Telephone," *Muhammad Speaks*, October 3, 1969, p. 5 (including illustration); Elijah Muhammad, "Mr. J. Edgar Hoover's Charges," ibid., May 31, 1968, p. 3; Elijah Muhammad, "Solve the Problem," ibid., November 7, 1969, pp. 16–17; and cartoon, ibid., October 22, 1969, p. 24.

30. William J. Grimshaw, *Bitter Fruit: Black Politics and the Chicago Machine, 1931–1991* (Chicago: University of Chicago Press, 1991), 115–40; Royko, *Boss*, 133–45; Rakove, *Don't Make No Waves*, 256–81; Biles, *Richard J. Daley*, 139–99, 221; Sullivan, *Legend*, 125, 167; and H. R. Haldeman, *The Haldeman Diaries* (New York: Berkley Books, 1995), 371–72.

31. The "mob action" statute was rescinded in March 1968. Jerry Lipson, "Fear and Force in Chicago," *The Reporter*, May 2, 1968, pp. 29–30; David Farber, *The Age of Great Dreams: America in the 1960s* (New York: Hill and Wang, 1994), 221–23; and Sullivan, *Legend*, 92.

32. "Cops Admit Destroying Spy Records," *Chicago Tribune*, October 27, 1976, p. 5; "U. S. Court Halts Further Destruction of Police Files," ibid., March 27, 1975, pp. 1, 15.

33. Philip Wattley and Robert Enstad, "Rochford Admits 'Spy' File," *Chicago Tribune*, March 26, 1975, p. 1.

34. Stanley Ziemba, "Daley Calls Spy Furor 'Political,'" *Chicago Tribune*, March 26, 1975, p. 4; "Chicago Police Used for Political Spying," ibid., June 19,

1977, p. 1; "Activists, Big and Small, in Police Files," ibid., June 20, 1977, pp. 1, 12; and "Police Spy Tradeoffs, Errors Make Big Trouble for Victims," ibid., June 22, 1977, pp. 1, 12.

35. "Police-Spying Curb Rejected by Senate Unit," *Chicago Tribune*, June 19, 1977, p. 18.

36. Clegg, *An Original Man*, 260–65; "Rare Interview with Messenger Muhammad!" *Muhammad Speaks*, January 28, 1972, p. 3; and James S. Tinney, "Black Muslims: Moving into the Mainstream?" *Christianity Today*, August 10, 1973, p. 44.

37. Theoharis and Cox, *The Boss*, 15; Daley's letter, *Muhammad Speaks*, April 12, 1974, p. 5; "The Achievements of Elijah Muhammad," *Christian Century*, March 26, 1975, p. 302; and "Daley Terms Muslim Leader's Death 'Loss,'" *Chicago Tribune*, February 26, 1975, p. 15.

38. Report—"Elijah Poole," November 29, 1974, sect. 15, p. 1a (E. Muhammad FBI file).

Part II

THE POLITICS OF
POLICE BRUTALITY

5

"What Did I Do to Be So Black and Blue?"*

Police Violence and the Black Community

KATHERYN K. RUSSELL

But that was not all there was to see.
—Toni Morrison, "Dead Man Golfing" (1997)[1]

Tyrone Guyton. This was the first name I connected with police brutality. Guyton was a fifteen-year-old Black boy who fled the scene of a robbery. He was shot in the back by a White police officer in Oakland, California, in 1973. I was twelve years old at the time. I knew Guyton had done something wrong, but even to my young mind, the punishment did not fit the crime. This was long before I was steeped in knowledge about police, race, and crime. Concepts such as "police brutality," "excessive force," "probable cause," and "racial profiling"—which I would later learn about in law school and in life—were unknown to me. Shot in the back by the police. I had a vague, yet distinct sense that a gross wrong had occurred. I did not know that Tyrone Guyton was just the latest in a centuries-long line of African Americans who had been killed by the police.

Twenty-six years later, reflecting on the ever-volatile relationship between the police and Black folks, I have a much clearer perspective. Even though the problem of police brutality is real, there remains a public haze, thick and oppressive, that surrounds the issue.

It is necessary to cut through this haze, chart a road map through the current discourse on police brutality, and in the process challenge what have been passed off as the social facts about police brutality. The above epigram by Toni Morrison concisely states the problem with mainstream analyses of police brutality and other race-related issues: they are narrow, one-sided, and ultimately misleading.

It's a Black thing. You wouldn't understand.

—popular 1980s slogan

There are some social terms and concepts that lose or gain currency over time. In some instances, the degree of the loss or gain is directly proportional to the term's "racial weight." This figurative weight is based upon how closely the public links a certain issue to a particular racial group.

Most people, for example, readily associate affirmative action with African Americans. Likewise, issues of race and crime almost never center on Whites and crime; rather, they typically refer to Blacks or Latinos and crime. This racial reductionism is nowhere more apparent than in media portrayals of welfare. The popular perception is that poor, lazy Black people are draining the nation's coffers with their monthly welfare checks.

Affirmative action, crime, and welfare have acquired their own racial baggage. More to the point, each has a Black weight. When an issue becomes a "Black thing"—something readily identified with Blacks and Blackness—a predictable set of events is set in motion. Like clockwork, the issue loses its public currency and is turned on its head. Once the issue becomes bogged down by Blackness, it quickly rises to the level of a serious social problem and, finally, leads to social, legislative, or political action (e.g., California's anti–affirmative action Proposition 209, President Clinton's "Mend it, don't end it" position on affirmative action).

The affirmative action debate offers the best example of this. Once the issue became characterized as a social policy set-aside for

Blacks, White males increasingly considered it a threat. The fact that White women were, and are, the primary beneficiaries of affirmative action programs carried no measurable weight. This led to the round of debates and discussions about the need for "color-blind," "race-neutral" legislation. Myths and anecdotes abounded that told of unqualified minorities who had taken jobs away from qualified Whites. Many Whites were said to have a brother or an uncle who lost out on a job or promotion (to which he was entitled) because his employer had to fill the position with a minority employee. A little thought, however, would have unmasked this argument as a numerical impossibility. How, in fact, could Blacks, Latinos, and Asians, who make up approximately 25 percent of the U.S. population, be responsible for "taking" jobs away from Whites, who constitute 75 percent of the U.S. population?

The process of recasting and relabeling social issues as Black problems, regardless of the established facts or findings, could be called empirical perversion. Debates about affirmative action, welfare, and crime fell prey to this game of racial twister. The same phenomenon is at work in the framing of police brutality. What was once a generic term used to describe police abuse against citizens has come to symbolize a confrontation between members of minority communities and the police.

Simply put, the public face of a police brutality victim is that of a young man who is Black or Latino. This racial link is the direct result of the disproportionately high number of Blacks and Latinos who have been assaulted by the police. Blacks report much higher rates of encounters with the police. For example, a 1997 household survey by the Justice Department found that Blacks and Hispanics were about 70 percent more likely to have had contact with the police than Whites. The survey also revealed that one-half of all the people who reported having been hit, pushed, choked, threatened with a gun, or restrained by a dog were Black or Hispanic.[2]

The racialization of police brutality has come at a high price. The fact that police brutality is represented as "Black" has relegated it to the bottom tier of social problems. A clear reflection of this is the public's yawning response to the escalating claims of police brutality offered by members of minority communities. Whether or not an issue is ghettoized has everything to do with how it is perceived. More troubling, the marginalization of police brutality may reflect a belief that there is something unique about Blackness that explains and justifies police abuse. This sends a subtle, yet clear, message: there is a reasonable link between Black skin and police assaults.

All told, the dismissal of police violence as a Black thing is not surprising. Historically, social problems that disproportionately affected Blacks were ignored. We need look no further than the sociopolitical inertia surrounding decisions to effectively address urban poverty and substandard inner-city schooling. The criminal justice system, courts in particular, has a dubious record of redressing its abuses against Black citizens. In fact, assaults against Black suspects have been at the core of seminal U.S. Supreme Court decisions—e.g., *Powell* v. *Alabama* (1932) and *Brown* v. *Mississippi* (1936). Racial scapegoating is not new. Contemporary examples of this age-old problem challenge us to ask, "How did we get here?" That is, how and why did we take this particular turn—a turn that results in collective fingerpointing aimed at Blacks?

Not only has police brutality been widely defined as a Black problem; it has been positioned as a problem for which Blacks are solely to blame. This sleight-of-hand reasoning mirrors arguments that have been offered to justify police practices that target minority citizens (e.g., "DWB"—Driving While Black). Some suggest that the disproportionately high levels of police abuse against Blacks and Latinos can be explained by their high rates of offending. Put another way, police brutality against Blacks and Latinos is dismissable as a byproduct of their high rates of involvement in crime.[3] The reasoning is as follows:

1. Blacks are disproportionately involved in street crime.
2. Police reasonably suspect that Blacks are involved in street crime.

3. Therefore, police are more likely to stop Blacks and, consequently,
   Blacks are more likely be victims of police brutality.

An unstated assumption of this deduction is that the high rate of
Black offenses gives police a legitimate basis for fearing Blacks. There
are several problems with this logic. Let's start with the most obvious. First, the argument is both circular and illogical. Blacks have
high rates of crime, therefore high rates of police abuse. End of story.
Where is the evidence that indicates that police violence against
minorities *is the result of* their high rates of offending? According to
this reasoning, all Blacks may be required to pay the debt incurred by
a tiny fraction of their group who are criminals. In this rigged lottery
system, Blacks always lose. This is not so much an argument as it is a
way of shifting blame.

This defensive chess move is reminiscent of an argument made by
James Q. Wilson after the 1992 Rodney King riots: if Blacks would
reduce their level of offending, White racism would decline.[4] This
statement raises as many questions as it answers. Applied to police
brutality, it suggests that Blacks must shoulder the entire burden of
solving the problem of police abuse. It implies that the police can
assault members of the Black community with impunity—that is,
until the rate of Black offending drops to zero.

A second, related objection to the above deduction is that it is
premised upon an argument of "statistical discrimination."[5] Blacks are
more likely to be targeted by the police than are members of other
racial groups because as a group they have high rates of involvement
in crime. Although racially disproportionate crime patterns are a
reality, it is not acceptable to use them as basis for public policy.
Taken to its logical limit, so long as Black offending rates are above
12 percent—the percentage of Blacks in the United States—it is per-
missible, in fact understandable, for the police to target, harass, abuse,
assault, and kill Black citizens. In other words, until there is a substantial reduction in the amount of crime committed by Blacks, all
Blacks should just accept that they too will be stereotyped as criminals and consequently may be assaulted, shot, or killed.

A look at the data on police killings indicates that the reality is more complicated than the attempts at racial finger-pointing would suggest. The table below provides figures for police killed in 1997:

Race of Killer

	Total	*White*	*Black*	*Other*
Police Killed by Citizens	71	35	29	7

Source: U.S. Department of Justice, "Law Enforcement Officers Killed and Assaulted," *Uniform Crime Reports* (1997).

As the above makes clear, most police officers who are killed by citizens are not killed by Blacks. This is not surprising, of course, considering that the majority of people police come in contact with are White.[6]

Given that police brutality is tacitly treated as a Black thing, the next question is, Why? The answer is that police brutality has not yet "crossed over," has not yet become an issue that concerns Whites as a group. Until police violence poses a threat to White communities, the threat of police violence to minority communities can easily be ignored.

The depth of this crossover problem is highlighted by the query "Where is the White Rodney King?" Is there a nationally known White victim of police brutality? Even in the absence of a White poster child for police brutality, where are the White victims on the local evening news? We rarely see victims of police assault who are White. Is it possible that there are no White victims of police assaults? This is implausible when we consider that each year Whites account for 67 percent of all arrests, indicating that every year millions of Whites come in contact with the police.

A second, more plausible response acknowledges that there are White victims of police brutality. For a variety of reasons, we are less likely to hear about these cases: police abuse cases with White victims are much less likely to raise issues of racism; police assaults against Whites are less severe than those against Blacks; Whites are less likely than Blacks to report incidents of police abuse; and Whites are less likely than Blacks to label police assaults as manifestations of "brutality," therefore, less likely to attract widespread media attention.

The Gidone Busch case provides a noteworthy example of this. On August 30, 1999, the mentally disturbed Busch was shot and killed by four New York City police officers. Law enforcement officers responded to neighbors' calls that Busch was praying loudly. According to police, Busch attacked them with a hammer. Police fired at Busch twelve times. News reports about the case have centered on his mental illness. Though there were explicit references to his religious faith, Orthodox Judaism, little attention was focused on his "Whiteness." No charges were brought against the officers.

What has to happen to get more Whites to view police brutality as their problem too? If there were five separate incidents involving the deaths of five innocent Whites at the hands of Black officers, it is easy to imagine the public outcry and concern. In the same way that the Littleton, Colorado, tragedy sparked a national conversation about school violence, a spate of White victims of police assault would likely be a catalyst for effective policy responses to the problem.

Our hands-off approach to police brutality stands in stark contrast to the empathetic treatment society usually reserves for innocent victims of crime. When blue crime is involved—unwarranted assaults by police officers against citizens—the reaction is different. We have the same litany of responses to minority claims of police abuse as we have to a next-door neighbors fight: let's not get involved; we really don't know what happened; let them work it out; there's probably a good reason that they were fighting; we don't know all of the facts; and it's none of our business. These types of rationales allow us to diminish the collective harm of police brutality. Police violence affects each of us, as individuals, as members of racial groups, and as members of society at large.

Interestingly enough, there are indicators that society's racial blinders are becoming much less effective at blocking out the problem of police brutality. There are clear signs that police violence is seeping into White consciousness. A winter 1999 issue of *The New Yorker* magazine indicates just how muted the racial lines around police brutality have become. The cover of the March 8 issue features a cartoon-like drawing of a White New York City police officer at a carnival shooting gallery. His gun, however, is not aimed at the usual suspects. It is pointed at White citizens, including a businessman talking on a cell phone, a small boy eating an ice cream cone, and an elderly woman hobbling along on a cane.

This magazine cover appeared in the aftermath of the Amadou Diallo case. In February 1999, Diallo was shot and killed by four members of the New York Police Department. Police fired forty-one bullets at the unarmed Diallo as he stood in his apartment vestibule. In effect, the magazine's cover announced that the NYPD had gotten so far out of control that even White people should be fearful. The message was that innocent White citizens might also be victimized by an out-of-control police force. It has taken several back-to-back, inexplicably excessive incidents of police force to shake some people out of their complacency. The public response to the Diallo and other cases supports the view that police abuse has to cross the racial void before it is perceived as a serious social problem.

> *Lamont*: Did you know that diabetes and heart disease are the leading killers of Blacks?
> *Fred*: I thought it was the police.
> —*Sanford and Son*, (TV series, ca. 1973)

For most of my life, I envisioned a lynching as a hanging. I visualized a Black man who had been rounded up by an angry mob of White vigilantes, who tortured him and, as their final act of indignity and domination, placed his head in a noose and hanged him. I was amazed to learn that there are more than a few ways to lynch someone. Beyond hanging, there is burning, beating, drawing and quartering, shooting, and dragging. Of course, a lynching victim might be subjected to a combination of these tortures. Common features of lynching cases include group participation in the death, which is motivated by twisted notions of justice or racial hatred.[7]

There has been a long-standing relationship between lynching and policing in Black communities. According to historical records, it was not uncommon for police officers to take part in the lynching ritual. Some of the well-known incidents of police brutality have the markings of a classic lynching. Examples include the cases of Jonny Gammage, Tyisha Miller, Malice Green, and Amadou Diallo. In 1995, Gammage was killed by Pittsburgh police following a traffic stop. Gammage, who was Black, was beaten and stomped to death by five White officers. The assault on Gammage was so brutal that it prompted one of the grand jurors to compare the case to a nineteenth-century lynching.[8] None of the officers were indicted, but they were subsequently fired.[9]

Given such violence, it is little wonder that for many Blacks police killings tap into long-held fears of unprovoked, random, brutal attacks, inexplicable except for their being of the wrong race, in the wrong place, at the wrong time. This historical legacy is directly linked to the visceral, negative reaction many Blacks today have toward the police. This fear, however, is not represented in mainstream portrayals of Black attitudes toward police.

Many Whites have no inkling of how afraid many Black people are of the police. The Black community's reaction to law enforcement is often presented in varying shades of bravado. This is particularly true for young, African American men. Media images, from the nightly news to rap videos, tend to portray a swaggering, "devil may care" Black male, ready to fight the police or anyone else who crosses his path.

A few years ago, I organized focus groups with young Black men who were college juniors and seniors. In describing their perceptions of the police, they did not actually use the word "fear." However, much of what they expressed were feelings of anxiety about the police. Many of the young men shared detailed stories of their encounters with the police. They described what it is like to be a member of a group that is under around-the-clock suspicion. One recounted his grandmother's warning "If I can't control you, the White man will."[10] There are, of course, a range of reactions to this reality, including anger, depression, and alienation.

The harsh truth is that young Black men have the highest probability of being stopped and, therefore, harassed by the police. This remains true whether they are driving while Black, walking while Black, running while Black, standing while Black, sitting while Black, bicycling while Black, or just being Black.[11] The ramifications of this social problem are magnified when we consider the predatory nature of the first interactions between Black men and the police. The "slave patrols," the earliest form of American policing, were designed to check and control Black movement. Southern White men, typically property owners, took rotating shifts to watch over Black slaves. These "paterollers" regularly inflicted corporal punishment to sanction errant slaves.

Furthermore, following emancipation, police also acted as silent partners in White attacks on Blacks. This frequently occurred in cases involving a Black man arrested on suspicion of sexually assaulting a White female. Sometimes a band of White men would *forcibly remove* him from police custody and exact their own brand of justice. The historical record is replete with instances where law enforcement officers winked, nodded, and enabled these assaults to take place. Given this brutal tradition, fear of the police is indelibly marked on the collective Black consciousness. Although this historical backdrop is rarely incorporated into mainstream analyses, its effect on contemporary sensibilities is readily apparent. Of course, this legacy coexists with the contemporary reality that police brutality is one of the many racial assaults that Blacks regularly face.

> Hey, did you see that?
> —response to the Roundabout dance

In far too many instances, an allegation of police violence is met with a series of predictable, you-can-set-your-watch-by-it, highly ritualized public responses. This is the police brutality dance or what I call the Roundabout. It is a lot like the cha-cha. Once you know the basic step, you have room to improvise. One version of the Roundabout goes like this:

- There is an incident of alleged police violence against a person of color.
- Expressions of outrage by members of the minority community are followed by calls for calm by the authorities (e.g., mayor, police chief).
- The authorities publicly classify the incident as an "aberration" and note that most officers do a good job and that the public should not rush to judgment.
- There are some attempts to portray the victim of the alleged police abuse as flawed or less than innocent. Attention may be drawn to a prior criminal record or the fact that the victim was engaged in deviant behavior at the time of the alleged assault.
- Community protests by the affected minority group (e.g., rallies) are met with further calls for calm by the authorities.
- A grand jury declines to issue a criminal indictment. No trial is held, and none of the officers involved in the assault is held accountable.

There are variations on these stages. For example, in a few instances the grand jury issues an indictment or the defendant enters a plea. Infrequently, the FBI intervenes. Case-specific variations notwithstanding, the fact remains that in most cases business as usual continues. Most problematic, the Roundabout—like the cha-cha, the hustle, the macarena, and the electric slide—simply repeats itself. Indeed, sometimes a new variation of the dance (another police assault against a person of color) begins before the prior routine has completed its course.

> I definitely do not like the Law.
> —Langston Hughes, *The Return of Simple* (1994)

In recent years, there have been several notorious cases involving a police assault against someone Black. As was noted earlier, well-known incidents include the Abner Louima case, in which police used a stick in a rectal assault (one officer, Justin A. Volpe, pled guilty during the trial; another, Charles Schwarz, was convicted of restraining Louima while Volpe sodomized him; two other officers, Thomas Wiese and Thomas Bruder, were acquitted); the Diallo case, in which four police officers fired forty-one bullets at Diallo as he stood in his apartment vestibule (the four officers were acquitted on all twenty-four charges against them on February 25, 2000); and the Tyisha Miller case, involving four policemen who fired eighteen shots, killing the unconscious woman as she sat in her car. The officers involved were not indicted, but subsequently fired.[12] These infamous incidents, however, obscure the more routine instances of police abuse—for instance, when a traffic stop is used to harass and berate citizens or when antiloitering laws are employed by police to target minority males.[13] It is such cases that account for the majority of police-minority interactions. They set the tone for the more egregious acts of police brutality.

Precious little attention—empirical, legal, political, or otherwise— is focused on the large-scale impact of this reality. What does it mean when a society ritually sacrifices the constitutional and civil rights of its racial minorities? Beyond the potential psychological consequences of such a decision, how does this reality influence the way members of other racial groups perceive Blacks? How does it shape how Blacks view themselves? How Blacks view Whites? Is it reasonable to expect that Blacks can and will shrug off this "Go directly to jail; do not pass go" mentality? Aren't we setting ourselves up for more racial grief and despair? As Randall Kennedy asks, what about the danger that "threatens all Americans when cynicism and rage suffuse a substantial sector of the community"?[14]

Most of us have watched passively as police brutality has more and more been framed as a Black issue. We have watched as variations of the Roundabout have been performed. We have observed incident after incident of police abuse. In fact, the number of cases we have read about, heard about, or experienced is mind numbing.

The toll of these incidents has been so overwhelming that it now takes a previously unimaginable police assault to rattle us. We are no longer shocked to learn that, in the hands of minorities, a candy wrapper, a key chain, or a cell phone may be fatally mistaken for a gun. This contemporary reality ensures that next week, next month, and next year, another twelve-year-old Black girl will hear about a police killing of a young Black man. It will be her Tyrone Guyton case. Only the victim will have a different name.

Notes

* Fats Waller and Andy Razaf (1930s blues classic).

1. Toni Morrison and Claudia Brodsky Lacour, eds., *Birth of a Nation'hood: Gaze, Script, and Spectacle in the O. J. Simpson Case* (New York: Pantheon, 1997), xxvii.

2. Bureau of Justice Statistics and the National Institute of Justice, *Police Use of Force: Collection of National Data* (n.p., 1997). It is noted that these data capture only one part of the picture. Some hard-to-count groups, such as homeless people, are underrepresented.

3. See, e.g., Jeffrey Goldberg, "The Color of Suspicion," *New York Times Magazine*, June 20, 1999, p. 51.

4. James Q. Wilson, "Race, Crime and Values," *Society* 91 (November–December 1992). For a full critique of Wilson's argument, see Katheryn K. Russell, *The Color of Crime: Racial Hoaxes, White Fear, Black Protectionism, Police Harassment and Other Macroaggressions* (New York: New York University Press, 1998), 124–28.

5. See, e.g., Michael Tonry, *Malign Neglect: Race, Crime and Punishment* (New York: Oxford University Press, 1995), 50: "Black Americans suffer from what social welfare scholars call 'statistical discrimination,' the attribution to individual persons of characteristics of groups of which they are members."

6. During the same period, law enforcement officers killed 353 citizens. FBI, *Uniform Crime Reports* (1997): 24 (racial breakdown of the victims was not available at submission).

7. Bureau of the Census, *Historical Statistics of the United States, Colonial Times to 1970*, pt. 1 (Washington, D.C.: U.S. Department of Commerce, 1975), 412.

8. See, e.g., "Coroner's Juror Compares Motorist's Death to a Lynching," *Washington Post*, November 15, 1995, p. A10.

9. *New York Times*, February 21, 1999.

10. Russell, *The Color of Crime*, 9.

11. Katheryn K. Russell, "'Driving While Black': Corollary Phenomena and Collateral Consequences," *Boston College Law Review* 40 (1999): 717–31.

12. *New York Times*, December 25, 1999, sec. A, p. 21; July 14, 1999, sec. A, p. 17.

13. See, e.g., *Chicago* v. *Morales*, 1999, No. 97-1121 (67 U.S.L.W. 4415).

14. Randall Kennedy, "Suspect Policy," *New Republic*, September 20, 1999, pp. 30–35.

6

Obstacle Illusions

The Cult of Racial Appearance

PATRICIA J. WILLIAMS

My friend Deborah was arrested in Chicago in the summer of 1999. Now, personally, I think Deborah, whom I've known since we were both students in law school some twenty-five years ago, is about as unlikely a suspect as you could find. After all, she's a law professor, a commercial expert lawyer, the coauthor of a textbook in contract law, and, to top it all off, a grandmother.

But here's how it happened. She was sitting in her car at a gas station, when out on the street she saw two policewomen searching a car and patting down two girls and two boys who appeared to be Latino. As she put it, "My son, who wears his hair in dreadlocks, was stopped on his way back to school after spring break because the light over his license plate was out. I didn't know why these teenagers had been stopped but it couldn't hurt to sit there, on private property, and just watch." But one of the policewomen saw her looking, came over, and ordered her to leave.

"I said very politely, 'I'd rather not.'"

A second cruiser was summoned, and Deborah was taken from her car, handcuffed, driven down to the station, and chained for hours to a bench. She was finally released on her own recognizance at one in the morning, with three charges lodged against her. The first was failing to wear a seatbelt. ("The car was stopped," she protested.) The second was described on the citation as "OBEDI-ENCE TO POLICE"—in big block printing as though to underscore the heart of the matter—followed, in parentheses, by the actual charge, "obstructing a driveway." The third claim was that Deborah had failed to register with the Illinois Secretary of State. (At the time, Deborah, a resident of New York, was teaching as a visitor at a Chicago-area university for one semester. The statute in question—who knew?—apparently requires anyone residing in Illinois for longer than ten days to register herself.)

Deborah is a child of the Civil Rights movement who, like me, came of age in a time when court watching and arrest witnessing were considered civic responsibilities as important as voting. "I tried to explain to the officers why I wanted to stay and watch. I guess I badly underestimated the touchiness of the police on the subject. But I hardly thought I would be arrested just for having an opinion."

Deborah paused as she told me the story, then laughed. "Oh, and then there was this really strange moment when the arresting police-woman was filling out one of several attempted reports of the inci-dent that she completed and then ripped up. Finally, she turned to me and asked with exasperation, 'What are you?'"

Deborah has one of those visages that suggests an ethnically, reli-giously, and racially diverse range, shall we say, of political possibility. "African American," said Deborah.

The policewoman, who appeared to be White, seemed incredu-lous and grew even more annoyed. "Why do you care what happens to Latinos?" She snapped.

With that, Deborah ended her tale on a note of resignation: "I decided that silence was the more prudent course."

About two weeks after Deborah was arrested, the Supreme Court of the United States handed down its decision in the case of *Chicago* v. *Morales*. In a 6–3 opinion, the court struck down Chicago's broadly worded antiloitering statute, allowing, as the *New York Times* con-cisely put it, "police to arrest anyone, who refusing an order to move on, remained 'in one place with no apparent purpose' in the presence of a suspected gang member."[1] It is good news, this ruling, but I am also a dissent watcher, particularly when the minority is composed of consistently conservative ideologues whose numbers could grow under a Republican president. So I paid close attention when Justice Antonin Scalia, who dissented, described his feelings from the bench: "I would gladly trade my right to loiter in the vicinity of a gang member in return for the liberation of my neighborhood in an instant."

Should Justice Scalia's view ever become the law of the land (rather than just practice, however prevalent), perhaps then it would become clear what is at stake when we do not care about Latinos, about poor African Americans, and about minorities who may one day find themselves in the majority. For the "right to loiter" is also about the right to stand in one place and just be; it is the right to look, listen, and witness. When we "trade" away that right, we effectively relinquish the ability to disagree in an orderly, political, and public manner. If indeed Justice Scalia's neighborhood is ever so "liberated," I hope that he—in fact, that we all—do not find ourselves regretting what has been purchased by such loss.

One of the most troubling parts of Scalia's pronouncement is that it doesn't address little matters of who gets defined as a "gang member," nor does it specify the point at which we might consider ourselves sufficiently "liberated" to allow random meandering on the public streets again. I guess I can't help thinking of the town of Littleton, Colorado, a very wealthy community that many would assume is pretty "gang free." Yet in the wake of the horrific events at Columbine High School in May of 1999, it might be fruitful to rethink what makes some people look dangerously "suspect," no matter how exemplary their behavior, while others bask in such benefit of the doubt that they can "con" others literally to death.

I don't presume to have any great comprehension of the madness in Littleton. But for what it's worth, here are a couple of things I will say. First, if gang members are often thought to identify themselves by wearing uniform clothing or headbands or tattoos, then Columbine High School must have had a ton of gangs—particularly if one thinks of gang "colors" as a kind of brand name. Indeed, the so-called "trench coat Mafia" appeared to be the only group at the school untethered to a corporate logo. The whole school seemed divided not just by personality or activity, like an athlete, but each group was clustered around a brand name, like pathetic little territorial flags. The nation-state of Gap over here. The empire of Abercrombie and Fitch. The tattered loincloths of the low-status K-Mart tribesmen, the Timberland types, and the Tommy Hilfigers. *Not* that this is a shallow matter of social demarcation. Consider the complications of Tommy Hilfiger alone; a white designer of colorfully preppy, Ralph Lauren–ish clothing who became wildly popular among Black teens. So many Black kids tried to "style" with Hilfiger's increasingly oversized logo that it soon became known as a black label. At which point, of course, it enjoyed renewed popularity among young White men hoping to look like rap stars. This is the sort of thing that has prompted some analysts to speak of the need for school uniforms. While I don't think uniforms will get at the underlying status anxiety, when listening to legions of traumatized adolescents speak—as though with designer clothing they had bones, volume, presence—one definitely got the urge to wrap them all in a sack cloth. There was a chilling *Amityville Horror* sort of conformity to their corporate allegiance that reminded me not so much of other recent school shootings as of the thirty-nine middle-aged, mostly White, clonish computer wizards of the Heaven's Gate cult— remember them?—the ones who committed suicide wearing purple shrouds and new black Nikes (Nike, I recall, issued a weird but very legalistic statement disclaiming any role in the suicide pact).

What an odd touch, those sneakers. Nike is so hyped as the brand of choice for inner-city youth that its name has become almost synonymous with thwarted Black male aspiration—broken hoop dreams of dribbling one's life course into alignment with a multimillion-dollar contractual rocket ship headed for the golden ether of some outer space. Young Black men found shot dead are always imagined to be wearing Air Jordans on their splayed, helpless, and upturned feet.

Consider the implications in another context: consider Federal District Court Judge Stanley Sporkin's ruling in 1998 striking down State Department "profiles" of foreign visa applicants that were actually based on skin color, ethnicity, looks, speech, and—remarkably enough—fashion sense. Judge Sporkin struck down State Department guidelines that explicitly encouraged "special handling" of those from Black areas and of those with Arab, Chinese, and Korean surnames. State Department manuals suggested abbreviations by which to sort applications, such as "RK = rich kid, LP = looks poor, TP = talks poor, LR = looks rough, TC = take care." The more dutiful consular agents justified rejections of applicants with such additional notations as "Slimy looking," "wears jacket on shoulders w/earring," and "No way . . . Poor, poor, poor."

Perhaps the State Department's bias is one to which Americans— fox smart, self-taught, and terribly insecure—may be peculiarly susceptible: we are afflicted with the class-jumping, hyper-vigilance of the embarrassed former peasant, trying to suppress the truth of exuberant family origins, when what is at stake is not a broken rule of etiquette but an entire sense of belonging in a yearned-for world.

The ritual dismissiveness of those "beneath" on the social ladder (however defined) too frequently mirrors the internalized admonishment of the anxiously newly arrived—right fork anxiety, left foot-in-mouth, the merciless rush to judge others because one's own humiliation is preordained. The self betrays itself when trying hardest. For the real rules are silent, so thoughtless, small as a detail—an earring, an inflection?—yet a matter of birthright, imparted in the nursery, hoarded until the grave.

This kind of class consciousness is troubling not only because of its overtness but because of its insistent orderliness, its authoritarian demand of obedience; it is troubling precisely because of the polite cleanliness of its cruelty. As Americans, we abandoned much of the sycophancy of European social hierarchy as a constitutional matter. But race has always been the great stumbling block to our most perfect union, and ever since the outlawing of explicit racial discrimination, economic classification seems to have reemerged as a kind of cipher for race, for ethnicity, for all manner of historic shortcoming. We are still a nation in which so many of the right things count—the rules for entries into most ordinary social realms are not unduly layered with arcane gestures of empty courtliness. But the ongoing imperative of the Civil Rights movement urges us well beyond the abolition of Jim Crow. As we reconstitute ourselves into a new global economic order, what some have called "nobility," we must be mindful of the mannerist's protean capacity for a barbarian's horde of resentments.

So. Let me shift gears and return to the Littleton tragedy. I want to go back and make a second observation about the dynamic there. I want to draw attention to the strikingly consistent protestations of the residents of Littleton, Colorado, in the immediate wake of the shooting: "it couldn't happen here," "we're not that sort of people," and so repeatedly, so unself-consciously, "this is not the inner city." (As certainly it was not. There were so few minorities among Columbine High School's two thousand impressively blond students that although the gunmen claimed they were aiming for minorities, it looked to me as though they ended up including in that category all the brunettes in town.)

The national conversation about "What went wrong?" pinned down the coordinates of our monstrous affliction of violence: Bombs on the Internet! Violent Videos! Single Mothers! Authoritarian Fathers! Guns! And, amazingly enough, Not Enough Guns!

If the denizens of the inner city, in particular young Black men like Amadou Diallo and a now heavenly host of others, have been made so fearsomely "suspect" that their reaching for their wallet can provoke a panic of "preventative" killing, privileged young Whites often seem to stumble through life as the victims of what I'll call innocent profiling. Dylan Klebold and Eric Harris seem to have been shrouded in presumptions of innocence—even after professing their love for Hitler, declaring their hatred for Blacks, Asians, and Latinos (on a public Web site no less), downloading instructions for making bombs, accumulating ingredients, assembling them under the protectively indifferent gaze (or perhaps with the assistance) of parents and neighbors, stockpiling guns and ammunition, procuring hand grenades and flak jackets, threatening the lives of classmates, killing thirteen and themselves, wounding numerous others, and destroying their school building. Still, the community couldn't seem to believe it really happened "here."

Still, their teachers and classmates all continued to protest that they were good kids, good students, solid citizens. Even their probation officers (assigned after Klebold and Harris were caught burgling a car) had released them to their parents while praising them as intelligent young men with lots of promise.

What is the force that drives this willful game of blindman's buff, this devotion to "mystery" and disbelief?

There was quite an astonishing little item in the paper recently about the sort of thing that makes me glad I grew up in the inner city: that is, the national proliferation of "assassination games" among mostly White, suburban, middle-class and upper-class youth. High school students across the country, even in the wake of Littleton, organize mock war games as a rite of passage—or of spring. "A.P. Assassination" is what one school in exclusive Westport, Connecticut, calls the hunting season that begins right after Advanced Placement testing. For approximately three weeks, students track one another around town with toy guns (at one school, five actual car crashes were attributed to the chase). The student left standing after this grueling process of elimination "wins." One exuberant eighteen-year-old who aspires to be a physics professor dismissed criticism as politically correct overreaction and likened the game to "playing cowboys and Indians" (no Indians were apparently available for comment).

As I read about this, it began to dawn on me why perhaps all those kids in Colorado could go on and on about how "normal" Eric Harris and Dylan Klebold were. I began to appreciate why the authorities might find it hard to pick out any further suspects from a student body whose poetic sensibility is suffused with the metaphors of blood lust. (Although . . . you've got to wonder . . . if "assassination games" were played in the inner city, I wonder whether those same authorities wouldn't have cordoned off entire neighborhoods?) Police have gone door-to-door searching people for less in Black neighborhoods—I remember the three thousand police sent to surround the few hundred people who showed up for the admittedly vile Mr. Khalid Muhammad's "Much-Less-Than-a-Million-Youth-March" in Harlem.

I think of the long tragic history of what happens to minority kids who wave toy guns in public. I think about Dylan Klebold tooling around Littleton in his BMW with its trunk full of bombs, and I can't help thinking about the Black dentist in New Jersey who was stopped by the highway patrol more than one hundred times in four years, before he finally traded in his BMW for something that was more drably utilitarian.

I don't know. Perhaps the power of what we call the normative to induce moral blind spots can be appreciated for its depth and complexity only when the world for some reason gets turned completely upside down. Perhaps, after all, it is not accidental that so many of these school shootings seem to occur in communities whose populations "fled" to the suburbs to "escape." Places where residents have been socialized to think of themselves in such automatic oppositions to "inner cities" and imagined "bad neighborhoods." Perhaps it is not surprising that the disgruntled children of such invested fears would choose to act out their community's worst fantasies by this sad, sad minstrelsy-in-overdrive. These sad White children rendering incarnate the ultimate black-masked, black-cloaked Superpredators Whose Guns Are Bigger Than Yours. As William Blake described such a psychic state,

> *The Bat that flits at close of eve*
> *Has left the brain that won't believe.*
> *The Owl that calls upon the night*
> *Speaks the unbeliever's fright.*

NOTES

1. *New York Times*, June 27, 1999, sec. 4, p. 4.

What's New? The Truth, As Usual

STANLEY CROUCH

Recent events such as the sodomizing of the Haitian immigrant Abner Louima by the New York police officer Justin A. Volpe in a Brooklyn station house make it very obvious that brutal acts by those who go to work with badges and guns must not be taken less than seriously. Bigotry and excessive force have been problems stretching across the history of how those in law enforcement respond to Black Americans. The numbers of those who have been mistreated, framed, crippled, and killed would be sobering if we went far back enough, and the feeble ways in which our system traditionally handled these cases might bring on a melancholic or bitter or angry mood, if not a feeling made up of all of those emotions. Negroes, quite simply, had a hard way to go when it came to authority and the meting out of both justice and injustice.

Beyond the racial angle, Americans have always resented police abuse. One of the things that distinguishes this nation from most places in the world is that the individual in the street has, over the long haul, gotten more and more respect from those who enforce the law, whether that person is rich or poor or in between. That is due not to sweetness in the halls of power but to agitation and the ongoing scrutiny of the press that is basic to our form of government, which has a built-in suspicion of power and functions with a certainty based in the human condition, a certainty that demands vigilance because of the inevitable twisting, bending, and breaking of the rules by some of those in stations of authority, elected and not.

I know a bit about this sort of thing. Almost thirty-five years ago, my younger brother, who was then about sixteen and liked to heckle and harass police officers whenever he had the chance, was standing outside of my mother's home in what is now called South Central Los Angeles, where the big riot of 1965 had taken place a year or two before. Two White cops were pursuing a Negro guy in a stolen vehicle who jumped out of the car, ran up the driveway, and disappeared over the fence into the next block. My brother was outside on the grass and began laughing at the cops and making fun of them when they came back from the chase with no suspect in cuffs.

According to the buddy of his who was with my brother, one of the cops got very angry and started talking to my brother as though he would arrest him if he didn't shut his trap. That wasn't my brother's way. He loved to poke at a lion through the bars of his cage, even if the cage was unlocked. His assumption was that, if the lion broke loose, fate would play a card in his favor and vanquish the beast. It had before, when he hosed down a couple of plainclothes cops with whom he got into an angry verbal exchange, as they were walking away. That was not long after the Watts riot, which made White cops wary of getting into physical confrontations during the day, while neighborhood people were looking on. This, however, took place perhaps a year later and at night. The rules were different. My brother, long, lean, and, from his point of view, deliciously arrogant, told the two police officers that they were on private property and needed go somewhere and see if they could catch somebody guilty of a crime before the night was over. That snapped it. The angry cop jumped him, and the two were tussling on the ground when I was called out of the house to see what was going on.

When they got up, the small blond cop with molten blue eyes was saying, "You're going to jail." My brother, meanwhile, was saying that he hadn't done anything and that he wasn't going anywhere. When the cop lunged at him again, my brother ran up the steps of the house, pushing some chairs behind him and throwing a flashlight at the cop's head, which missed its flesh-and-blood target. The blond one's partner was an older cop. Throughout the whole scuffle and during the shouting, he had been trying to calm things down and moved around to the back of the house to see whether my brother was fleeing that way. He wasn't; he was inside.

My mother, hearing all the commotion and trying to make sense of my brother's absolute rage, was alarmed now. When I went into the house, she wanted to know what happened. The cops remained in the front yard talking. The one struggling with my brother was hopped up; the older cop was calm but seemed caught in the middle of something he would have preferred to be out of. Both were eyeing the front door. Then they came to the steps.

As my mother talked to the older cop, the younger one, still saying my brother was going to jail, put his foot in the door so that it couldn't be closed. The two cops wanted her to send my brother out. While this talk was going on, back and forth, with my brother standing behind my mother and me, cop cars arrived in swarms on the street and the blue wave started trotting up the walkway to the porch. Before anything else could be said, they had swept through the door and grabbed my brother. They pushed him backwards— from the dining room to the living room and past a bedroom and the bathroom—all the way into the kitchen, where he began resisting, screaming for them to take their hands off of him. Having followed this blue-and-white burst of muscle, leather, pistols, and helmets into the kitchen, I watched with my mother as a couple of cops, their hands on their guns, held us at bay. The others were really putting it on my brother—billy clubs and fists—snatching him by the hair, snapping on handcuffs, and dragging him back to the front door of the house, onto the porch, and into one of the cars. With the whole mess of cops gone, sharp tweaks of violence remained in the air.

My brother was supposed to be arraigned in juvenile court on the following Thursday, which was a few days away. When my mother, our lawyer, and I got there, we were told that he couldn't be brought to court, because of a mixup. According to my brother, they had beaten him so badly that his destination on the night of the arrest had been changed en route. The two cops who were transporting him took a look at all the proof of excessive force and, intending to protect their fellow peace officers, erased the original destination on the transferal document and entered that of a facility where he couldn't be photographed. As they arrived there with him, he recalled, the guy reading the document laughed about their changing it and they all chuckled together conspiratorially. The reason why he wasn't in court when he should have been was that there was a holiday that Friday, which made it a long weekend. By Monday, his bruises would have gone down enough to corroborate the official version of the arrest and the struggle, not his.

In juvenile court, my brother was found guilty of assault with a deadly weapon—the thrown flashlight that had missed the hot-headed officer—and resisting arrest. An ample number of neighborhood witnesses had seen the whole business in front of the house, the younger cop arguing with my brother and then leaping on him, which clarified how out of control he had become under the weight of his own anger. That didn't do it. While the older cop, who was obviously conflicted, couldn't go so far as to say that he had seen the flashlight bounce off the face of his partner, he did lie in his testimony and say that his fellow peace officer had sustained an easily observable bruise beneath one of his eyes from the assault. Along the way, it didn't help that the lone judge deciding the verdict in juvenile court wasn't really a trained jurist and didn't take too well to our lawyer's pointing out a number of things he had to look up in the law book on his desk. Nor did he like it when my brother's version of the incident was read in court and he referred to the officer who had attacked him as "a pure one, with blond hair and blue eyes." The air was soon heavy with the smell of a goose cooked in excrement. The White folks had done it again.

I was told by another lawyer at the time that it would have been rough on the older officer if he had not backed his partner and instead told the truth. The LAPD was supposed to have had ways of disciplining those who refused to adhere to the idea that the police were the thin blue line between civilization and chaos, which meant that you did not go against your partner over something as trivial as smacking someone around who didn't know when to keep his mouth shut. In fact, a few years before my brother's trouble, a veteran cop I had met in downtown Los Angeles was directing traffic and being moved from one intersection to another all day, which required him to quick-step his way in order to avoid being written up for doing a bad job. He was White and had intervened one night in his station house when a prisoner was getting roughed up. Soon after that, he was out of a squad car and back on his feet as a traffic cop.

Three years later, I too was picked up outside my apartment house and taken to the station, supposedly because I talked too much stuff when the light was shone in my eyes. While I was being booked, a drunken Mexican guy in a cell was going on about how Colorado, Texas, New Mexico, Arizona, and California were rightfully the land of Mexico. This was the late sixties, and the imperial histories of non-European countries—including slavery, female genital mutilation, foot-binding, and slaughters of the innocent—were less important than similar things, or exactly the same things, in Western countries such the United States. What the guy was proclaiming had been said many, many times but, as we learned, could have an irritating sting. You people have it now, all these states, you know, all of this land, he continued, but someday, *someday*. A small White officer with dark hair and a dark mustache said that he had heard enough. He took off his gun, put it on his desk, and opened the cell. The Mexican lifted up his dukes and stepped out, expecting a chance to let the gringo have it. The cop gave him the first martial arts drop kick to the head I had ever seen. When the man went down, the peace officer continued beating and kicking him for a while. Then, satisfied, he dragged the prisoner back into the cell, straightened himself up, and went back to work. If anything, I was sure the Mexican would be charged with assaulting a police officer and there would be plenty of uniformed witnesses to back the story.

In Los Angeles, things historically were that way because, on one plane, the police force has long been too small: the very large number of people it had to handle stretched out over a sprawling landmass.

As in imperial Rome at the height of its expansion, the sea of authority was broad but not very deep. That had become the burden of law enforcement in an enormous two-story town. The tactic that evolved into convention was to intimidate with confident ferocity so that the people would never think too much about how many more of them there were than cops. A protocol existed to end all disagreements by immediately arresting the apparent troublemakers or disputants and leaving the area in a puff of exhaust. Such tactics helped avoid small riots and made people think twice about arguing with a member of the LAPD. Another problem in Los Angeles, at least from a racial perspective, was that the police were often recruited from the South, as they were in Oakland, California, where the Black Panthers made their name. Southern cops and Negroes were not always a good mix. When things got nasty and the smoke cleared or calm had returned, those who bore the greatest part of the burden were not the ones who wore the badges.

That is, even so, only part of the story. Over the last thirty years, much has changed for the better. We have seen more than a few cases in which police officers who had stepped across the line in dealing with Black people were brought to justice, sometimes many years after an incident. We have recently had to soberly look at the corruption in the Philadelphia Police Department that, uncovered, might result in hundreds of inmates being released from prison because of planted evidence. In New York, just a few years ago, we saw Francis X. Livoti found not guilty in a criminal trial for the wrongful death of Anthony Baez, whom he killed by using a chokehold that the NYPD had outlawed. We also saw Livoti investigated by the department, fired after the findings came in, and called an unapologetic disgrace to law enforcement by Howard Safir, the commissioner of police. Finally, Livoti was found guilty of trampling on Baez's civil rights, and he now sits behind bars. In the Louima case, the fellow officers of Justin Volpe testified quite strongly against him; the accused then changed his plea and confessed to having sodomized Louima with a stick. Volpe was sentenced to thirty years in prison. Louima, as things go, will become some version of a millionaire when his suit against the City of New York is resolved. That's a very hard way to make a buck, but, as we all know, in Haiti, where Louima is from, there would have been no case at all.

That is exactly why the alienation between the police and the community has a very serious genesis. I heard it put most eloquently when I was a member of the task force that Mayor Rudolph Giuliani appointed soon after the Louima case became front-page news in and out of New York. In a meeting at City Hall in which a cross section of Brooklyn's Haitian community was invited to talk with and be questioned by Giuliani, Safir, and the task force, a noble and voluptuous woman in her forties said that *whenever* a police officer commits a brutal, justified act against a citizen, there is a very deep feeling of betrayal—betrayal by one who is supposed to be on your side, working to protect you from the anarchy of the criminal world.

That sense of betrayal, she said, does not deny the greater danger of criminals but brings with it a different kind of hurt, a disillusionment and a resentment. One might conclude that such incidents have created a predictable set of rhetorical flourishes in which, exaggeration being the demon that it always is, police are depicted as the central danger to life and limb in the black community. I don't believe that. Something else is going on when we hear such distortions, since people actually know better, even those who you assume would take the conventional liberal position of totally condemning law enforcement. For instance, Senator Dianne Feinstein, of California, who is not a card-carrying but a billboard-carrying liberal, cosponsored in 1999 the Violent and Repeat Juvenile Offender Accountability and Rehabilitation Act (S254)[1] because, over a two-year span, more than three thousand Californians had lost their lives as a result of gang-related violence.

This statistic reflects a situation we can only look at in horror. Let me give you a historical comparison. Between the end of Reconstruction in 1877 and the turn of the century in 1900, there were three thousand lynchings, the highest number in the history of the country. This period witnessed the most sustained brutality experienced by Negroes outside of slavery (an institution, by the way, that would not have countenanced the killing of what were considered three thousand rather valuable work animals; more often than not, other measures would have been taken). So, in sunny California, the activities of Black and Mexican gangs resulted in more people's being murdered over a two-year period in this state alone than were lynched over a thirty-year period in the entire country.

How do these kinds of body counts compare with the numbers of so-called minority citizens who meet their ends through police homicides? Well, on the average, in even the largest cities, police homicides average between fifteen and thirty people annually. This is fifteen to thirty people too many, but ten to twenty times fewer than the number of civilians murdered by those who do not wear badges.

Does this mean that, when the cops go across the line, we should just look at some statistics and forget about it? Not at all. What it means is that we need new angles of discussion; and we have to face the fact that antipathy between the community and the police works to the advantage of criminals with and without badges. A gang-banger or a dope dealer or a rapist or any other kind of criminal enjoys much better odds against being removed from the streets when the people and the police distrust or dislike each other. This is equally true of the rogue cop, who is clearly no more than another kind of criminal. The community bad guy and the bad guy in law enforcement can both count on that alienation working in their favor, since the community will not cooperate with the police, and the other cops, feeling that the community hates them anyway, will neither take the actions certain situations call for nor speak up when they see one of their own do something disgraceful. So the worst among both groups are liberated.

The problem continues because those who claim to speak for the community do not at all give an accurate report of community attitudes. When I was on the post-Louima task force appointed by Mayor Giuliani to examine police-community relations, I was confronted by the same attitudes that I had encountered talking with Negroes in high-crime communities across this country for the last twenty-five years. A common complaint made by the community residents was that their male children suffer greater risk of being harmed by the police than by anyone else. They say that when their sons leave home, they hope and pray that the young men will not be shot dead by police officers. When one moves the questions up into the arena of specificity, they admit that far, far more kids have been killed by other kids than by the police and that their largest fear is actually that their children, male *and* female, might become gunshot victims of gang violence, intentionally or accidentally. The next point they make is that they want the bad cops removed from their communities as soon as possible—yesterday, in fact, if anyone could bring that off. Then, given the ways in which their lives are oppressed by crime and violence within their communities, they go on to say that they want *more* police. Right: *more* police.

Is this because Negroes are confused? Not exactly. What happens in our society is that many of us repeat what we have heard over and over, even if it doesn't actually apply to us. Pavlovian recitations. Yet few of us are so removed from our own realities that we cannot be reminded of what we actually think and feel and have experienced. For instance, no one hates violent Black youth criminals more than Black youth, because these knuckleheads are the people who might attack or kill a kid for something as trivial as "eye fornication"—looking at them in a way that they don't like. These are the people who bring unrest to school campuses and who, as reported by my daughter, who was at a 1994 party in Los Angeles, angrily went out to their car, removed their pistols, and shot through the windows because they weren't invited and weren't allowed in to the event. Such violence, I maintain, has created learning difficulties among some of the Black kids in Chicago whose defensive brains now retain only as much as necessary because of the great hurt experienced through the trauma of witnessing someone wounded or killed by a firearm. The stories go on. That is why no one hates these people more than do other young people from the same backgrounds. What all of those young people know is that the overwhelming majority of them don't brutalize or murder other people, which is why they don't buy all of the sociological mumbo jumbo. *If more than 90 percent of us can come through this and not sink down into this kind of buck wild behavior, they could, too—IF they wanted to act right.* That is the attitude one encounters from coast to coast, and it is quite reasonable. In short, barbaric behavior is the result of more than poverty or the problems that can arrive as a result of skin color.

But let us look at how things actually occur when young Black men are stopped and searched by the police. From the perspective of the cop, the idea is that if a kid who *looks* as if he's carrying an illegal gun is stopped, searched, and arrested because the kid *is* armed, the case might be thrown out of court on the basis of insufficient probable cause. But it is justified by the fact that one more potential murder weapon will be off the streets. Shouting about such harassment by those who purport to hold the freedoms of our system quite high are not to be ignored. That is why the cops know they will be lectured in court for stopping those guys and hope that, on a good day, both the kid and the next gun he has might be removed from circulation. They don't assume that any circumstances other than the martial law attending a riot will make it acceptable for them to stop young guys on the basis of "a gut feeling." They see this as an expedient way to address a problem that has *everyone* climbing the walls, especially those who are usually the receiving ends of the bullets, so-called minorities themselves. In short, this is a nonviolent way of handling violent people.

What community people think about this tactic is fairly consistent. You hear the same thing over and over. As one example, a cab driver in East New York—one of the most crime-plagued areas of the city before the cops clamped down—told me that he was glad the cops were putting so much pressure on the kids out in the street. He no longer heard gunfire all night and had overheard a number of them say that they had stopped carrying their pistols into the streets for fear of an automatic year in jail if the issue of probable cause worked against them. Were the police to pull him over and search him from out of the blue, his tune might change, or it might not.

Another element of law enforcement that Black, brown, and yellow people have known for some time is that the most dangerous cop is one of their own on a bad night. It doesn't seem to matter what the racial composition is, either. It used to be that there was surely no rougher police officer than the Black one coupled with a White partner. This guy could go out of his way to prove that he wasn't showing any favoritism, which amounted to treating a Negro worse than he might be treated by a Day-Glo redneck. Two Black cops working together usually had no patience whatsoever for any line of jive and were known for whipping heads when they didn't like what they heard or were suspicious of what they saw. Although there are now organizations for cops who are not White, those kinds of encounters, like those between White cops and Black people, have in general not gone away, simply because those ethnic groups have complaints about the racial nature of behavior in the departments across the nation.

What is needed now, as much as it ever has been needed, is a strong alliance between the civilians and the police. In New York, at the Police Academy, one can attend classes and watch all the role-playing cops who now recognize they must learn how to deal with many different cultural attitudes in order to keep things from boiling over into chaos or physical force. Cops of different ethnic backgrounds conduct classes and help these trainees come to understand that loud talk doesn't always mean the approach of violence and that one has to develop ways of speaking to people that lower the intensity and defuse prickly situations. The same is true in firearms tactics, which is taken very seriously. The types of drills rookies are taken through demand solid thinking on one's feet. None of these things, however, will eliminate the arrival of the bad cop any more than genius IQs and affluence prevented Leopold and Loeb from murdering their cousin.

But if police departments make community relations a central function of each precinct house, allowing precinct commanders to have highly visible feelers in the community who go about the job of discerning how each neighborhood works and developing relationships of respect and trust with community leaders, we might finally see a reduction of the double alienation that works against the quality of civilization. It is imperative that we have police. It is imperative that the people the police are hired to serve and protect become so confident in law enforcement that they fully cooperate with those who have what is possibly the most demanding, noblest occupation. Full cooperation is surely something like a golden dream, but so, after all, is the idea of justice. We must persist in attempting to get closer to that dream, which is the ultimate identity of our democracy.

NOTES

1. *New York Times*, May 21, 1999, sec. A, p. 1.

Part III

POLICING

THE POLICE

8

From the Inside Looking Out

Twenty-nine Years in the New York Police Department

LIEUTENANT ARTHUR DOYLE (RETIRED)

It was an ambition of mine going back to high school to join the police department. My family lived on 115th Street and Lenox Avenue, and I was born in Harlem in 1943. My father was a laborer, working at Fordham University. My mom was a housewife. When I was about seven, we moved to the South Bronx, where I went to Prospect Junior High School and then Morris High School. I graduated in 1960, a few years after General Colin Powell.

As a youngster, I was sort of a joiner. I joined the Police Athletic League (PAL), where they had sports I could engage in. An officer from the Forty-first Precinct, a patrolman named Officer Thomas, coordinated PAL. He was African American, one of the few such cops around then. He encouraged me to consider joining the police force.

Basically, I saw cops making things right. No people appreciate the selling of drugs in their neighborhood. Not that that was a big problem in the 1950s in the South Bronx, but I saw police act on things like that. It wasn't that I had any relatives or friends who were police; I simply felt it was something I could do.

I graduated from high school when I was seventeen, and two weeks after that I was on my way to a four-year enlistment in the Marine Corps. Although I liked the Marine Corps, I didn't forget my thoughts about becoming a police officer. In 1963, home on leave, I decided to take the examination.

Right away, I ran into problems. I passed the written part of the exam, and I asked for and received a ninety-six-hour pass from my base down South to come up and take the physical exam. I'd been in the Marine Corps, a pretty tough outfit, and was in good shape, so I wasn't worried about the physical. I thought I'd done pretty well. But the department told me I had failed. The reason? I was missing a tooth. That's something that occurs in my family; some of us are missing teeth. It hardly seemed like a reason to deny me entrance to the police force, though.

I took this rejection letter back to the base dentist, a U.S. Navy captain, and he read it. He examined my teeth and got very upset at the rejection I had received. He said, "Your teeth are excellent. They are good enough that if you had applied to the Naval Academy, you would be accepted without question." The captain wrote a letter to the Department of Personnel in the city. It was a pretty strong letter, mentioning my record in the Marine Corps. The next thing I knew, I got another letter, saying I was accepted and on the list.

Months later, at the graduation ceremony from the Police Academy, I turned to smile at another officer, a White man, standing right next to me. He smiled back. His teeth were all rotten—falling-out rotten.

That was my first experience with recruitment discrimination. I got another one right afterward, involving my own family.

My brother-in-law, who had moved to New York City from Tuskegee, Alabama, was very interested in joining the police department as well. At that time, I was already actively recruiting African Americans to join. My brother-in-law took the exam and did very well, too. But the department investigated him thoroughly. He had never known his father. He had been raised by his grandparents back in Alabama. The police personnel officials told him he had to go back to Tuskegee, find three people who knew his father, and have them write letters attesting to his father's good character. My brother-in-law was humiliated and frustrated. There was no way he could get those letters. So he just went to work for the post office instead.

Those kinds of rejections frustrate people when they occur at ages like nineteen, twenty, or twenty-one. Most of them are not going to fight back. The department seemed to have ways to frustrate people it didn't really want. In my police class of five hundred, there was a handful of other Blacks. I found that several had similar stories. One had been put through a tough hearing about a distant relative he knew nothing about, who had been arrested many years earlier. This sort of thing didn't happen with other officers.

It was obvious that minority recruitment was not really a goal in the department. Somebody should have prevented that dental rejection. Someone should have circumvented the demand that my brother-in-law find people in Tuskegee to vouch for his father's character. For my part, I was humiliated. But where would I go to confront the problem? To whom would I talk about it?

My initial assignment was to the Forty-fourth Precinct in the South Bronx, near where I grew up. The first real lesson I learned was that the police department has both a formal and an informal leadership structure. Most people pay greater attention to the informal structure, where leaders have their own rules. In the police department, the informal leaders may be other cops and not necessarily ranking officers. They are the ones who lay down the rules.

One rule I learned was that any suspect who assaulted a police officer in any way was never supposed to be able to walk into the station house on his own. He was supposed to be beaten so badly that he couldn't walk. If you did bring a prisoner in who had assaulted you or another officer and he was still standing, you were admonished by your colleagues, sometimes by supervisors.

This happened to me several times. It led to some bad feelings. I refused to accept prisoners who had been beaten while handcuffed. I made it clear I wouldn't tolerate that in my presence. It was really not a humane or manly thing to do. But it was not uncommon to see officers take advantage of the fact that they were police officers and abuse that power, because that's what the informal leadership structure demanded.

For a while, I worked with youth gangs in the Bronx. There was one particularly tough kid. He was part African American, part White; they called him Red. This kid had a long criminal history and had assaulted police officers in the past. It was indicated he was involved in a double homicide.

My partner and I accosted Red on the sidewalk. We arrested him, and he came along with us without a problem. We walked him into the precinct. Within minutes I was called aside by another cop. "Hey, why is this kid walking in?" this cop asked.

"Because he is my prisoner and that is not my thing," I replied. He backed off, but I could see he didn't like it. At other times, if I saw someone else beating a prisoner, I stopped him. They didn't like it, but I insisted.

A similar unwritten law covered chases as well. If an officer had to chase someone, by car or on foot, the person would invariably be beaten when captured. After a long chase, the officers would be pumped up, angry. They would want revenge for having put their lives in danger. That was the case in the Rodney King situation. It was taken to the extreme.

At the trial in Los Angeles, we all saw that video for days on end, and the officers were found not guilty. The system came to their defense. They weren't portrayed as bad cops, within either the law enforcement community or the larger community. Analysts argued that the force used was within departmental guidelines, even though the whole world had seen this man, lying prostrate on the ground, hit over and over and over again. Those cops were out of control. Although a supervisor was present, they were still completely out of control. One needs a supervisor on the scene who keeps his cool, who holds the officers back. Why have a sixty-five-mile-per-hour chase down crowded streets, with the risk of injuring innocent people, over a traffic incident? Better to call off the chase.

But the system came to their defense.

The informal leadership structure that I've described almost demanded that kind of response. Officers were more or less encouraged to be abusive, as long as they stayed within certain parameters. If they did, the system would give them the benefit of the doubt. Even if they went outside those parameters, the system would still come to their aid.

In my first few years on the force, we were often called out to handle civil disturbances. The Harlem riots erupted the same day that I was discharged from the Marine Corps in 1964, and there were frequent incidents in the ensuing weeks and months, some in Harlem, some in the Bronx. They almost always followed the same sort of scenario: unnecessary force, indiscriminate use of the nightstick, unnecessary brutality. The goal was supposed to be to stop the riot or the disturbance and to arrest those who were actively participating. Not to wantonly corral people, or corner them. When you cornered people, you invariably had a group of cops on one side and angry people on the other who defended themselves. At those times, it looked as if it was just one mob chasing another mob.

Later on in the 1960s, I was assigned to a lot of anti–Vietnam War demonstrations. I was also assigned to Columbia University in 1968, where a group of students had taken over a building. The police were called in to clear it. I saw these officers wildly clubbing these kids. I was surprised. That these were White kids offers another clue to the nature of brutality: race does not necessarily have to be a part of it. The only crime of the White students was to have taken over and occupied a building at a prestigious school. Even though there was some provocation—some things were thrown out of windows, and I think a student jumped from a window onto a cop—that sort of response was not necessary. The retaliation, the violence, far outweighed the provocation. I believe this happened because most cops thought the system would protect them if they went overboard.

I learned a different sort of lesson on the job as well, one that drove home to me the need for greater minority recruitment in the police force. Many times, my presence alone at the scene of a confrontation was enough to ease tensions. Having a Black officer as a witness on the scene seemed to discourage officers from abusing people. I think they couldn't be sure whether or not I would report it, and they may have been reluctant to go out of control.

That was particularly true on the few occasions we would encounter interracial couples walking in the city. White officers I worked with became highly perturbed at that sight.

There was a White man whom I generally liked and considered a good cop. Once when we were working as partners, he spotted an interracial couple walking down the street. He was behind the wheel and, without saying a word about what he was doing, he proceeded to drive around the block three times, slowing up each time we came abreast of the couple and glaring at them. At one point, the young Black man hugged the White woman he was with. He bent her back—almost as in a Hollywood swoon. I thought perhaps he had noticed us and was determined to make the point that no one was going to interfere with him. My partner became so outraged that he punched the car dashboard over and over. But he didn't do anything. I have absolutely no doubt that had I not been there he would have gotten out of the car, approached this man, and goaded him into some sort of confrontation.

Partly because I was from the community and had shown a rapport with kids, I was named to a youth aide position in the Bronx. Everyone called it the youth squad. It was a citywide unit, with each division having its own, separate youth squad. We would patrol juvenile delinquents. Our job was to get to know the kids. If there was a graffiti problem, if cars were being broken into, or if juveniles were committing certain other crimes, we would patrol those areas and investigate.

It was during that period that I endured one of the most humiliating personal experiences. I remember it was a very hot August afternoon—hot in the way only the South Bronx can be. The streets were baking. To top it off, the city was in the midst of a water shortage. It was my responsibility, as a youth patrol officer, to drive around with another officer and someone from the city's Department of Water

Supply and turn hydrants off. We were on Union Avenue, where the kids had turned on a lot of hydrants. The other officer, a White man, turned to the city official, who was also White, and said, "Let's get them all off. Turn them all off. I want to make life as miserable for these bastards as I possibly can."

I guess he forgot I was even there in the same car with him. Or he didn't care. The man from the water supply department looked at me. I could tell he was embarrassed. Here I was, a Black officer who had grown up in the South Bronx, a boy who had relied on these hydrants himself for relief in hot summer weather, and here was this guy making a comment like that right in front of me.

I was steaming, but tried not to show it. I quickly reminded him that the European Americans on the Lower East Side and in other parts of the city also lived in tenements and projects and also turned hydrants on. He didn't say a word—he just sat there, looking at those kids as though he hated them. I thought, "If this officer can express that kind of hostility with a Black officer in the car, you can imagine what goes on in other places." He and I both had youth squad assignments, where one of the requirements was supposed to be that you had an interest in young people.

There were other incidents like this, not as dramatic or venomous, but they let me know what some of my colleagues really thought. One day when I was headed out on patrol, I realized I had left my wallet at home. I was in a plainclothes unit then and lived on Olinville Avenue, not that far from the station house. I asked the two officers I was working with to drive with me to my home so that I could get my wallet. They did, and when I came back out, one of the officers looked up at the building and asked me, "How can you live in a building with all these Jews?" That was a shock to me. I thought, "If he can make a comment like that to me, I wonder what he is saying about Blacks and Latinos behind my back?" It was a wonderful building, and we had wonderful neighbors, much like those where we live now.

Other things that happened also disturbed me. There would be disparaging remarks on the police radio. Racist graffiti in the station house. Photographs of wanted posters with the names of Black suspects scratched out and the name of a Black officer written in. There were racial jokes, ethnic jokes.

During a locker room bull session with other cops while I was in the youth squad, I made a comment about being Black on the police force. I said that I had spent four years in the South with the Marine Corps from 1960 to 1964—and it was really the pre–Civil Rights South—and I still felt more comfortable with those White Marines than I did with my White colleagues in the New York City Police Department. I still feel that way today. In the Marine Corps, you might once in a while hear something like, "I'm just not used to taking no orders from no colored folks." But that was more comical than anything else, and we would all laugh.

The atmosphere in the squad must have been bad, because we had an old-timer, a lieutenant, who called me into his office. He asked me whether I felt uncomfortable in the squad and wanted a transfer. He was aware of the level of racism that was prevalent there. But I said no, I wanted to stick it out.

The majority of cops were good, hardworking, conscientious individuals. They cared, and they wanted to do a good job. But there were enough bad cops—not one rotten apple, but several rotten apples—to give law enforcement the taint it had received.

My experiences with discrimination after my first few years on the job were enough to make me doubt whether I really wanted to stay on the force. I had a friend, a public school principal, who suggested that maybe I should become a teacher. He offered to make me a teacher's aide while I worked on getting the necessary certification. I did that part-time for three months, but teaching wasn't for me. I decided I could promote change and be a more positive force by working in the police department, as opposed to running away from it.

A key part of the work we did involved the juvenile reports. These were informal reports prepared by officers who encountered youngsters committing minor offenses and certain misdemeanors. An officer had the discretion to prepare a report rather than arrest a youth. It was our job to investigate those reports.

The entire system allowed enormous discretion in the way cops could handle things. I saw that minority kids, Blacks and Hispanics in particular, were never given the benefit of the doubt. If cops could arrest them, they would do so. Other youngsters got the old story from the police: "I'll drive you home and knock on your door and tell your father that this is what you've done,"—that type of discretion.

If a cop wanted to be particularly venomous, he could escalate the situation, by taking what was essentially a misdemeanor and writing it up as a felony. Nobody questioned it. That kind of discretion I found particularly disturbing when children were involved.

One view of minority communities seemed to be almost passed down from generation to generation in law enforcement: that *these people* condoned and tolerated criminal activity in their neighborhoods. Of course, that was simply untrue, as any cop doing his job found out. Most of the serious crimes in those neighborhoods got solved because somebody in that neighborhood informed. That was how a detective solved crimes. People informed, because they wanted to rid their community of crime. Resident in all communities wanted the same thing for their children. Still, the attitude was almost, "Why don't they police their own community" Well, why doesn't anybody police his or her own community?

In my ten years in the youth squad, I developed such a reputation that nowhere did people confront me with abusive, racist behavior, because I wouldn't tolerate it. If I saw somebody abusing a prisoner, or getting ready to abuse somebody, I would stop him. I figured it was easier to do my job well than to do it the other way.

During that time, officer sometimes went into gang clubhouses and destroyed them. Part of my job with the youth and intelligence unit was to try to persuade these kids to stay out of trouble, and keep an eye on what they were up to. I said to the other cops, "Listen, at least we know where they are when they're in the clubhouses. They're not in trouble if they're in the clubhouse."

The kids themselves began to respect us. We would take kids to doctor's appointments, act as advocates for them in school, and talk to their parents. When there were gang murders, we went to the kids and got the information. Kids would call my office and surrender to me and me only, because they knew that they would be treated fairly, that this was the way I operated. They feared that other cops would beat them up.

The period 1969–1971 saw a rash of shootings of Black plain-clothes cops, both on- and off-duty police officers, by White police-men. Several were badly wounded, and a Black detective was shot dead by White officers as he was holding a suspect at bay. The police commissioner at the time convened a focus group at Arden House upstate. It included many Black, Hispanic, and White offi-cers—patrolmen as well as superior officers, a cross section of the department.

Officers were randomly selected to share rooms, and two White officers refused to share rooms with Black officers. They slept in the lobby. I thought, "How can we be here to deal with this problem, and this attitude surfaces?"

Some good did come of the conference, regarding the problem of how we could identify officers who were wearing civilian clothes. After considerable discussion, we hit on the idea that at the begin-ning of each tour, in each precinct, the "color of the day" would be announced. Plainclothes cops would all don that particular color on a sweatband, and this would supposedly protect them from the peril of mistaken identity.

That conference in 1971 showed that when you forced police offi-cers to sit down and brainstorm about a problem they could come up with some solutions. I don't recall a similar effort being made to deal with more recent problems of police brutality.

Of course, the conference didn't end the mistaken-identity prob-lem. It saddens me that this problem occurred in 1971 and that just a few years ago (in 1994) we had another incident in the subway. A Black plainclothes officer who had just turned out from the six-to-two tour was shot during a chase by some of the same officers he'd just finished working with.

Right now there are all these touchy-feely sessions and highly paid consultants, but I question how much impact they have on preventing police brutality. It is my conviction that discipline is the strongest motivator to change. If you know that discipline is going to be sure and certain, you are going to refrain from certain kinds of behavior. Discipline can force you to leave your attitudes in the locker, if it is made clear that you will get into a world of trouble if you take that attitude onto the job. When you get off duty, you can put on your racist hat if you want to, but in the meantime, you had better leave it in that locker.

In the early 1990s, during the development of the "Safe Streets, Safe City" initiative and the disturbances in Washington Heights in upper Manhattan, I was given the go-ahead to put together some sessions on police-community relations. We took ten adults from the community and ten randomly selected officers from the precinct. We had consultants come in to help push the discussions along, but it wasn't a touchy-feely thing. At those sessions, police brutality was the subject that always generated the most discussion. People expressed their feelings and named names. After two days, the community residents came away with a real understanding of what it was like to be a cop in their neighborhood. The police officers got a better understanding of what it was like to live in that community. That program was expanded to several precincts, and I think it proved very successful.

During my years on the police force, people frequently complained about police brutality. If they told me about instances involving other officers, I would tell them to go to the precinct and fill out a form, and if they couldn't do it, I would help. People who went to the station house on their own were often treated discourteously. Sometimes they would get frustrated and just walk away. That old informal leadership structure came into play, and if those informal leaders in the precinct had racist attitudes, these attitudes set the dominant tone there.

I was on the police force during the early 1970s, the years of the Knapp Commission hearings and the subsequent Knapp Commission Report on Police Corruption, released in 1972. The investigation was prompted by revelations of brutality and corruption by the police officer Frank Serpico. Just about every major unit in the police department was touched by this scandal, with the exception of the youth squad, where I was working. I don't know whether police brutality and other forms of police corruption go hand in hand, but I suspect that if you are going to take the opportunity to engage in other illegal activities, you are going to take the chance to be brutal as well.

Just the same, I know from my own experience that not every complaint about police brutality is true. I had my own encounter with a false accusation.

On a sweltering summer afternoon on the Lower East Side, some kids playing at an open hydrant sprayed an African American man coming home from work. He got mad, went to his house, came back out with a .38 revolver, and started firing shots indiscriminately in the air. There were hundreds of kids and people in the streets. I was about a block away when the call came in. A kid on a moped pointed the man out to me. I got out of the police car, drew my weapon, and ordered him to drop the gun. Instead, he put the gun in his jacket pocket and froze. He just stared at me. I got closer and closer and then tackled him. We went rolling around on the sidewalk, I reaching for his gun pocket and he holding on. Cops were coming from everywhere because citizens had called in that a man was shooting at cops. It was a wild scene. The man wouldn't let go of his gun, and another cop came running up, pulled a knife, cut the pocket, and pried the gun loose. Well, he cut the guy's hand in doing so, though not seriously.

Three months later, I was called to the Civilian Complaint Review Board because I was the subject of a citizen complaint. This guy had filed a complaint against me. I could have shot him, and I would have been within department guidelines on using deadly force. He had used a gun; I saw the gun. I had witnesses pointing him out as the one with the gun. He refused to relinquish the gun. The investigator at the hearing even told me, "You could have shot him. It would have been a clean shooting."

I was promoted to detective after I was transferred to the Runaway Squad. My partner and I patrolled the Times Square area. We would look at the area where prostitutes worked and try to pick out the very young faces. We found this one kid who was really young and appeared to have been beaten by one of the pimps. We put her in the police car and drove her back to our office. She took it very hard, not saying a word. We had to take her up to the Spofford Juvenile Center. She suffered like that for two days. Later we learned that her pimp had really beaten her; she had broken blood vessels in her eye. Half her jaw was broken in three places. It took her that long to come around and call her father, who, it turned out, was an influential person upstate. We ended up getting the coveted gold shield for that work.

In 1979, I was promoted to sergeant. I was briefly assigned to the Seventh Precinct, on the Lower East Side, on Pitt Street. I was then one of about seventy-five Black sergeants in the department, out of about twenty-five hundred sergeants in all. It was police department procedure that the sergeant in charge of patrol had an officer assigned to him as he went around supervising officers on patrol. Word got back to me by way of some sympathetic officers that there were a couple of White officers who were saying they wouldn't "chauffeur this nigger sergeant." The ones saying that were older officers, but I'm not sure that a lot of other cops didn't feel that way too. Although I didn't seek out any confrontation with these people, I certainly didn't back down. When the situation arose in which they had to drive, they did.

After I became a sergeant, some people were reluctant to speak to me, reluctant to follow orders—nothing flagrant, nothing that I had to take to another level, but I was disappointed. This wasn't the 1950s in Birmingham, Alabama; this was the 1970s in New York City. It was another example of what we called the "Black tax," the extra tax we paid on the police force for being Black. We were the last to get good assignments, the last to get steady radio cars. We suffered from overzealous supervision by some supervisors.

The biggest change on the police force that I witnessed was the influx of large numbers of female officers in the late 1970s. These officers had a calming influence. They were particularly effective with community people and children. Many were African Americans and Latinas who came directly from that community. Many had children and knew how to communicate with kids. That was crucial, because the inability to communicate is often what leads to aggravation between cops and kids.

I come from a well-disciplined, strong family background. One word out of line, and my father would correct me. Most cops have such a background. It is a big change to go into the inner city and say, "Hey, you, kid, come here." The kid's answer may be different, but there is no crime in being disrespectful. I think the female officers understand young people and have a real impact in dealing with them.

In other respects, the police department hasn't changed nearly enough. There is the joke about the southern sheriff who pulls the Black body out of the river. The body is wrapped in chains and a 300-pound weight is attached to it. The sheriff gets the body on shore and says, "Well, there is a clear case of suicide."

That scenario is supposed to be out of the 1920s or 1930s. But look at the venom surrounding the Abner Louima case, where a man was beaten and sodomized with a broom handle in a station house. The cop who changed his plea to guilty in the middle of the trial, Justin A. Volpe, had the same attitude as the old southern sheriff. In his opening statement, Volpe's lawyer, Marvyn Kornberg, said that the severe internal injuries to Mr. Louima's rectum and bladder were the result of consensual sexual activity[1] prior to his altercation with the police, and that he would introduce evidence to prove that such activity had taken place. Of course, he never did, because his client, Officer Volpe, admitted before the trial ended what he had done. Still, how far removed are that cop and that lawyer from that story about the sheriff? How far have we really progressed?

These kinds of situations are not the rule, but they do happen. Although the vast majority of officers today are well trained, committed to the job, some still tend toward brutality. In a way, this attitude is more frightening today because it is more subdued. Officers know that the likelihood of being disciplined and punished is now far greater. Citizens are more likely to make a complaint, and their complaint is more likely to be acted upon. The momentum is starting to build in the department to address the brutality issue. The Louima case and the Diallo shooting are forcing the department to take a harder look at itself.

I have always been an active recruiter for the police department. It offers a good job, and I can't understand why it doesn't attract more minorities. Now, even though retired, I tell youngsters to apply. As part of my volunteer work at a local high school, I try to set up summer youth employment program slots. These funded positions require only that you get an employer to agree to sponsor them. But I still have difficulty getting kids placed in the police department. Why not invite these kids into the precincts and make them a part of the force? They might want to make it a career.

In talking with kids about the police force, I use several raps. I tell them it's not boring. I never had a boring day in twenty-nine years. The pay, though not the best in the world, is certainly adequate. I put my daughter through Cornell and my son through Wesleyan—and I was a dead-honest cop. We drive a car that is twelve years old, but at least we have a car. I got a great deal of satisfaction and a sense of accomplishment in the police department, especially from my work with kids. And there are the retirement benefits: somebody who joins the force at twenty-one or twenty-two can retire at forty-two or fifty.

The key to meaningful change is minority recruitment. More ethnic diversity on the force would mean less brutality. I have seen it happen. It is a natural thing, because you identify better with the people you are dealing with. But minority recruitment becomes a front-burner issue only after some highly publicized incident of police brutality.

We don't need to lower standards to improve minority recruitment. Nobody in any community wants to see that happen. On the other hand, we should not set artificially inflated standards in the recruitment of police officers. When the U.S. armed forces moved to become an all-volunteer force, the guys in charge realized up front that they would have to establish a level playing field and make the armed forces attractive to minorities as a matter of national security. They said, "Whatever it takes to do that, we are going to do." And they did. They continue to do it and to do it well. Why can't the law enforcement people follow that example? Why can't they do it? Apparently, they don't feel the same sense of urgency.

NOTES

1. *New York Times*, May 5, 1999, sec. A, p. 1.

Thanks to Tom Robbins for his assistance on this essay.

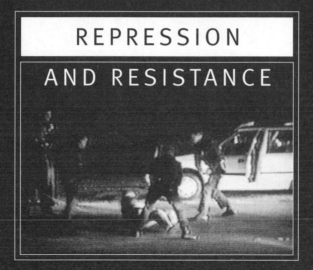

Part IV

REPRESSION

AND RESISTANCE

9

Another Day at the Front

Encounters with the Fuzz on the American Battlefront

ISHMAEL REED

Three African American writers, Patricia Williams, Lee Hubbard, and Cecil Brown, have complained about taking younger relatives to see George Lucas's *The Phantom Menace* only to have these children exposed to stereotypical images of African Americans. I'm actually glad that the children saw this movie in the company of these writers, because movies provide an opportunity for them to prepare for the combat they must wage in a society where media, including Hollywood, television, and newspapers, present African Americans as the enemy.

These media portrayals, fictional or otherwise, are not unlike the portrait of Asian Americans found in *Faces of the Enemy: Reflections of the Hostile Imagination and the Psychology of Enmity* by Sam Keen. This work deals with propagandistic portraits of the Japanese, who, at that time, were engaged in hostilities against the United States. They could just as well be those of African Americans, who are often shown as inferior and simian, their males a threat to European women. A poster showing a Japanese soldier dragging a nude White woman over his shoulder is consistent with the images thrown up by the Bush candidacy's Willie Horton commercials during the 1988 presidential campaign. The image of Horton, a Black man who raped and beat a White woman while on prison furlough, was projected as emblematic of all Black men. This is not an infrequent occurrence. Each day, African Americans confront hostilities from their fellow White citizens, who see themselves as unofficial deputies for an occupying army: the police. I experienced two such incidents while working on this essay.

The first incident occurred on July 6, 1999, while I drove to the home of the author Cecil Brown, whose encounter with the police at a swimming pool used by the University of California faculty inspired him to write a poem entitled "Strawberry Creek," which I published in my zine, *Konch*. The University of California police subsequently charged that Cecil Brown had been a menace to the White women bathers at the pool, a strange allegation since on the day of the incident, when Brown asked the supervisor of the pool why the pool personnel had called the police, the supervisor couldn't give a reason. The police put out this story, I believe, because they wanted to cover their embarrassment at having harassed Brown, a Berkeley faculty member, because he had the temerity to use this pool, where one rarely sees a Black person.

When I arrived at Brown's apartment building at the Emeryville Watergate, I didn't find his name listed on the directory of the building. This was unusual because it was the building where I had met Brown in the past when we walked around the Emeryville Marina and where, from time to time, we were put under surveillance by the Emeryville police. I returned home to call Brown and was informed that he'd forgotten to tell me that he had moved to another apartment in the building and that he hadn't received a directory number.

We decided to meet in front of the building. During my first trip there, I'd noticed a police car parked at the end of my block. When I left the block to meet Cecil, for the second time, the car followed me, changing lanes when I did and finally making a dramatic left turn when it was parallel to the left side of my car. I saw my encounter with the policeman as a skirmish. A strafing. A little like when an innocent passenger airplane enters unfriendly territory and is buzzed by fighter jets.

These policemen are descendants of the White patrollers and citizens' councils whom Booker T. Washington and others have historically complained about. Throughout history, their job was to regulate the comings and goings of African slaves, just as the UC Berkeley police and the policeman on my block were regulating Cecil Brown and my comings and goings. The irony is that I have been the neighborhood block captain, and as part of my job I have complained to the police and to my councilperson about the activities occurring in a house at an intersection located near my home, without response. It continues to be a safe haven for drug dealers and small-time criminals.

An exterminator who rid my house of rats said that the infestation had begun at this pest house, because of the young owner's unsanitary habits and the steady flow of young men who could be seen entering and exiting the house at any time during the day and night. My oldest daughter, Timothy, a novelist, had been harassed by a young man as she walked past the house. This situation has been going on for a year, without official response, yet the police found the time to tail me. This is a fact of everyday life in the inner city. Meanwhile, across the country, the people who sit on their fake, genteel behinds in their Upper West Side apartments, paid for by their intellectual treachery, and earn their living by writing "tough love" op-eds for the *New York Times* haven't the slightest idea about what goes on in these neighborhoods, the subject of their fatuous musings.

UNLIKE THAT of those Black children watching *The Phantom Menace*, my first scary experience with the representatives of a population that is hostile to African Americans and treats them as members of an enemy nation was more immediate. It was not with the propaganda arm, the television and motion pictures whose job it is to keep the White population mobilized against African Americans by recycling stereotypes in the same manner that the Nazi media aroused hostile passions against unpopular minorities.

It occurred on Elm Street in Chattanooga, Tennessee, when I was about three years old. The police had been called, ostensibly to get rid of a pack of dogs that had been disturbing the neighborhood. We were told to remain inside. The police invaded the neighborhood and began shooting up the place. It didn't occur to me at the time, and none of my relatives read anything into it, but looking back upon it I now see that these were war games. The police wanted to demonstrate their firepower to a neighborhood that might become troublesome. This was an act of intimidation. Most, if not all, of the riots that occurred during the 1960s were the results of a police incident. These uprisings should be viewed as stateside *intifada*.

After having grown up in Buffalo, where I moved from Tennessee, I, like most Black male youngsters I knew, was often stopped by the police. I never gave it much thought, but it occurs to me now that these were checkpoint incidents. Small-scale border incidents. In many countries where the majority is at war with the minority, minority members must constantly show their IDs to the occupation forces located in their communities. When these minorities venture from their neighborhoods and are found to be in enemy territory (which is where Cecil Brown and many other Black men regularly find themselves), they must show proof of who they are, just as during slavery free African Americans constantly had to show their papers. Sometimes, when I am driving through White California towns, I find myself being followed by the police from the time I enter until the time I exit town. It's as though the Black codes of the late nineteenth century were still in operation.

I lived in Buffalo from the time I was four until I was twenty-two. I became fully conscious of the role of the police when I began working for a newspaper, the *Empire Star*. I was thirteen and worked as a "printer's devil" under a staff of Black intellectuals led by A. J. Smitherman. A former newspaperman in Tulsa, Oklahoma, Smitherman had been charged with inciting a riot and run out of town during the famous Tulsa riots of 1921. It was at the *Star* that I became acquainted with the historical and contemporary legacy of being Black in the United States. African American newspapers, which I used to deliver, filled in the gaps about Black issues that weren't covered by my "formal education."

While attending the University of Buffalo in the late 1950s, I became acquainted with the relationship between interracial encounters and police brutality and surveillance. Black and White bohemians began to intermingle and would sometimes party together. I remember on several occasions our cars being tailed by the Buffalo police. Like the "patrollers" of old, they knew their mandate—to confine Black people to Black belts and to monitor any signs of integration. White women have told me stories of being stopped by police when out on a date with Black men.

In 1960, I began to write for the newspaper for which I had worked as a teenager. We reported about police brutality, segregation, and politics. I wrote one story about the Buffalo police's attack on Black prostitutes. "Cops and Dogs Attack Innocent Girls on High Street" was the headline. The police were offended and got a Black councilman to try to get me to soften my views about the police. I didn't budge.

My experience with the Buffalo police was mild in comparison with an ugly event that would take place in New York, where, in 1999, the dictatorial mayor Rudolph W. Giuliani endorsed the actions of an elite patrol, the Street Crime Unit, a sort of White tonton macoutes, which has stopped and frisked thousands of Black and Hispanic men. Giuliani gets credit from White nationalist journalists for lowering the crime rate, even though this trend was begun under David Dinkins, whose administration saw the New York crime rate significantly reduced after the hiring of seven thousand new police officers following 1990. (Even the *New York Times*, which inflames its White readers with generalizations about African Americans in almost every section of the newspaper, gave credit to Dinkins for lowering the crime rate.[1] Yet reporters erroneously reported that crime had gone up during Dinkins's term.)

It was in New York that I discovered the historical ethnic divisions that colored the relations between the police and Blacks and Puerto Ricans. The cops were members of the Irish and Italian American upper underclass, who, as one former police commissioner said, were from authoritarian backgrounds. I also found that Whites, no matter how radical, were generally treated better by the police than Blacks. The late Abbie Hoffman said in the *New York Times Magazine* that he had a nephew-uncle relationship with the commander of the precinct located on the Lower East Side. Ironically, this was the same precinct where I, and other Blacks, men and women, were being beaten up.

When I first arrived in New York in the early 1960s, I was standing on a street corner in Greenwich Village, talking to some friends, and a Black policeman told us to move on. I said something clever, and I'll never forget the hatred in that cop's eyes. He banned me from ever returning to Greenwich Village, a demand I of course ignored. Another day we were sitting in Pee Wee's, a bar, located on Avenue A on the Lower East Side, and the police came bursting in, guns drawn. When they found that no crime had been committed and that there was no disturbance, one of them said, "We just wanted to be ready."

Ready for what? To wage an all-out ethnic war against Black Americans? No matter how prosperous a Black American, he has, in the back of his mind, the knowledge of what happened to the Native Americans.

WHILE LIVING in New York, I worked in factories and hospitals, as well as a couple of times on the *Daily News* straw poll and at the New York State Department of Labor, where I was a clerk. I'd spend my leisure time writing poetry and socializing at Stanley's, a bar on Avenue B, where artists, writers, and musicians would hang out. Some of my friends were members of the Umbra workshop, a group of Black novelists and poets who met weekly to examine one another's work. I can recall an incident in which, in 1973, Calvin Hernton, a poet, and Duncan Roundtree III, a sociologist, and I were walking down Avenue B. We were in a jovial mood. I had been reading about police corruption that had been exposed by the Knapp Commission. One memorable line I recalled was, "They're taking bribes in low places." When I saw two cops carrying something wrapped in paper bags out of the Annex bar, which was owned by the late Mickey Rushkin, I turned to Calvin and said, "They're taking bribes in low places." I said it within the earshot of the two police-men, but didn't think they'd heard me. We kept walking, and Calvin said something to a woman who was walking on the other side of the street. I don't remember her saying anything, but she wasn't offended. In fact, she smiled.

The next thing I knew, the patrol car was speeding toward us. The police leapt out of the car and put the three of us in the back seat. They took us to the police station, which was commanded by the man who Abbie Hoffman said reminded him of an uncle. I was put into a separate room at the request of the cop—let's call him Officer Shrunk—who, on the way to the station, kept going on about how he didn't want Black guys dating his wife or daughter. Even the other cops looked at him funny. The cop said he wanted to deal with the "nigger" who was wearing the blue shirt. That was me. Shortly after this, I was isolated from Calvin and Duncan. The cop came into the room and began punching me out. I burst into tears because I was frustrated. My urge was to smash him as one would a termite or an ant, but I had enough sense to restrain myself. He had the guns. I knew that if I struck him, I could be killed or accused of resisting arrest. These are some of the tricks that the police use to add more Blacks to the prison population, one of the many facts ignored by people like James Q. Wilson, who believes that Blacks are genetically prone to violence.[2] (Wilson is provided with a forum by CNN to broadcast his views to two hundred countries.) That police officer had the power, while I had nothing but my wit, which ultimately would get me out of this jam. This miserable human being was intent upon ruining us, because I had made a dumb remark, and he searched us, hoping to find some reefer so that he could really stick it to us.

Shortly thereafter, we were taken from this station, where White cops had called us "niggers" while the Black cops went about their work. Officer Shrunk came into my cell at the Tombs, a city prison whose gothic style mirrored the state of our racist and primitive criminal justice system. By contrast to the fierce person with the contorted face who'd beaten me at the police station, the man before me was very polite. He said that if I would plead guilty to disorderly conduct, I would only spend a weekend at Riker's Island, the medieval facility where New York prisoners are stored. I told him that I wasn't going to plead guilty to anything. Years later, I learned from a British documentary about the New York criminal justice system that indigent Blacks were urged to plead guilty whether they were guilty or not, another factor in the high incarceration of Blacks.

Officer Shrunk got mad and left the cell in a huff. I learned later that the details of the incident had gotten around, and when we were released, some Black cops asked us to tell the story about the incident that led to our being jailed. They thought it was funny. A Catholic priest, whom I shall never forget, visited my cell and asked if there was someone he could call on my behalf. I gave him the number of the woman I was living with. We had been charged with disorderly conduct—the kind of all-purpose charge that's used to satisfy a policeman's Blacks and Hispanic quotas, similar to the Black codes that the South used to contain African Americans. Duncan Roundtree had to spend the weekend in jail, but since I was obviously the target of the policeman's malice and hatred, I raised the bail for him. I borrowed the money from the daughter of one of New York's most prominent capitalists, who had devoted time and effort to the Civil Rights struggle only to become cynical. She told me in the mid-1960s that most White people don't care whether Blacks live or die. She was right.

They kept postponing our trial because Officer Shrunk failed to show up. This, I was to learn later, was a vindictive way of running up our lawyers' bills. When the day of the trial finally arrived, I put on a three-piece pinstriped suit and sat patiently until our case was called. When it was, the charges against Calvin and Duncan were dismissed. I was obviously the target, and I took the stand. This was about a month after one of the first demonstrations against the Vietnam War had taken place in Times Square. Seated behind me were about thirty cops, who were there to testify against the demonstrators whom they had arrested.

I pointed to the two cops who were sitting below the judge's bench and told them that I'd seen them taking bribes out of the Annex. After I had called them on it, they had arrested us and beaten me. My narrative got good to me, and some of the Black people and Puerto Rican people in the courtroom began to make sounds of approval, egging me on. I was venting all of the rage that had built up inside me for months. The Blacks and Hispanics knew what I was talking about because a number of them had also been set up, victims of what amounted to relentless paramilitary search-and-destroy missions. I was calm and precise and pulled up a strength that I didn't know I had. When I finished, the two officers, who at the beginning of the trial were smirking, were now glaring at me.

When I sat down, I felt a wave of hostility aimed in my direction from the thirty or so cops who were there to testify against the anti-war protesters. They'd probably lie too. When I was asked to stand to hear the judge's verdict, I was prepared to take what was coming to me. The judge said, "Guilty." But when my lawyer asked for the sentence, the judge almost ran from the courtroom! My lawyer stood with his mouth open. He was stunned by the sight of the judge fleeing the courtroom without sentencing me. He said he'd never seen anything like it. Flo Kennedy, the feminist advocate and lawyer, who was seated in the courtroom, said she'd never seen anything like it, either. I know I was convicted of disorderly conduct, a misdemeanor, but to this day, I have no idea what my sentence was. Suspended? Time served? Who knows? I was just happy to get out of the courtroom. We were in a celebratory mood when we left, and some of the Blacks in the audience came up and congratulated me. The two cops were obviously angry. They had their guns and their other toys, but I had the words and had beaten them with the words.

THIS EXPERIENCE, though time-consuming, was worth more than a year at a university. It taught me how I stood as a Black man in the

United States. Whites had their government, with its three branches and innumerable services. The police were my government. They could regulate my comings and goings with all of the leeway accorded the modern-day patrollers that they were. They could request an ID check with or without cause. They could invade my home without a warrant, and the criminal justice system would tolerate this invasion with a wink and a nod. They could arrest me without cause, judge me, and in some cases carry out the sentence. Sometimes, this system decides that the penalty is death. Though some Black males and feminists are still engaged in an intellectual war of words, these cops have never heard of a gender war; they shoot Black women as well as Black men. Though Black men are still public enemy number one for many White Americans, Black women are becoming a growing part of the prison population. In the end, the experience taught me that the Bill of Rights did not apply to me.

When Calvin Duncan and I were marched into the Lower East Side station, I said, in my foolishness, "Thomas Jefferson wouldn't approve of this." A detective who was passing by said, "Fuck Thomas Jefferson."

How right he was. Most Whites enjoyed their "rights." The rest of us lived in a police state, a crude backward nation within this great democracy, presided over by primitives like Officer Shrunk. He could violate my "rights" whether I was an ordinary person or a celebrity football player beloved by millions. He could plant evidence on me, and if I was of little material wealth, he could force me to plea-bargain for a crime I didn't commit. If I did have some means to hire a lawyer, he could get up in the stand and testify his ass off. When I left New York, I was no longer the innocent idealist I'd been when I arrived in 1962. I knew a thing or two. But if my most serious encounter with the New York police was bizarre, an encounter with the Los Angeles police was even more so.

IN THE SUMMER of 1967, a few months before the publication of my first novel, I moved to Los Angeles. During the week I worked on my second novel, *Yellow Back Radio Broke Down*, a hip takeoff on the old yellow backs from which the cowboys derived their style. It had taken me a while to adjust to the automobile culture of California, and I didn't get a driver's license until the early 1970s; one day, I was nearly arrested for walking while Black.

It had been my custom to walk downtown to the Los Angeles library to do research for the novel. I was passing through a Black neighborhood when a police car pulled up and some police in plain-clothes piled out of it. They rushed up to me and snatched the pouch in which I carried my notes and books. A crowd of African Americans who had gathered about the scene began to laugh when they removed the contents from the pouch. Some books and a notebook. The police said they thought that it was a lady's purse that I had stolen. The pouch didn't look anything like a purse.

I said for the crowd to hear, "Gee, you can't even go to the library any more." The cops were humorless, though, and piled back into their car and sped off. It did not occur to me then that I could have been beaten or shot for acting smart.

My encounters with the police were minor for years, which for a Black man means that there is no physical confrontation, no threat to his life. I'd get followed sometimes when going to work at the university, especially when a Black criminal had committed some crime and was at large. This happens frequently. All Black men come under suspicion when the police are after one Black man, usually when that person has committed an offense against a White person. A typical incident happened a few years ago when I was seated in a restaurant. A police car drove up, and the occupants, a White girl and the police, stared at me for about thirty seconds. I said nothing about it to my dinner companions, and the policeman and the White girl drove away. All the time that they stared at me, I was trying to reconstruct my whereabouts for the previous week, just in case.

In 1983, while I was producing a television version of my play *Mother Hubbard*, I had dropped off Jason Buzas, a New York director, and was returning home. As I drove down Shattuck Avenue in Berkeley, I was stopped by the Berkeley police, who came down on me, red lights whirling, like gangbusters. They checked out my registration and told me that they stopped me because a robbery had been committed. I was tired and told them that I didn't feel like robbing anything. When they discovered that I worked at the University of California at Berkeley, they got nervous. One of them said that they had stopped me because I'd been drinking. They were trying to get their lies straight. I was a teetotaler then, as I've been ever since.

MY NEXT ENCOUNTER with the police occurred after Kofi Nataumbo, the poet, had invited me down to the California Institute of Technology to give a lecture. We had exited from the John Wayne Airport and were walking in the parking lot when three plainclothes White men approached us. They identified themselves as members of the Airport Narcotics Security or something or other. They wanted to know why I had used an exit different from the one the other Southwest Airlines passengers used. I didn't have any baggage, so I had departed from the main exit while those with bags went through the baggage claim exit. They were very tense.

I had heard one of the many White experts on Black things, appearing on Terry Gross's National Public Radio show, *Fresh Air*, say that the police hassled only the Black underclass. I thought of this when I identified myself as a senior lecturer at the University of California at Berkeley in town to give a lecture at the California Institute of Technology. That only made them more uptight. They asked me to produce a ticket, which I did. I figured that if I exercised my rights and refused, I would have been arrested and my briefcase planted with narcotics so that they could make a charge. Many Whites believe that Blacks are crazy when they accuse the police of planting evidence, yet they're the ones who are crazy, bewitched by the media, which too often serve as a kind of public relations annex for the police, creating and reinforcing the belief that American crime is Black or brown, even though over 70 percent of arrests in both cities and rural areas are of Whites. In fact, according to recent FBI statistics, it is White adult crime that's on the increase. People are programmed and manipulated by the media, seduced by an education that traffics in expensive lies. They live in an intellectually and culturally confined world that's similar to the one inhabited by Truman Burbank, the character in *The Truman Show*, who has no idea that the world in which he lives is no more than a media construct.

At the turn of the last century, Booker T. Washington complained about the media's coverage of African Americans when he said that the media emphasized the "weaknesses" of African Americans. According to Barry Glassner, things haven't changed. In his book *The Culture of Fear*, he criticizes the media for stigmatizing Black men: "Thanks to the profuse coverage of violent crime on local TV news programs . . . night after night, Black men rob, rape, loot, and pillage in the living room."[3] The media do their part in influencing the attitudes of the White public so that such warlike measures against Black people by the police are tolerated. Mass media provide modern, sophisticated tools of propaganda that Joseph Goebbels would have envied.

I have had only one police incident since then, as bizarre as the others. I appeared on *Nightline* in a discussion of police brutality and said that one solution would be for the police to live in the communities they served. The next day, I pulled up in front of the Bank of America at Lake Merritt in Oakland and was immediately accosted by the searching eyes of a policeman. I figured he had seen the program and was about to provoke an incident. I was right. As I got out of the car, I put on my headphones. He came up and told me that it was illegal to wear earphones while driving a car, although I hadn't been wearing them while driving. I said something like, "Thank you, officer, for informing me of that," and went about my business. For Black men, it often seems like a victory to escape from encounters with the police unscathed and have the last word.

We must understand that the police wouldn't be able to wage war against the Black population without the collusion of the majority of Whites. In criticizing the growing prison industry, by which Blacks are treated as merchandise and free labor just as they were in slavery,

Jerome G. Miller writes in *Search and Destroy: African-American Males in the Criminal Justice System*,

> To the inner cities, all this criminal activity brought a war mentality, destructive strategies, and vicious tactics, which exacerbated the violence and fueled social disorganization far beyond whatever negative effects might hitherto have been attributed to single-parent homes, welfare dependency, or the putative loss of family values. The White majority embraced the draconian measures with enthusiasm, particularly as it became clear that they were falling heaviest on minorities in general, and on African-American males in particular.[4]

The majority of Whites endorse the Gestapo tactics of the police as long as it keeps Black people out of their hair. The support for the presidential candidacy of General Colin Powell, according to one right-wing fan, was based upon his ability to handle "crime" and "welfare," which in the American vocabulary are synonyms for "nigger." Whites want Colin Powell to be the Head Overseer for Black Americans. Ronald Reagan was elected and David Duke received a large percentage of White votes in Louisiana because the public perceived that they would put Blacks back in their places.

AN INDICATION of how little most Whites care about how Blacks and browns are treated by the police comes from a poll about police brutality after an incident in 1997 when a New York policeman sodomized a Haitian American named Abner Louima with a broken broomstick. Most Blacks and Hispanics felt that police brutality was a problem; most Whites didn't. When NBC broadcast the poll results, it left out the fact that Hispanics agreed with Blacks as a way of isolating the Black population as malcontents and paranoids who are devoted to political correctness, when in fact their views are shared by other people of color.

In Northern California, an Asian American was recently shot to death because, according to the police, he was threatening them with martial arts moves. A Hispanic man, caught in the border wars now being waged against Hispanics and Indians in the Southwest, described his ordeal on Pacifica Radio news after being stopped by the border police. He was stopped at 9:00 P.M., and when he told the officers that he was the town's mayor, they said, "That don't cut no ice with us."

It didn't cut no ice with them, because they knew that in the eyes of the Anglo population, they had more power than the duly elected Hispanic mayor. On October 22, 1998, the National Council of La Raza issued a news release that complained about police brutality aimed at Hispanics. Groups ranging from Amnesty International to the Mexican American Bar Association to the National INS Raids Human Rights Watch have documented countless incidents of law enforcement abuse and excessive use of force.

Here again, the legion of writers who get paid by places like the *New York Times*, *The New Yorker*, the *New Republic*, and the *Atlantic Monthly* to coast along the familiar clichés about race and crime show their incompetence in analyzing such issues as police brutality. It's not single-parent households that get you into trouble with the law enforcement; Hispanics are often praised by the same writers for their strong family ties. It's your Black or brown skin that marks you, as the Star of David and the pink triangle marked Jews and gays in Nazi Germany.

From the very beginning of American history, when Africans were stored on ships and held in jail, innocent of any crime, while waiting to be sold, prison has been a second home for Blacks. Even Supreme Court Associate Justice Clarence Thomas, a Black man and the most conservative member of the Court, acknowledged, while watching a prison bus full of Black prisoners, "There but for the grace of God go I." Thomas knows that he too can be injured by a policeman to whom all Blacks are the same. Recently the police detained the son of Detroit's mayor and a few years ago, in New York, the son of Earl Graves, publisher of *Black Enterprise* magazine. Some psychotic New Jersey policemen held a famous African American dancer to the ground, until they saw that he was on the cover of that week's *Time* magazine.

There is a facelessness, a randomness, and a potential powerlessness and violence that defines many of Black people's interactions with White people. Leaving the Oakland Civic Center, I mistakenly got off at the basement of the garage, used by monthly patrons. I was wandering about, trying to find my car, an activity that goes on throughout America each day. A White woman walked toward me. When she saw me, she hesitated, a scene that occurs throughout America each day when a Black man and a White woman are alone in a public space. I ignored her and kept searching for my car. While walking through one aisle, I noticed her at the other end of the garage, staring across at me. Hers was the same stare of terror and hate that has gotten thousands of Black men incarcerated, maimed, or lynched and whole sections of the Black belts wiped out and their inhabitants massacred.

In an everyday situation like this, a White woman has more power than a Black woman or a Black male millionaire. When I came down another aisle of the garage, confused because I wasn't aware that I was on the wrong floor, I noticed a White man, whose job was apparently that of filling the cars with gas. He was standing, frozen, glaring at me. His fists were clenched. He had deputized himself as a patroller. He was ready.

Suddenly a security guard approached me and demanded that I produce a ticket. (I guess they sent a Hispanic because if I was a really dangerous Black man and harmed him, it would be no big deal.) I told him I had left it in the car. He said that it was probably upstairs. He escorted me there and followed me until I located my car. Unlike those kids who were disturbed by *The Phantom Menace*, I take all of these incidents in stride. You see, I'm a veteran, and this was just another day at the front.

Notes

1. *New York Times*, October 11, 1993, sec. A, p. 1; August 11, 1995, sec. A., p. 29.

2. Jerome G. Miller, *Search and Destroy: African-American Males in the Criminal Justice System* (New York: Cambridge University Press, 1996), 205, 217.

3. Barry Glassner, *The Culture of Fear: Why Americans Are Afraid of the Wrong Things* (New York: Basic Books, 1999), 109.

4. Miller, *Search and Destroy*, 241.

10

Under the Veil of Suspicion

Organizing Resistance and Struggling for Liberation

RICHARD AUSTIN

> If we're going to talk about police brutality, it's because police brutality exists. Why does it exist? Because our people in this particular society live in a police state.
>
> —Malcolm X

Summer 1989. South Ozone Park, Queens. My best friend and I are just leaving his home on a quiet tree-lined street in the urban jungle. The shadow of a police patrol car greets us at the curb. The police officers slowly drive past us with a dubious glare. As we are about two hundred yards from my friend's house, he realizes that he has forgotten his watch. We turn around and begin to walk back to his residence. Before we are able to move a foot, the patrol car stops, and the officer in the passenger seat calls out to us. "Where are you two going? What are you doing around here?"

The sight of two Black men leisurely walking down a residential block is not an acceptable one for this cop. Since I have been distrustful of cops for as long as I can imagine, I do not answer the cop. Instead, I silently gaze at the patrol car. My friend walks over and attempts to explain the situation. "I live here," my friend calmly tells the cop, pointing to his home.

"Well, do you have any proof that you live there?" the cop asks smugly. "We just got a report of a robbery. The victim said that the suspect was a Black male wearing a bright yellow shirt," he continues with a strong hint of disdain in his voice.

My best friend is wearing a dark green shirt, and I have on a tri-colored shirt with a sliver of mustard yellow in it. I am astounded and angered at the de facto pass laws that exist in postslavery America. It reminds me of Reconstruction, when Black people were required to carry identification cards that allowed them to pass through to certain sections of the country. Officials could ask them for ID and the reason for their travel at any time as a result of these pass laws. This cop's comments seemed to echo behavior of the distant past.

During this encounter, my friend makes a move toward his house to verify his status as a resident of the block. But it is obvious that they aren't interested in seeing any proof of our right to be there, because the cop offers one more snide remark, and then they drive off. My friend is nonplussed, I am still seething, and we both walk away with the feeling of having been violated.

This incident, which some might view as innocuous and even commonplace, strongly disturbed me. At this juncture, the idea that a Black man could not stroll the streets without a cloud of suspicion constantly hovering above him crystallized for me. Although I had been involved in other unpleasant exchanges with the police, usually being told to move off a corner with a group of friends, this episode was especially disturbing. I was raised to believe that the police harass only criminals, those who are guilty of illegal acts or who look suspicious enough to be interrogated. But this interaction totally altered my conceptions. We were two innocent young Black men who were off to enjoy a beautiful summer day. The life lesson was learned in a painful instant. It was one of many to come.

Spring 1995. One o'clock in the morning. The spring night is crisp and clear. My roommate and I, both students at New York University, are restless and famished. We decide that it is time for another late-night food excursion. Our dormitory, a former hotel in Manhattan facing Union Square Park, is a couple of blocks from our favorite deli. We have made that trip over a hundred times in an uneventful manner, and we do not expect anything unusual to occur. As we head to the deli, we joke and talk about our plans for graduation and the summer. We buy our usual greasy meals and head back to our dormitory room. Our cheerful banter enlivens the otherwise quiet surroundings. As we are about to cross the street, a squad car with its lights flashing and its siren blaring pierces the peaceful night air, and catches the corner of my eye. Before we can step off the sidewalk, the squad car, going the wrong way on a one-way street, cuts us off. "Stop right there," barks a gruff cop. The two cops exit the vehicle, guns drawn, grab my roommate, and push him against a wall.

"Where are you going?" The same pass law question is once again uttered.

"We live right there," I reply coldly, pointing to our residence hall.

"Well, we got a report about a burglary suspect. He's a dark-skinned Black male with a beard," the cop angrily retorted, as he patted down my stubble-faced friend.

Having completed their daily quota of tormenting Black men, the two police officers depart without the slightest hint of an apology. My roommate and I are both perturbed. Once we enter our room, he lets out a string of obscenities. I vicariously feel his sense of humiliation. But I recognize that at that moment I can do nothing to console him. His sense of autonomy, his feelings of safety, and his dignity have been obliterated. "This has to stop. Our rights must be respected, and the NYPD has to learn that this kind of power-mad behavior is unacceptable," I think with a new sense of determination.

These two incidents were significant markers of my experience under the shadow of suspicion. Each case reflected how the image of the Black male has been criminalized and continually defiled. We are constantly pilloried in the media and in many social circles. Drug dealer. Gang member. Absentee father. High school dropout. These are a few of the labels used to describe Black males. Although it has been stated numerous times, the situation for the young Black male is dire. We benefit the least from higher education, and are targeted the most for incarceration and violent acts at the hands of the police. The numbers are startling and bleak:

- Black males make up less than 7 percent of the U.S. population, yet they make up almost half of the prison and jail population.[1]
- An analysis of the jail system in Duval County (Jacksonville), Florida, in 1993 demonstrated that 76 percent of the Black males living in Jacksonville in 1990 would be arrested before they reached the age of thirty-six.[2] One out of every three Black men between the ages of twenty and twenty-nine in the entire country was under some form of criminal justice supervision (in prison or jail, on probation or parole) in 1994.[3]
- African Americans seem to be disproportionately the victims of police abuse, given the overall racial composition of New York City. Statistics published by the Civilian Complaint Review Board, an oversight agency that receives complaints from citizens against the police, indicated that about half (50.3 percent) of the people who lodged complaints with the CCRB from January to June 1995 were African American.[4]
- A California study concluded that, in Oakland, unfounded arrests of African Americans occurred at twelve times the rate of Whites.[5]

Young people of color, particularly Black males, form a distinct group that has been targeted by law enforcement under the guise of investigative profiling. Law enforcement officials have continually stated that they stop Black males because they fit a distinct profile of a suspected criminal. They say that the majority of criminal perpetrators are Black. Therefore, their argument goes, a greater number of Black males will be stopped and searched. The practice of racial profiling is illegal, but that has not kept a large number of police departments nationwide from employing it. Moreover, this stain of criminalization doesn't end with the police. As Black men enter department stores or walk down an affluent block in any city in the United States, many people clutch their purses tighter or cast a suspicious eye toward them. Whether in a three-piece suit, or baggy pants and a hoodie, Black men are affected by this incessant shroud of suspicion.

A great deal has been written about the emotional and economic burden on the Black community of having so many Black men incarcerated or otherwise under the auspices of the criminal justice system. The financial struggles of single-mother households and the feelings of abandonment many children experience have been well documented. However, there remains a dearth of information in regard to the psychological struggles of Black men and their loved ones caused by the specter of criminalization constantly cast over them. That is, a Black male, whether incarcerated or free, innocent or guilty, must carry the stigma of "suspect" as he attempts to survive in this society. A great number of Black men have experienced the degradation of being forcefully frisked by the police as they are told that they match the "description." Many of them have been pulled over and brutalized by overzealous cops who cannot fathom a young male of color driving a luxury vehicle. Such stresses begin to take a toll on the psyche of Black men, who come to approach life differently. For instance, a Black male is more cognizant of news reports describing a wanted suspect. I recall many times when I watched the evening news and a description of a suspect was posted. Sometimes, I noticed that I shared some features with this person (e.g., height, weight, hairstyle). But with the broad range of physical descriptions generally used, a large number of Black males fit the given profile. I immediately became uneasy at the thought that someone could tab me as the suspect and I could be dragged to jail. There have been too many accounts of such events for me to discount this notion as a mere overreaction. I don't believe that White males need to employ such thought patterns.

Given this state of affairs, we must raise our young sons in a different manner. Black males must have the police interaction procedure drilled into them. As my parents lectured me, "If a police officer stops you, don't make any sudden moves, don't talk back to him, and do all that he says." My parents' concern, like that of many mothers and fathers, is to ensure that their children survive such confrontations with police officers. We have a heightened sense of danger when police officers are in the vicinity. The concern is no longer to preserve our manhood but rather to escape with our lives. Moreover, the consistent devaluing of their image may provoke Black males to hate themselves. For instance, Black males are routinely cast as drug dealers or gang members in movies. Also, news reports consistently examine the high incarceration rate of Black males in such a way as to hint at their "natural" criminality. This constant projection of their deviance causes many to accept their place in society as that of a social pariah. The belief is that there is no brass ring to reach for, since not much is expected of us. While a certain amount of responsibility for how they are perceived rests on the shoulders of Black males, the influence of psychologically debilitating external factors, such as stereotyping, negative media characterizations, and constant harassment by the police, in impeding the creation of a healthy self-concept must be acknowledged.

I am not unusual in feeling unsafe walking down the street when I see a police vehicle cruising by me. My "fight or flight" response is always heightened. That is, my palms get sweaty and my adrenaline starts to flow as my body prepares itself to deal with a potentially dangerous situation. I have strong, hostile feelings toward police officers and the system they represent, and often feel angry about the ordeals that young Black males must undergo every day in order to survive in this world. Although I have become accustomed to the constant surveillance when I am in a store, it still exasperates me. It always disgusts me when a salesperson or a security guard obviously watches my every move. Some Black males believe the fallacy that because they are accomplished to some degree—have the credentials of, say, a doctor or a lawyer—police officers will recognize their lofty social standing and not harass or brutalize them. However, I know that, despite my credentials, I'm just another Black male suspect to the common cop on the beat. So, whether in a store or on the street, I am always on guard and aware of the possible dangers that I face as a young Black male. And while I am oftentimes bitter about having to live this way, I realize that the only way to change things is through organized action.

The challenge to Black males is to retain their sanity under this far-reaching net of mistrust. One can easily feel overwhelmed and extremely angry by constantly being targeted for harassment. But we must analyze the forces that are working to maintain this image of the Black male as the "perennial criminal perpetrator." We must realize that the attacks on the image of the Black male benefit those who wish to maintain the status quo of the social caste system in America. This system mandates that there be an underclass that is reviled and feared. Black males, particularly poor, young ones, make up a good portion of this underclass. The fear engendered by this segment of the population serves as a diversion for the citizenry to spend less time thinking about the inequities and injustices of this country. In addition, this pervasive "threat of the Black male" construct allows people to use Black men as scapegoats to literally get away with murder.

For instance, Charles Stuart, a Boston resident who murdered his pregnant wife in 1989, could fabricate a story of a Black male assailant killing his spouse, and have the Boston police force subsequently invade Black neighborhoods to threaten and interrogate all Black males who vaguely fit the phantom suspect's description.[6] Then there was the case of Susan Smith, a young mother from South Carolina convicted of killing her two children in 1994, who concocted a tale of a Black male carjacker stealing her car and her kids, and had a national manhunt initiated in search of the nonexistent perpetrator.[7] These two incidents exemplify how people can take advantage of the much maligned representation of the Black male.

As disturbing as this omnipresent cloud of distrust over the heads of Black men is the premise that any Black male brutalized or killed by the police somehow deserved his fate. Oftentimes, an aura of criminalization is automatically created to justify the assassination of Black males. Two cases out of many in the recent sordid history of New York Police Department officer shootings highlight this phenomenon. On June 13, 1996, Aswan "Keshawn" Watson, a twenty-three-year-old Black man from the borough of Brooklyn, was shot twenty-four times by two undercover cops, Officers Keith Tierney and James Gentile, as he sat in a car. The cops claimed that he was in a stolen vehicle and that he reached for something. Yet Watson was unarmed, and eyewitness accounts asserted that he had his hands raised when the cops approached him.[8] Despite these conflicting reports, the spin immediately coming out of the NYPD headquarters was that Watson was wanted in connection with an unsolved murder. This disclosure seemed to intimate that because Watson was a possible suspect, he clearly was dangerous, and deserved his fate. When Kevin Cedeno, a young Black male from the Washington Heights section of Manhattan, was shot in the back by Police Officer Anthony Pellegrini on April 16, 1997, the police department quickly announced that Cedeno had a criminal record, and it speculated about his intentions on the fateful night he was killed.[9] In both instances, the release of information in regard to the victims' alleged past behavior marked an attempt by the NYPD to debase the images of these young men in order to create the appearance that they were threats to society whose murders were justified. In both cases, the legal protection of "innocent until proven guilty" was discarded. The NYPD served as the judge, jury, and executioner. The line emanating from City Hall and the police commissioner's office, in New York City as well as across the United States, seems to be that if a man has committed any transgressions in the past, he is fair game to be beaten up, maimed, or slaughtered at the hands of "officers of the peace." While still under investigation for the shooting of Cedeno, Pellegrini was named "Cop of the Month" by his colleagues in the Thirty-third Precinct.[10] The officers involved in the Watson and Cedeno cases were not indicted for the shootings of these young men.[11]

The prevailing notion appears to be that in order for a victim of police brutality, or the families of victims killed by the police, to obtain justice, the victim must have been a virtual saint. The case of Abner Louima, a Haitian immigrant who accused four police officers from the Seventieth Precinct in Brooklyn of brutalizing and later sodomizing him with a broken broomstick in 1997, offers a perfect example of this belief and a fine contrast to the two previously mentioned cases. In the initial, as well as during later, stages of this case, one member of the defense team suggested that the injuries Mr. Louima suffered to his rectum and his intestinal area were "not consistent with a nonconsensual insertion of an object into his rectum."[12] This calculated move was an attempt to tinge Mr. Louima with the "Black male as depraved individual" hue by tapping into the rampant homophobic attitudes of this society. The attorneys for the accused police officers then hired private investigators to examine the victim's past to cull any morsel of information that could portray Louima in a negative light. Despite all their efforts to soil this man's reputation, the officers and their defense teams failed to find any evidence that would be useful for their contemptible purposes.

As the case progressed, it became increasingly clear that Police Officer Justin A. Volpe, the one whom Mr. Louima accused of having sodomized him, was guilty of this reprehensible act. When some of Mr. Volpe's fellow officers testified against him, and his defense team was unable to damage their credibility, he suddenly decided to cop a plea, admitting to the sodomy and assault charges. In the remainder of the trial, one other officer, Charles Schwarz, was convicted of holding Louima down while Officer Volpe sodomized him. The other accused officers were acquitted.[13] Volpe was sentenced to thirty years in prison. Schwarz is awaiting sentencing in state court and planning an appeal, at least partially based on statements Volpe made after his confession that it was not Schwarz, but Officer Thomas Wiese, who was present during the attack on Louima. On March 6, 2000, Schwarz and Officers Thomas Bruder and Thomas Wiese were convicted in federal court of conspiring to obstruct justice in claiming that Schwarz was not present during the attack on Louima.

Lost amid the euphoria over the guilty plea, and the subsequent conviction of one of the officers, was a troublesome underlying message: hardworking, family men, like Abner Louima, with spotless records deserve justice, but young Black males like Aswan Watson and Kevin Cedeno, because of their alleged criminal pasts, do not.

Unfortunately, many people, including members of the Black community, are strong advocates of this position. They have bought into the law-and-order mentality of this society. This nation projects the notion that crime is the central challenge facing this country, particularly inner cities. Therefore, the rationale goes, if you eliminate crime by locking up the criminals, our world will be a much better one. People are perpetually bombarded with the idea that their safety is always at risk if criminals are not stopped. The roots of such criminal behavior, and the racial biases in terms of law enforcement and criminal prosecution, are rarely examined, however. Thus, a great number of Black people are convinced that their lives are in jeopardy until lawbreakers are put away. As U.S. prisons continue to overflow with Black bodies, and the lives of our children are consistently snuffed out, the general consensus is that if a person is in jail or if the police kill or assault a Black male, he more than likely did something unlawful. It is evident that many people are manipulated by fear and a general cynicism regarding the value of young Black male lives, but we must not be fooled or intimidated. Aswan Watson and Kevin Cedeno had as much a right to live as Abner Louima had to not be assaulted and sodomized. All human beings should have the privilege of life and the benefit of the doubt in regard to their actions until a valid investigation takes place. No law enforcement agency or government institution should be able to trample on such rights with impunity, and when it does so, such actions must be addressed.

It may seem that our future is extremely dismal. However, hope is forever on the horizon. Oppressed communities are constantly faced with the challenge of addressing the conditions of their existence. We have a responsibility to our children and to our elders to improve their surroundings and way of living. While I recognize that there is no panacea for what ails our communities, I've chosen to struggle for social justice and the liberation of my community through the path of revolutionary activism. My understanding is that we must all decide how to confront obstacles to true freedom. Freedom from incessant police brutality and murder. Freedom from economic exploitation. Freedom from poor housing and faulty education. My work as an activist is to engage people in meaningful dialogue. The goal is to participate in a mutual relationship with others who believe that our circumstances are deplorable and must and can be changed. Therefore, my work is based on the construct of collectivism. I recognize that no one can alter reality alone. Therefore, I have decided to struggle within the framework of the revolutionary Forever in Struggle Together (FIST) Collective, a people of African descent, grassroots organization based in central Brooklyn.

FIST is the outgrowth of the Student Power Movement (SPM), a student of color organization formed in response to the budget cuts to higher education in New York State in 1995. As SPM, young activists of color were able to organize mass opposition to the decimation of the City University (CUNY) system and call attention to other campus issues, such as the introduction of armed SAFE officers on school grounds. Through direct action such as rallies, speak-outs, and political education study sessions, SPM was able to influence the debate about the need for people of color to access higher education. SPM also did extensive work in the summer of 1995 on the campaign to save the life of the political prisoner Mumia Abu Jamal, a death row inmate in the state of Pennsylvania and a former Black Panther Party member. SPM was heavily involved in many different aspects of the liberation struggle and developed a strong membership base. However, as the leadership of the SPM began to graduate, and leave its respective campuses, a reevaluation of the organization's best position within the movement for social change took place. Recognizing the transience of student struggle, and understanding the leadership's inability to effectively influence campus issues after departing their schools, SPM decided that a more long-term focus and identity was necessary. Thus, FIST was born to reflect the membership's belief in the protracted nature of struggle.

In addition to operating a feeding program in central Brooklyn and organizing various other community projects, FIST has been dedicated to addressing police brutality and its impact on our communities. It has attempted to combat police misconduct and brutality through a variety of methods, with the strategic aims of educating oppressed communities about their rights and redirecting community control back into the hands of residents. FIST has used a multifaceted approach in order to attain these objectives. First, in the area of education, the collective has organized "Know Your Rights" workshops that feature information about the appropriate procedures one should use when confronted by the police. For instance, carrying valid identification and attempting to memorize the badge numbers of the officers involved in the interaction are two advisory items discussed in these workshops. Role-playing of potentially inflammatory situations with the police is also used to provoke meaningful dialogue about the problems of police-citizen interface. Finally, the workshop concludes with a question-and-answer segment where participants can ask a lawyer specific legal questions in regard to their rights in a confrontation with police. FIST also has created *Know Your Rights*, a pamphlet that summarizes the points covered in the workshops. The pamphlet also provides a list of the names and contact information of legal institutions and community organizations where people can seek assistance in filing a police brutality complaint or obtaining legal counsel.

Second, FIST has been involved in the discourse concerning alternative means of protecting our communities. The organization takes the position that the mission of police officers is to protect property, not people, in disenfranchised communities. FIST believes police brutality is a systemic issue, not a case of a "few rotten apples." The police department and its members are the military arm of a capitalist state that directs it to regulate a population it wishes to keep contained. The comments often presented to FIST members are that the police are needed to apprehend criminals and that, sometimes, safety can come at the expense of civil rights. Thus, many people perceive police brutality as an unfortunate yet bearable part of protecting our communities from unlawful elements. The response of FIST members is that the true necessity is an entity that has a vested interest in protecting our communities. For a long time now, the police have been viewed as this force, no questions asked. However, FIST espouses the notion that members of neighborhoods and populations that suffer the most under the brutal measures of law enforcement must engage in dialogue about alternative ways of securing our own well being. Therefore, FIST has talked about the possibility of cop patrols modeled after the Black Panther Party. The Black Panther Party gained a great deal of its early notoriety for following police officers in Oakland with guns and a copy of the California penal code that detailed mandatory police procedures in suspect detainment. This was an attempt by the Black Panthers to address the dilemma of Oakland's Black citizens being assaulted by the police on a regular basis. In early 1998, the Black Panther Collective, a grassroots organization based in New York City, updated the idea of copwatch patrols by using video cameras and other surveillance equipment to shadow police officers in the Washington Heights and Harlem sections of Manhattan. FIST supported such measures, and our members accompanied the Black Panther Collective on some of their patrols. FIST has also considered initiating such a patrol in the central Brooklyn area, where it does much of its organizing.

Another way of improving safety in our neighborhoods is to create a stronger community response to illegal activity. We should acknowledge that only a small segment of our communities are engaged in criminal activities. The majority of citizens are hardworking, law-abiding folks. However, conditions have allowed that small segment to dominate our neighborhoods, and there is a sense of fear and isolation among a large number of people living in poor, oppressed communities. They feel under constant attack from drug dealers, gang members, street hustlers, and brutal police officers. Many of them do not realize the power of the majority, and instead exist under the tyranny of the minority. FIST understands that people must gain a sense of power in dictating the happenings in and around our communities.

We seek to increase dialogue about developing stronger block and tenant associations that will organize citizen patrols of their respective locales. These patrols should establish a presence that will deter criminal behavior. They should be able to respond to, and when possible resolve, interpersonal issues such as incidents of domestic violence and neighbor-to-neighbor disputes. Community residents must trust one another to handle internal community issues without police intervention that can exacerbate the problem and result in the death or unjust detainment of residents. Community pressure must exhort drug dealers to discontinue their blood trade. We must also take some responsibility for creating spaces where our children can play unharmed, and our elders can sit and talk of better days into the late evening, without fear of attack. We must realize that some of the criminals who are demonized and portrayed as almost subhuman are our children. It is crucial to our collective growth that we provide guidance through education and engagement. We have to produce and utilize a code of acceptable behavior in the streets. It is vital that we learn to deal with our own before the police manhandle and murder them. Intergenerational links must be established as elders impart to younger generations critical information on how to handle and overcome life barriers such as police brutality and murder. Young people should also seek the wisdom of the elders about how to raise families properly, how to create more engaging neighborhoods, and, in general, how to reach our goals successfully. Mutual respect should be developed between generations as the views and ideas of younger folks are acknowledged by our older role models. Essentially, we must once again begin to make the meaning of community a part of our everyday lives.

Next, the harsh economic realities of many communities and its causes should be studied. Most crime is influenced by the lack of access to jobs. A *New York Times* article of May 23, 1997, that detailed the upsurge of employment for Black males with only a high school education reported that the unemployment figure for Black males of all education levels was 17 percent. That is twice the rate for their White male counterparts. An analysis of the tools necessary to alleviate this problem should be undertaken. Finally, the economic exploitation of disenfranchised populations is an essential component that we must investigate in order to improve the financial health of these communities. Many people settle into our communities without having its best intentions on their agendas. From parasitic landlords who ignore tenants' pleas to improve building conditions to unscrupulous merchants who cheat consumers with high prices and shoddy goods, the elements in our midst that are harmful to our economic development should be challenged through constructive dialogue and protest, if necessary. If they are unresponsive to our concerns, we should set up a mechanism to force them to leave our communities.

All the aforementioned proposals are subsumed under FIST's concept of developing "liberated territories." FIST envisions a time when community control will be a genuine reality. The economic, political, and social thrust of our communities will then truly be shaped and dictated by its residents. These "liberated territories" would be built around the collective interests of the neighborhood members, and would be free from the obstruction of persons or forces that are toxic to its vitality and prosperity. While it may sound quixotic to some, it is, when carefully examined, simply the authentic notion of a democratic, humanitarian society. We have been led to doubt and discount our abilities of self-determination because many would stand to lose their fiefdoms if this idea were effectively nurtured. From entrenched bureaucrats to disingenuous corporations to brutal police officers, these individuals, in order to thrive, need us to feel dependent on them. The "liberated territory" construct allows every individual to feel efficacious in contributing to the outcomes of his or her daily existence in some manner, unhampered by such unhealthy subordination. FIST believes that the movement for the birth of liberated territories is gaining momentum, and a discussion of the topic is crucial.

FIST also recognizes the need for alliance building to strengthen our vocal opposition to police violation of our communities. Toward that end, FIST became one of the founding member organizations of the New York City Coalition against Police Brutality (CAPB), a collection of youth-oriented, grassroots organizations of color. CAPB was established in 1996 to build a progressive front to address the epidemic of police brutality in New York City. In addition to FIST, the other founding organizations—the Audre Lorde Project, CAAAV Organizing Asian Communities, the National Congress for Puerto Rican Rights, and the Malcolm X Grassroots Movement—serve African diaspora, Asian, Latino, and Lesbian, Gay, Bisexual, Two-spirit, and Transgender (LGBTST) people of color communities. Since 1997, CAPB has organized Racial Justice Day (RJD), a rally and march held in New York City, as a day of resistance and solidarity with the victims of racial violence and their families. Racial Justice Day was started by the National Congress for Puerto Rican Rights to commemorate the death of Manuel Mayi, a Dominican college student who was brutally murdered by a White racist gang in the Corona, Queens, section of New York City. Racial Justice Day usually occurs on or near March 29, the date of Mayi's death in 1991. CAPB asserts that police brutality is one of the greatest forms of racist violence, and some of the goals for RJD are to reach out to a diverse range of communities to expose how police brutality is perpetuated, and to stand united in our collective demands for social change and justice.

The New York City CAPB has also organized a campaign to address the issue of NYPD-trained officers in city public schools. In the fall of 1998, the New York City Board of Education, with the support of the schools chancellor and the mayor, and without consulting parents and students, voted to transfer control of school safety to the NYPD. Given the NYPD's poor track record in dealing with young persons of color, who are the majority of the public school system population, CAPB vigorously opposes this measure; it has attempted to organize parents, students, and other concerned citizens to possibly overturn this measure. Some members of CAPB work directly with the victims of police brutality and the families of the victims killed by police in attempting to gain justice through the legal system while providing a support base for them. CAPB is unique in that it links a diverse group of populations that are disproportionately affected by police brutality and is led by an array of visionary, young activists of color. Members are able to exchange ideas and sharpen skills within the CAPB space, which serves as a fruitful training ground for anti–police brutality activists. The potential of this coalition is endless and will continue to grow as the struggle against police brutality escalates.

FIST and CAPB both recognize that it is especially important to get young people involved in the battle against police brutality and the overall struggle for liberation. I have worked with youth of color in some manner for the last twelve years. Whether in mentoring young boys in Harlem or counseling high school students in a dropout prevention program in Brooklyn, my experiences and interactions with young people of color have lead me to conclude that their view of the police is mostly negative. Unfortunately, these youngsters have accepted police harassment as a part of their daily routine. They usually express a sense of powerlessness and hopelessness in terms of defending themselves against police brutality. As one of my former students stated, "Cops are always gonna harass us no matter what we do." Young people are disenfranchised in so many areas, particularly in educational institutions and in accessing employment, that it is critical that they believe in their ability to decide the course of their daily interactions. They must not feel frustrated and upset every time they walk the streets, anticipating being badgered by police officers energized by their dominion over young people. The aim of FIST and CAPB is to get youth involved in activist work to understand their capacity to dictate their own destinies. From being trained as workshop leaders to being co-leaders of a work committee to participating in a study group, youth develop a greater sense of self-confidence in guiding the direction of their lives.

While the feelings of disempowerment in the face of police authority are found in greater proportions in young people, they are not restricted to this population; rather, they pervade all segments of oppressed communities, where the concept of the police as an occupying army is very widespread. Usually, it is young White males with guns and a macho attitude guided by fear and loathing who are sent to control neighborhoods that they don't understand. Their interactions with the community are brief and rough. Although the nature of repression is much more sophisticated and subtle than it was in the past, it can be debated whether many people of color are just as frightened now by the sight of an approaching squad car as they used to be of roving street gangs. It is vital that we assist in changing this attitude. Members of our communities have to feel a sense of power in determining their safety, both from criminals and from the infringement of their rights and the battering of their bodies by police officers.

The war against police brutality must be fought on many fronts. First, we must address the immediate concern of removing and punishing brutish police officers while getting justice for the victims of police brutality and the families of those murdered. Next, citizens, particularly young people of color, must fully comprehend their rights when approached by a cop, and be cognizant of what recourse they have in a hostile situation. Internally, oppressed communities of color have to take the initiative in developing viable options to ensure their own security instead of depending on the police. We must also fight the tendency to criminalize our youth, particularly our Black males, while attempting to create a more positive image of them. The root causes of police brutality must be frankly discussed. A comprehensive analysis of the economic inequities mandated by capitalism and its link to crime and punishment must be tackled.

While these steps do not have to occur in such a linear fashion as I've detailed, it is essential that each be dealt with. Obviously, a number of formidable tasks must be addressed by those who are dedicated to stopping police violence. I concede that it is a huge challenge to implement all these proposals. However, I believe that they can be accomplished through collective determination, strength, and commitment. With the knowledge and the spirit of those warriors who preceded us, and through the use of a variety of effective strategies, liberated territories can be developed that are relatively devoid of police brutality and murder, and rich with vigorous growth. We must either make it happen or face the continued decimation of our communities. We at least owe our elders, our children, and ourselves the possibility of a better existence through a hard-fought battle.

> Let our legacy be that with our every waking breath, we challenged the status quo. Not for our own personal gain, but so that our progeny would know a more just and humane society than we ever did.
>
> —FIST (Forever in Struggle Together)

Notes

1. Steven R. Donziger, *The Real War on Crime* (New York: Harper Perennial, 1996), 102.

2. Ibid., 112.

3. Marc Mauer, *Young Black Americans and the Criminal Justice System: Five Years Later* (Washington, D.C.: Sentencing Project, 1995).

4. *United States of America: Police Brutality and Excessive Force in the New York City Police Department.* New York: Amnesty International, 1996.

5. Donziger, *The Real War on Crime*, 104–5.

6. *Boston Globe*, January 10, 1990, Metro, p. 1; September 25, 1990, p. 16.

7. Associated Press, November 9, 1994.

8. *Village Voice*, June 17, 1997, p. 43.

9. *New York Daily News*, April 10, 1997, p. 6; *New York Daily News*, July 2, 1997, p. 4.

10. *New York Times*, May 28, 1997, sec. B, p. 1.

11. *New York Daily News*, July 2, 1997, p. 4; *New York Daily News*, May 3, 1997, p. 8.

12. *New York Tiimes*, May 5, 1999, sec. A, p. 1.

13. Ibid., June 9, 1999, sec. A, p. 1.

Point No. 7:*
We Want an Immediate End to Police Brutality
and the Murder of Black People

Why I Joined the Black Panther Party

FLORES ALEXANDER FORBES

It was another warm day in the summer of 1968 in San Diego. I hooked a U-turn on Imperial Avenue in order to pull my parents' 1960 Mercury in front of what appeared to be the local office of the Black Panther Party. I was sixteen years old, and after having read the Black Panther newspaper and most of my older brother's Black history and literature books that he had brought home from UCLA, I was convinced that this was my calling. I had heard from my brother and his college friends that the brothers up north in Oakland had a program to deal with the "man." Maybe I thought this new program would get the "man" off my ass too.

In general, I wanted to be a Black Panther so that I could help my people overcome the oppression they and I were experiencing. In particular, I wanted to get back at the San Diego policeman who had been harassing me since I was twelve.

Back in 1964, when I was twelve, I was riding my brand-new Schwinn Sting Ray bicycle up the hill from my parents' home on Forty-seventh Street, in southeast San Diego. As I reached the intersection of Forty-seventh and Market, I could hear the tires of a car slowly following behind me or just off to my right on the gravel of the adjacent parking lot. As I came to a stop at the red signal light, I heard a man's voice with a distinctly southern drawl call out, "Boy, come over here."

The sound of the voice scared me. So I froze for a few seconds. By the time I recovered and turned around, I saw two White policemen getting out of their white cruiser. The officers came over to me and said, "Would you come with us for a ride?" I was horrified and looked around for help. My mouth was so dry that I couldn't shout or speak—not one word would come out. I was petrified as I straddled my bike. I couldn't even raise my arms to wave and draw the attention of the people who were passing by, many of them friends of my parents. Cars passed and the people in them were just looking at this scene as if it were normal. The policeman took my bike from me and put it in the trunk of their car, opened the back door, and told me, as one of them squeezed my arm, to get in. Like a frightened fool and the innocent I was, I hopped in.

They drove me up the hill on Market Street toward downtown San Diego. After a ten- or fifteen-minute ride, they pulled into a residential area just short of downtown and drove up to several other police officers and a young White couple. The car stopped, and the cop on the passenger side got out and walked over to the group of people. After a few brief words, which I could not hear, the officer pointed toward me sitting in the back seat, explaining something to them as he pointed. The cop and the couple walked over to the car and peered in. By this time my entire body was shaking with fear. All I could think about was going home and never riding my bike again. They looked at me in the back seat, conferred, and looked again. The couple looked at each other and spoke a few more words I couldn't hear (they never rolled the window down). The White man stood back from the window, shaking his head from side to side. He then took his woman by the hand and walked back toward the six or so policemen and they huddled again. The policeman returned to the car. They drove me back to Forty-seventh Street and pulled into the parking lot where I had been kidnapped.

A huge crowd had gathered in the parking lot, and standing in the center was my mother. The policeman stopped, got out, went around to open the trunk and got my bike, while the other cop opened the back door to let me out. Man was I glad! My mother, with the crowd of neighbors in tow, approached the cops asking, "What are you doing with Flores? Did he do anything wrong?"

The cop who had my bike told my mother, "Back away, bitch, this is official police business." My mother stopped in her tracks. This was the first time in my life that I saw my mother kill someone with a look. I grabbed my bike as fast as I could and ran with it to my mother's side. The police car pulled off, spinning its tires in the gravel and dirt, kicking up rocks and dirt as it sped into the street and drove away.

This was strike number one for me and my encounters with police harassment. I was young and had just taken a ride in a police car. I did not know then that my life was in danger, but I would never forget. The second strike came just two years later.

It was nighttime, and I was jogging around the track at Lincoln High School, which was about two long blocks from my home. At the time, I was playing Pop Warner football, and it was Friday night. According to the weight standards for my division, I was two or three pounds overweight. So that evening, I put on my workout gear and underneath wrapped my body, from the waist up, in dry cleaners plastic so that I could sweat the pounds away. I ran hard up the hill on Forty-seventh Street to Lincoln (Saturday was game day, and I wanted to play badly). At the top of the hill sat Lincoln High School. On another corner, where the old Hudson Department Store used to be, was now a dance hall for young people. As I ran by, I could see it was packed with dozens of young Black men and women dancing inside and milling around outside. I could just barely hear the latest Temptations record, "It's Growing," over the outside speaker. I turned left at the intersection of Imperial and Forty-seventh Street and carefully crossed the street and headed toward the track. I crawled under the fence surrounding the track and began sprinting to burn off the two or three excess pounds.

I had been running for about fifteen minutes when I saw dozens of police cars racing past the track heading for the dance hall. The young Blacks at the dance were restless; maybe a fight had broken out. They started throwing rocks and bottles and what have you at the policemen. The police were taking up positions behind their cars for cover. Apparently, the police swooped on the crowd, and everyone outside of the dance hall began to scatter and run down Forty-seventh Street and in both directions along Imperial Avenue. Many headed toward the track, where I continued to look and run at the same time. As I continued running, a spotlight started tracking me as I rounded the backstretch. Unsuspecting and, yes, very innocently, I continued to run and run, thinking only about making the weight and showing Coach Wallace that I was not the "lazy slob" he had called me at our last practice.

All of a sudden, I could see cop cars lining up along the fence just above the depressed athletic field I was running on. Several San Diego policemen in beige uniforms began climbing the fence. I heard one of them shout, "Here's one here, running down the track."

I did not realize he was pointing me out. I thought they could clearly see I was not at the dance and that I was not dressed for the dance. I kept running and as I made another turn could hear footsteps and hard breathing coming up on me. I also heard the jingling of several police utility belts clanging against their sides. Out of the corner of my eye, I noticed this one cop gaining on me. As he got nearer, he hit my legs with his baton. The blow knocked me off my pace, and I stumbled and then rolled over onto the ground. I was hit with another club again and again as I squirmed to avoid the blows and protect my head. Some of the cops started kicking me as I tried to roll away, onto the grass, in an attempt to avoid their blows. Then they stopped. From the ground I could see several of the cops with flashlights, clubs, and scowling faces looking down at me pointing and calling me names. Several of them restrained the cop who had run me down. He was yelling something like, "No nigger can outrun Joe," or something to that effect.

They started to move in again, but then a Black cop intervened. It was the father of a classmate of mine, Mr. Cunningham, the first Black policeman I knew of in San Diego. He walked toward me quickly and pulled me up and toward him with one hand. With his free hand he pulled my sweatshirt hood off my head while flashing his flashlight in my face.

"What are you doing up here running from us?" he asked.

"I'm trying to make my weight for the game tomorrow, Mr. Cunningham," I said almost crying through my trembling lips.

The other cops, especially Joe, continued to pull at me and jostle me until Mr. Cunningham said, "My God, fellas, this is the Forbes boy. He goes to school with my kids."

Upon hearing this, the other cops seemed to calm down and then one of them shouted directly in my face, saying, "Get out of here, boy, and run home as fast as you can."

I immediately broke any grip they had on me and ran to the fence, scaled it in no time, and ran toward home. I could hear them laughing. My heart pumped with fear. I felt as if my heart was still pounding the next day at the game. I made my weight.

Two years later, in the summer of 1968, I joined the Black Panther Party. I was sixteen. Work in the party was to be my career for the next ten years. My reasons for joining were simple: I wanted to help my people and myself by ending the police brutality I had experienced. I wanted to stop the police tendency to murder Black people with impunity. The Black Panther Party's Ten-Point Platform and Program addressed this issue in point no. 7, which jumped out at me as I reviewed the program line by line upon my first visit to the San Diego office. However, the paradox of my youthful career choice was that joining the Black Panther Party to fight police repression would place me squarely in harm's way. Doing something to help my people meant that I would put myself in a position to be killed, imprisoned, made a fugitive, and/or for long periods of time receive the brunt of police or state-sponsored repression by placing myself between the police and my community. I understood this in the beginning, and I understood it in the end. I accepted the challenge and dealt with it with my eyes wide open.

There was no illusion brought on by psychedelic drugs, nor was there a White Communist-led conspiracy organizing Black people to respond to this menace. What it was for me, as it may have been for other young Black men and women at this time, was a strong belief that White policemen were engaged in activities that were deliberate, clear attempts at genocide against the Black race. Being under siege convinced me that the only way to gain freedom was to fight and fight hard.

The harassment and brutality that I experienced while in the Black Panther Party was intense, consistent, and severe. However, my experiences within the organization were extremely broad and fruitful. I participated in every functional area of work that the party had to offer. I sold Black Panther newspapers seven days a week, organized and served free breakfast to hungry schoolchildren, and worked in the Ministry of Information as a community news reporter and as a leaflet developer. I was the officer of the day (OD) in one of our Los Angeles offices as well as the OD in one of our offices in San Francisco. I helped bag groceries for food giveaways and worked in various capacities in the large "Free Huey" rallies and on other issues as well. As time went by and I became more experienced and more trusted, I was promoted up through the ranks. In 1974, I was appointed the assistant chief of staff of the Black Panther Party. However, regardless of my area of work or rank, I was still subjected to the same intense and consistent harassment and brutality for the entire ten years.

During these same ten years, I also experienced geographic diversity in the party. I was stationed in San Diego, Riverside, Los Angeles, East Oakland, San Francisco, and, finally, Oakland. In each of these cities, the party and the individuals that made up a particular chapter or branch were subjected to police harassment, murder, and brutality on a daily basis. Without exception, though, no party chapter or branch experienced the type of harassment, brutality, and murder that was experienced by the chapter located in Los Angeles.

In Los Angeles, I was stopped by the LAPD while selling Black Panther newspapers almost every single day. The cops insulted me, beat me, and, usually, dislodged my papers from under my arm, causing them to fly all over the streets of South Central Los Angeles. Even when I invoked the principles and guidelines of the *Pocket Lawyer of Legal First Aid*, the cops would bristle. One told me emphatically, "Nigger, you, your momma, and them other Black motherfuckers in this country have no constitutional rights that we recognize."

As time went on, the harassment got even hairier. For example, one of our offices was a victim of a police drive-by from a regular "black and white" that zoomed past our office at Seventy-eighth Street, firing a barrage of rounds from an automatic pistol. The office was riddled with bullets; luckily no one was hurt. However, following the drive-by, the LAPD made a move against us at Seventy-eighth Street that was so intense that almost half the Panthers stationed at this office deserted over the following week.

It was late afternoon on a Saturday in 1971, and the office was full of comrades returning from selling papers in the field. The officer of the day, Shelton Jones, had left his desk and walked outside into the front yard for his routine visual patrol of the streets in front of the office to see whether there was any unusual police activity. Our office was typical of the homes in this section of South Central Los Angeles: single family detached, one story with an attic, three bedrooms, a living room, kitchen, one bathroom, and a dining area. (We had moved our offices into residential areas because it was safer and less isolated there than in the storefronts we had inhabited earlier in our history.) The front yard was expansive, with the main house set back about thirty-five feet from the sidewalk and the street. In the front yard, there was a powder-blue sign with black lettering and the Panther logo designating this site as a Black Panther Party Office, Southern California Chapter. In the center of the front yard, bordered by a manicured green lawn, was a long sidewalk that went from the front gate to the steps of the porch. The entire front yard was enclosed by a wire fence about four feet high.

This may have looked like a normal house to the untrained eye, but once you stepped inside, you easily noticed a difference. Since I joined the party in 1968, the LAPD and other agents provocateurs had to my personal knowledge killed eleven Panthers. Therefore, as proponents of self-defense by any means necessary, we were intent on surviving whatever the LAPD threw at us, because we knew there was a revolution to be fought in the future. We had been "tunneling for freedom" for the past two months. We dug straight down through the floor of a closet in one of our bedrooms for about ten feet and then hollowed out an area, like a vestibule that had two tunnels heading in different directions. The entry and the tunnels were all braced with plywood and two-by-fours. Each of the tunnels went directly to an exit under our neighbors' homes. Large planter-like boxes were constructed in the living room, bedrooms, and dining area. The boxes were rectangular and had frames made of two-by-fours that were built out from the drywall of the house. The frame was then covered with plywood on all sides, including the top. Prior to being sealed, the boxes were filled with the dirt from our tunnels. (We did this so the police could not see us bringing in the dirt.) The boxes were either painted to match the office paint or decorated with wallpaper. They extended out from the drywall about eighteen inches. We had been assured by our resident engineer that no bullet could penetrate that distance. (The engineer was one of the brothers who fortified the office at Forty-first and Central. This was the scene of the December 8, 1969, shoot-out, which marked the first time the LAPD had used its new SWAT team. The gun battle lasted six hours, and no Panthers were killed, so we had a great deal of confidence in the brother's skills.)

In the attic, Simba, one of the many Vietnam veterans in the party, constructed an "eagle's nest." This station was sandbagged and would be used as an elevated firing position. Under the house was a trench system that faced the front yard, backyard alley, and the two short sides of the house. This system had eight reinforced gun ports that were protected with wire mesh and sandbags. Finally, in one of the bedrooms off the kitchen in a locked closet was the gun cabinet, stocked with riot pump shotguns, one AR-180, and an assortment of handguns.

Shelton was outside by himself, packing a .45 automatic, as was customary for the officer of the day. The OD at different intervals walked down the sidewalk to the front gate to look up and down both sides of the street to check whether the police were forming, which could be a sign of a raid or direct assault. (Our office was located just two blocks from the LAPD's notorious Seventy-seventh Precinct.) All of a sudden, one of the sisters pointed out the front door and shouted, "The pigs have Shelton."

Shelton was standing just inside the gate with his hands in the air, surrounded by six to eight policemen, all with their guns trained on him. The police disarmed him and pulled him over the fence. They did not come in the yard or rush the door. I started to hear the pounding of feet and the jingling of keys on the right side of the office. The police were outflanking us and taking up positions in our neighbor's yard. I could also hear the heavy engines from LAPD squad cars roaring through the alley. They literally shook the house. I noticed, as did everyone else, that the police in the front street were positioning themselves behind their cars with revolvers and riot shotguns.

I did not feel anxious, having experienced these fake assaults dozens of times. But I was somewhat alarmed at the speed with which everything unfolded and with the precision displayed by this particular group of cops. I asked myself a very personal question, "Was this it?" Damn, I was only nineteen years old. The defense captain came from the back quickly with a key in his hand and went to the gun locker, unlocked it, and started handing out the weapons to the Panthers, who had begun lining up to get their piece. One brother slammed the large reinforced front door and slid the two-by-four we used to secure the door between the metal L-shaped braces that snugly cradled the long board, making it more difficult for a police battering ram to knock it down. As the defense captain handed out the weapons, he reminded each Panther what his or her preassigned position was. When I got my riot shotgun and bandolier from him, he shouted directly into my face, "What's your position?"

"I'm in the trench, northeast corner," I shouted back at him.

"Right on," he responded. "And keep your head down."

"Right on," I said in response.

I could sense from the defense captain's body language and the stern look on his face that he might not believe this was a drill, either. (This sort of harassment, dubbed a "Mexican standoff," or almost a shoot-out, happened to every office we had in LA on either a weekly or biweekly basis.) I moved quickly through the dining area, into the hallway, and around the corner to the tunnel-trench system. There was a short line, so I waited my turn to climb down the ladder. When my turn came, I went down the ladder and slipped, landing hard on the plywood floor. Yes, I was a little nervous, but steady. I followed the trench that led to my position under the northeast corner of the house. It was dirty and hot down there. The dust was flying, since so many bodies were moving around, and this made my breathing, and I assume everyone else's, difficult. I started to sweat profusely. Nevertheless, I loaded the shotgun, chambering the last round—a rifled slug. I set my bandolier down in the dirt and waited, still sweating. From my vantage point, I could see our front yard, grass level. I removed the screen from my gun port, exposing the wire mesh that remained to protect me from tear gas canisters. I put the barrel of my shotgun near, but not completely outside of, the gun port. Everything got quiet in the office, which made me believe we were all in position and ready to defend ourselves. To me at that moment, this was what it was all about: taking a stand and letting the state know that somewhere in our community a group of people were prepared to fight and die, if necessary.

The house started to rattle. The trees in our yard and across the street started to swirl. The once still grass began to flutter. It was the LAPD's chopper descending slowly and then drawing to a hover over the office. In the street outside the office and over the sound of the chopper, I could hear hundreds of our neighbors shouting and yelling at the police, who had once more invaded our community as if they were an occupying army in a foreign land. The police did not move, and we did not move. Upstairs, the cocoordinator of our chapter called the local press, our lawyers, and the Seventy-seventh Precinct's watch commander to ascertain the purpose of their actions. We remained like this for about thirty minutes. I was still sweating, coughing, inhaling dirt particles, and glancing over to the persons next to me, looking into their eyes to see if they were as nervous as I was becoming.

After this brief pause, there was movement outside. I tensed up, ready for something to happen. The police started to pull back. It was over. We stayed at our positions until all of the police had moved beyond our sights. It was at that point that the message to stand down was passed down to the trenches. I waited my turn and moved slowly down the trench and up the ladder. Everyone was quiet as we lined up to return our weapons to the defense captain.

The next day, Shelton was bailed out and charged with possession of a loaded firearm.

Over the next week, four of the ten Panthers stationed at Seventy-eighth Street deserted. One year later, we officially closed down the LA Chapter, and I and the two dozen or so Panthers left were transferred to Oakland in February 1972.

The remainder of my career in the Black Panther Party, a period lasting from 1972 to 1977, would be spent in the San Francisco–Oakland Bay Area. During those six years, I matured into a full-grown adult Panther, achieving the rank of assistant chief of staff and a position on the party's central committee, which meant taking on enormous responsibilities. Fortunately for me, these responsibilities brought me into direct contact with the two men who founded the Black Panther Party, Huey P. Newton and Bobby Seale.

From 1972 to 1977, I wore many hats while in the Black Panther Party and served almost simultaneously on the staffs of Huey P. Newton and Bobby Seale. Moreover, during the period in which

Bobby ran for mayor of Oakland, from 1972 to 1973, I lived in the same house with him and his family. On most days, I would have a conversation with either man about our struggle, strategies, and tactics and just the basic routine of surviving in a country that has oppressed us for several hundred years. But there were also those times when the conversation was sparked by my curiosity regarding more mundane subjects. The biggest of these issues for me was the beginning of the party. How and why did it start? The most interesting aspect of my inquiries had to do with how they developed the Ten-Point Platform and Program in general and how they came up with point no. 7 in particular, which was the reason for my joining the party.

To my delight, both men loved to talk about the beginning. Both Huey and Bobby said they didn't make this stuff up. They said they went into the neighborhoods in the San Francisco–Oakland Bay area and canvassed the young brothers and sisters, asking them various questions on a broad range of issues. As Bobby put it, "We kept getting one overwhelming response from almost every question that began with 'What do you want?'" Almost to a person, he said, their response was related to the police and how they behaved toward and treated Black people in their own communities. "We have the right to defend ourselves as we have the right to Revolution," Huey said. But they would always reiterate one of the main issues: "This program was created by the demand of our constituency. They said they wanted an end to police brutality and the murder of Black people."

The people most directly involved as victims of police brutality were usually people just like me: Black, young, and tired of getting their asses kicked by people other than their parents. My opinion, that Black people should use force to end their oppression, represented a viewpoint that was developed over several years of harassment. It was enough time, however, for me to realize that the response and solution to my problem rested in the program and actions created by Huey P. Newton and Bobby Seale. Moreover, there were many people during those early years, 1969 and 1970, who held the same opinion as I did, whether they joined the party or not. They thought that the Black Panther Party's response and actions mirrored their beliefs.

The approval ratings gleaned from the official survey of support for the Newton and Seale program was in my estimation confirmed by the creation and evolution of the organization that was the Black Panther Party. However, in 1970 the Louis Harris polling agency conducted a survey that asked a representative sample of Black people various questions regarding their attitudes toward, support of the ideas of, and sympathy for the Black Panther Party.[1]

To the question "Do you personally feel the Black Panther Party represents your views or not?" 43 percent of those asked responded by saying yes. To the question about whether the Panthers gave the individual as a Black person a sense of pride by standing up for the rights of Black people, 66 percent said yes. In response to the attacks from 1966 to 1970 on the party that left nineteen Panthers dead[2] as a result of conflicts with the police and other law enforcement agencies, the survey asked whether the individual believed these agencies were attempting to wipe the party out. Sixty-two percent said yes. To the question "Even if you disagree with the views of the Panthers, has the violence against them led you to believe that Black people must stand together to protect themselves?" 86 percent replied in the affirmative. Finally, to the question "Do you feel that the Panthers are gaining sympathy among Black people you know?" 50 percent replied yes.[3]

I had always thought that I would remain a Panther for life or until I was dead. The latter almost came true when I was seriously wounded and my best friend killed in one of the many covert operations I was responsible for in October 1977. From 1977 to 1980, I was a fugitive. In 1980, I turned myself in and was subsequently convicted of Felony Murder and served four years, eight months, and nine days in the California Department of Corrections. I had to reinvent myself while in prison. I started planning a new life without the party; that included forming a personal business plan to focus my activities after my release and completing three semesters of college work in a special prison program. I was released on August 9, 1985; the Black Panther Party as I knew it had been defunct since 1982.

I was absent from the day-to-day operation of the Black Panther Party for five years. If I were to suggest a reason for its demise, I would thus only be speculating. Most people believe that it was COINTELPRO. I didn't learn what this acronym stood for until I was a fugitive. If it was this FBI program, I would still be guessing because when one was out of the loop in the party, one had no idea what was happening. Other people say it was bad internal management. Again, I would respond by saying that if you weren't there, you would find it difficult to pinpoint the exact cause.

As for myself, I outgrew the need for a disciplined organization. So by the time I learned of the party's demise, I had already moved on with my life. I did not need the comfort of numbers to shape my ideas any longer. The menace of police brutality will, in my estimation, be with this society as long as the system continues to view Black people as beings less than human.

I would not change, however, the path I took. The Black Panther Party, in its short history, educated millions of people and myself about a country that is violent and brutal toward its so-called citizens who happen to have red or Black skin. It is because of the Black Panther Party that the buzzwords "reverse discrimination" are today synonymous with "Manifest Destiny."

In 1986, I completed my undergraduate education and moved to New York City to study urban planning at New York University as a Patricia Roberts Harris Fellow. One evening, in 1989, I was leaving NYU's law library and started walking down Washington Square South toward the main library when out of my left eye I noticed a blue and white NYPD vehicle pulling up on the sidewalk to block my path. Two White officers got out of their car and approached cautiously. They told me they had received a call from a local resident identifying me as a local drug dealer in Washington Square Park. I was a little shocked at their "Keystone Cop" antics and decided not to follow the guidelines of the *Pocket Lawyer*. I would play it straight.

I told them they must be mistaken because I was a graduate student doing research in the law library, where I had been for several hours.

They responded, "Oh yeah, right! You go to NYU?"

"Yeah! I'm working on my master's degree . . ."

One of them cut me off and said, "If you don't have a valid NYU ID card, I'm taking your Black ass to jail."

I looked at both of them before responding. I had no flashbacks or anything like that. "I'm going to reach into my book bag and get my ID," I said. They glanced at each other as if I was mocking them and motioned for me to proceed. I produced my ID as they snickered. They seemed to be unhappy that I was being truthful.

One of them said, "Okay, you can go, but watch it." They pulled off.

Instead of going on to the Bobst Library I went back to my dorm room, muttering to myself, "Not much has changed."

I WANT AN IMMEDIATE END TO POLICE BRUTALITY AND THE MURDER OF BLACK PEOPLE!

Notes

*Point no. 7 of the Black Panther Party's Ten-Point Platform and Program.

1. *The Harris Survey Yearbook of Public Opinion*, 1970 (New York: Louis Harris and Associates, 1971).

2. Ibid., 260.

3. Ibid., 257.

12

The Crisis of Police Brutality and Misconduct in America

The Causes and the Cure

RON DANIELS

The police killing of Amadou Diallo, an unarmed twenty-two-year-old street vendor from Guinea, West Africa, by officers of the New York Police Department (NYPD) on February 4, 1999, was the proverbial straw that broke the camel's back. The forty-one shots fired at Diallo, nineteen of which hit his body, reverberated around this country, Africa, and the world, a telling sign that something was terribly wrong in American society in terms of police-community relations. The killing of Diallo provoked such a firestorm of reaction because his death was the tip of the iceberg of police brutality and misconduct in this society. The acquittal of the four officers who killed Diallo does not mitigate the outrage in communities of color. America is in the throes of yet another epidemic of police violence and abuse—an epidemic that is generating outrage all across the country, particularly in Black communities and communities of color. In my capacity as executive director of the Center for Constitutional Rights (CCR), virtually every conversation I have with people about the most critical issues facing their communities includes police brutality. It is once again a major problem in communities of color in this country.

The growing crisis of police brutality and misconduct first came to our attention at CCR in 1996. During regular monthly meetings with representatives of community-based organizations through CCR's Movement Support Resource Center, the issue of police brutality began to dominate the discussions. Whether the scheduled topic was workfare, environmental justice, or poorly performing schools, police brutality would find its way into the conversation, particularly if young African Americans and Latinos were participating in it. At the request of participants of the MSRC, we decided to convene a series of special meetings dealing exclusively with the issue of police brutality and misconduct.

At the first meeting, the conference room was packed with people, the overflow spilling out into the hallway. What unfolded was a picture of young people relentlessly harassed through random stops and frisks and massive sweeps of Black and Latino neighborhoods in New York. Worse still, people complained of an increasing incidence of police beatings and use of deadly force. During one of these special sessions, we heard an urgent appeal for help from a group that was then called Mothers against Police Brutality (later renamed Parents against Police Brutality). It was at this meeting that I first met Iris Baez, whose son Anthony Baez was killed by an officer administering a chokehold, and Margarita Rosario, whose son Anthony Rosario and nephew Hilton Vega were both killed execution style by officers of the NYPD as they lay face down on the floor. Mrs. Baez and Mrs. Rosario would emerge as key leaders in the struggle against police brutality in New York.

These special meetings led to a call for CCR to convene a national conference to bring activists and lawyers together to assess the extent of the problem of police brutality nationally and to explore strategies for police reform and accountability. The sentiment was that the conference should be held in New York, which many activists believe to be the police brutality capital of America. Among the New York/New Jersey–based organizations that agreed to assist with the local and national mobilization for the conference were the National Congress for Puerto Rican Rights, the Committee against Anti-Asian Violence, the Black Panther Collective, the December 12 Movement,

Black Cops against Police Brutality, the Malcolm X Grassroots Movement, Jews for Racial and Economic Justice, the New York chapter of the National Lawyers Guild, Refuse and Resist, the NAACP Legal Defense and Education Fund, and the Asian American Legal Defense and Education Fund. In terms of the national mobilization, CCR reached out to Amnesty International, the National Black Police Association, the National Coalition for Police Accountability, the National Lawyers Guild, the National Conference of Black Lawyers, Concerned Citizens against Police Abuse in Syracuse, United Concerned Christians at Work in Pittsburgh, and the Coalition against Police Abuse in Los Angeles.

On April 25–27, 1997, more than seven hundred people from fifty-two cities and sixteen states gathered at Hunter College for the National Emergency Conference on Police Brutality and Misconduct. The testimony at this crucial conference validated what civil and human rights activists suspected. What could only be described as police terror was on the rise around the country. One of its most frightening manifestations was a dramatic increase in police killings of African American, Latino, and Asian American youth, mostly men. From virtually every community represented at the conference came stories of controversial cases of police killings that had sparked local protests. The tragic list of police killings spanned every region of the country:

- In Pittsburgh, Jonny Gammage, a cousin of the Pittsburgh Steelers defensive lineman Ray Seals, was asphyxiated by police in 1995 after they stopped him in his late-model Jaguar in a predominantly White suburb of the city. The officers involved claimed that Gammage, who was unarmed and had no prior police record, was acting suspiciously.[1]
- Archie Elliot, a twenty-four-year-old Black man, was killed in 1993 in Prince Georges County, Maryland. He was shot fourteen times by two police officers while his hands were handcuffed behind his back as he sat in the front seat of a police cruiser. The

officers said that Elliot was able to get his hands on a gun and was threatening them.[2]

- Rudy Buchanan, a twenty-two-year-old Latino man, was killed in a housing project in Phoenix, Arizona, in 1995. Buchanan was fatally wounded when thirteen officers fired a fusillade of eighty-nine shots at him.[3]
- Malice Green, a Black man, was killed in Detroit in 1992 by two White police officers who kicked and punched him after he allegedly refused to comply with their orders. Other officers at the scene failed to stop the beating. Green suffered a seizure and died on the way to the hospital.[4]
- Kim Groves, a Black woman, was executed in 1994 in New Orleans by Officer Len Davis, a Black man, who learned that Groves had filed a police abuse complaint against him.[5]
- Esequiel Hernandez Jr., a Latino man, was killed in 1997 in Redford, Texas, by four U.S. Marines on drug patrol. This case triggered a national debate about the role of the military in civilian policing.[6]
- Ivory McQueen, a forty-three-year-old Black woman with a history of mental problems, was killed when she was shot multiple times by sheriff's deputies in Cumberland County, North Carolina, because she was holding a kitchen knife.[7]

But it was New York City that surfaced as the epicenter of the crisis, with scores of cases of police beatings and killings in the last decade. The case of the torture and sodomizing of Abner Louima, an emigrant from Haiti, in 1997, focused the national spotlight on New York, two years before the police shooting of Amadou Diallo. It was in New York that Mayor Rudolph W. Giuliani, a former federal prosecutor, assigned himself the task of innovating a strategy for crime reduction that he hoped would be emulated nationally. The essence of his approach is to promote "aggressive policing," targeting "high crime" neighborhoods in Black and Latino communities. These neighborhoods are subjected to extensive random stops and frisks and massive dragnet-type sweeps, ostensibly to get guns off the streets and to capture drug dealers and petty criminals.

According to data published in the *New York Times* on February 15, 1999, the NYPD's infamous Street Crime Unit (it was officers from this unit who killed Amadou Diallo) conducted some 45,084 reported stops and frisks in 1997 and 1998 in search of guns. (It is important to note that these are reported stops. Officials of the NYPD admit that only 1 in 3 or 1 in 5 or even 1 in 10 stops are ever recorded. Using the most conservative estimate of 1 in 3, this would mean that nearly 150,000 people were actually stopped by the NYPD from 1997 to 1998.) Of the 45,084 reported stops, 9,546 people were arrested. Of those arrested, some 5,000 cases were dismissed. About 40,000 innocent people were stopped solely on the basis of the fact that they either lived in a "high crime" neighborhood or fit the "profile" of a "probable suspect."

A random survey conducted by the New York *Daily News* on March 26, 1999, in selected Black and Latino neighborhoods found that out of one hundred people interviewed, eighty-eight had been stopped and frisked by the NYPD. On March 8, 1999, the Center for Constitutional Rights filed a federal civil rights class action lawsuit against the NYPD, seeking to shut the Street Crime Unit down. The suit argued that the practices of this unit violated the Fourth Amendment protection against unreasonable search and seizure and the equal-protection clause of the Fourteenth Amendment because of the use of racial profiling.

In addition to stops and frisks and massive sweeps, Giuliani launched a campaign of "zero tolerance" of "quality of life" crimes. These included consuming alcohol in public, being a squeegee person (offering to clean car windshields for money), aggressive panhandling, and jaywalking. The theory behind the zero tolerance campaign is that petty infractions of the law eventually lead people to commit more serious crimes, hence the need for stringent enforcement of laws dealing with any and all violations, no matter how petty. Under the Giuliani administration, the NYPD has come to encapsulate much of what is wrong with policing in America today in the minds of advocates for police reform—crime reduction strategies that trample on the constitutional rights of people of color and the poor and give police officers the green light to brutalize and even kill "suspects" with impunity.

In discussing the crisis of police brutality in America today, I have deliberately referred to "the most recent wave" of police brutality and misconduct. It is no secret that police brutality has been a persistent problem for Black people and other people of color in this country. Those of us who grew up in inner-city ghettos developed a fear, suspicion, and distrust of the cops because all too often they behaved like a corrupt, occupying army, terrorizing and exploiting our community.

Because of the "we against them" fraternity mentality and the "blue wall of silence" within police departments, it has always been difficult to prove police brutality cases. Police officers often refuse to come forward to expose brutal and corrupt fellow officers. Police departments seldom vigorously investigate allegations of police misconduct. Police officers are also invested with a special dispensation of trust, which affords them the benefit of the doubt in court proceedings. When a police officer arrests a person or testifies in court, there is an automatic assumption that he or she is telling the truth. Although police brutality has always been a fact of life for people of color, we have often felt powerless to do anything about it.

Race and class distinctions also contribute to the problem. Much of White America has an entirely different experience with and perception of the police. Cops do not behave like an occupying army in middle- and upper-class White communities. The view of the police is radically different in these communities. If the Rodney King police beating had not been captured live on videotape, most White Americans would never have believed that the police were capable of such violent and deplorable conduct. Even so, the officers were acquitted of criminal charges. As happened in the case of the Rodney King police beating, Black people and other people of color have periodically risen up in rebellion against persistent patterns of police brutality and misconduct. Indeed, the 1968 Kerner Commission Report, which examined the causes of urban rebellion in the 1960s, concluded that with few exceptions these insurrections were triggered by acts of police brutality. The angry reaction across the nation to both the death of Amadou Diallo and the acquittal of the four police officers who killed him clearly suggests that attitudes in the Black community and other communities of color have reached the boiling point again in terms of the tolerance level for police brutality. This is the cumulative effect of years of escalating abuse at the hands of policing authorities.

The crisis of police brutality and misconduct that is making headlines throughout the country is the bitter harvest of nearly two decades of misguided public policies. As the conservative backlash and counteroffensive against the gains of the Civil Rights movement of the 1960s deepened, right-wing politicians mounted a furious campaign demanding the implementation of one-sided, punitive policies ostensibly aimed at combating crime and lifting the burden of government off the backs of the middle class. Cleverly utilizing code words and negative images cultivated by mass media, the "burden of government" and "crime" increasingly became associated with Black people and other people of color in the consciousness of much of White America. The consensus on the goals of the Civil Rights movement forged by a "coalition of conscience" involving Blacks, Jews, labor and liberal Whites was shattered. In addition, the national concern for the plight of the poor that was the foundation for the War on Poverty, Model Cities, and other social programs gave way to "empathy fatigue" in the face of the conservative tide that swept the nation. This tide was fueled by latent and overt racism, which the right wing successfully tapped to attack programs that were effective in meeting the needs not only of people of color but also of poor and working-class people in general. Racism was used as a wedge to divide and exploit.

As the conservative tide gained momentum, the social safety network, which provided basic relief for poor people in this country, was shredded. Programs for the hungry and homeless were dismantled as attitudes toward the poor became less tolerant. Indeed, blaming the victim gained new currency as a twentieth-century form of Social Darwinism became popular in conservative circles. The American people were told that, to the degree that poverty was still a problem in this country, it was because poor people either chose to languish in poverty or suffered from cultural or ethnic defects that make them incapable of breaking the "cycle of poverty." Similar arguments were propagated to fuel the assault on affirmative action and other civil rights programs. Racism against Blacks was declared a problem of the past. According to conservative propagandists, the real problem was "Black racism" and "reverse discrimination," which was encroaching on the rights of decent, hardworking Whites—taxpayers whose tax dollars were paying for ill-conceived civil rights initiatives and social programs that benefit people of color to the detriment of White people.

Finally, conservatives told the American people that the same groups that were benefiting from unnecessary social programs and civil rights initiatives were disproportionately inclined toward violence and crime, hence the increase in crime and lawlessness in urban ghettos. Crime and lawlessness came to be perceived as a threat to "our cherished American way of life." Who can forget the sinister Willie Horton commercials used by George Bush during the 1988 presidential campaign. The image of a dark and dangerous Black male parolee, who betrayed the public trust by failing to return from a forty-eight-hour furlough and subsequently beating and raping a White woman, reinforced the deepest stereotypes and played to the basest fears of White America about Black people in general and Black men in particular. Indeed, the symbol of Willie Horton became a metaphor for the demonization of Black men in the media and society at large. In the law enforcement community, virtually every Black man became a "suspect"—a potential "menace to society" who could legitimately be stopped and frisked, harassed, intimidated, and brutalized, if necessary, in the interest of maintaining public safety.

Simultaneously, it became expedient for aspiring politicians to exploit the law-and-order, get-tough-on-crime issue as a tactic for gaining or retaining public office. Serious analysis and deliberations about the root causes of crime became a casualty of political demagoguery. Shallow and self-serving analysis was followed by shallow and self-serving prescriptions for solving the "problem": the addition of hundreds of thousands of new police officers across the country, tougher sentencing, the federalization of more crimes requiring the death penalty, and the construction of more prisons. The police were unleashed against our communities, and people of color, particularly Black and Latino young men, became chattels and commodities for one of the fastest-growing sectors of the American economy, the prison-industrial complex.

In that regard, the "war on drugs," perhaps more than any other single factor, has contributed to the current wave of police brutality and misconduct. As one commentator put it, "The War on Drugs is a war on us."

When the highly addictive and relatively inexpensive drug crack cocaine burst onto the market in the 1980s, it set off an alarm bell in the law enforcement community at all levels. No one can deny that many impoverished inner-city communities were racked by dramatic increases in crime, violence, and fratricide as drug dealers, large and small, and rival gangs battled for control over the illicit drug economy. It is important to note that the rise in crack cocaine trafficking in inner-city communities coincided with the calculated deemphasis on urban policy and the systematic gutting of social and economic support programs designed to ameliorate the plight of poor people, a disproportionate number of whom are people of color.

This shift in public policy was directly related to the pronounced drift to the right of both political parties in response to the conservative tide sweeping the country. As a consequence, the interests and aspirations of inner-city communities, which are heavily populated by people of color, were sacrificed as politicians curried favor with outer-city and suburban voters, most of whom are White. Rather than advocating investment in inner-city communities to alleviate poverty, unemployment, and underemployment, public officials deemed it far more popular politically to propound get-tough-on-crime strategies that called for major increases in allocations for police and prisons.

As Timothy Egan observed in an article in the *New York Times* (February 15, 1998), "In the 1980s crack cocaine scared the country, and the criminal justice system has never been the same." The "scare" produced dramatic changes in policing strategies, sentencing policy in the courts, and the growth of prisons and jails. When I testified at a national summit on police-community relations convened by Attorney General Janet Reno in June 1999, I pointed out that what distinguishes the current epidemic of police brutality and misconduct from previous crises is racial profiling and the militarization of the police. The war on drugs is in large measure predicated on the presumption that stopping drug trafficking in communities of color is the key to "victory."

The adoption of the "war" paradigm of policing has led to the creation of paramilitary special units like narcotics squads, the Street Crime Unit in New York, and heavily armed SWAT teams. These units employ quasi-military tactics, such as the targeting of "suspect" populations and the "pacification" of high-crime areas through the cordoning off of neighborhoods and the use of massive dragnet-type sweeps. Commenting on the trend toward the militarization of the police, in an article entitled "SWAT Nation" in the May 31, 1999, issue of *The Nation* magazine, Christian Parenti wrote, "Throughout the nation, paramilitary, SWAT or tactical policing—that is, law enforcement that uses the equipment, training, rhetoric and group tactics of war—is on the rise." Parenti cited a study by the sociologist Peter Kraska indicating that "the nation has more than 30,000 such heavily armed, militarily trained police units."

The deployment of these paramilitary units in communities of color in cities and locales across the country, and the targeting of their residents, with an emphasis on Black and Latino youth, is a key source of tension and conflict with the police. Racial profiling is an integral component of the war on drugs. The notorious practice of racially based traffic stops or "driving while black" (DWB), is part of a racist drug interdiction strategy widely utilized by policing authorities across the country. The practice of racial profiling in traffic stops and the targeting of people of color communities have also transformed the complexion of the prison population in the United States. Timothy Egan further observed that "more whites than blacks use crack, according to surveys, but as the war on drugs focused on poor city neighborhoods, blacks went to prison at a far higher rate." The war on drugs *is* a war on us.

The problem of police brutality must be understood in a larger social, economic, and political context. As Jerome Miller, president of the National Center on Institutions and Alternatives, asserted in an article on increasing rates of Black imprisonment, in the February 28, 1999, issue of the *Boston Globe*, "Over the past 20 years there has been a terrible propensity on the part of politicians to deal with difficult economic, social, family, and personal problems with a meat axe approach to the criminal justice system." The policy of more police and prisons has been used as a substitute for policies that promote social, economic, and racial justice for people of color. This formula of ill-conceived public policy and policing practices has produced a highly combustible situation in communities of color throughout the nation.

Frederick Douglass once declared, "Power concedes nothing without a demand. It never has and it never will. Find out just what people will submit to, and you have found out the exact amount of injustice and wrong which will be imposed upon them. And these will continue until they are resisted with either words or blows, or both. The limits of tyrants are prescribed by the endurance of those who they oppress."[8] After almost two decades of largely tolerating the intolerable in terms of blatant neglect and escalating police abuse, the police shooting of Amadou Diallo galvanized Black America and people of conscience and good will to cry out, "Enough is Enough!"

It is not that there was no outrage and protest in the country prior to the death of Diallo. As we discovered at the National Emergency Conference on Police Brutality and Misconduct, numerous organizations had been engaged in protest demonstrations and lobbying local officials for change around the country. In Pittsburgh, the police killing of Jonny Gammage provoked a protracted struggle for justice. In November 1996, thousands of Black high school students staged a massive walkout, marched to the heart of downtown, and called for a boycott of the city by tourists and conventiongoers. In St. Petersburg, Florida, the Black community erupted in rebellion in response to the 1996 killing of eighteen-year-old TyRon Lewis, who police claimed lunged at them with his car when they directed him to stop. In San Francisco in 1997, Bay Area Police Watch led a series of rallies and marches at City Hall, demanding police reform in response to a rash of incidents of police brutality and police killings. On October 22, 1996, a broad-based coalition staged demonstrations across the country and launched the Stolen Lives Project, which produced a book that documents police killings nationwide since 1990.

In New York City, the National Congress of Puerto Rican Rights, working in concert with a coalition of police reform advocates, was at the forefront of fighting for justice in the Anthony Baez case; it also organized family members of victims of police brutality to fight for police reform. The December 12 Movement continued to agitate around the case of Aswan Watson, an unarmed Black youth who was shot twenty-four times by three White officers in Brooklyn. The National Action Network, under the leadership of the Reverend Al Sharpton, took up the cause of Kevin Cedeno, a sixteen-year-old Black youth who was shot and killed in 1997 by a police officer who claimed that Cedeno lunged at him with a machete (the medical examiner's report indicated that Cedeno was shot in the back).[9] The officer responsible for the shooting, Anthony Pellegrini, was not indicted.[10] And there was the mass mobilization around the case of Abner Louima, the highlight of which occurred when more than ten thousand people marched across the Brooklyn Bridge to One Police Plaza, the headquarters of the NYPD, in August of 1997.

The slaughter of Amadou Diallo, however, became the defining moment, a critical turning point in the struggle against police brutality and misconduct in New York and the nation. On February 25, 1999, Hugh Price, president and CEO of the National Urban League, convened an extraordinary press conference at the National Press Club in Washington, D.C. Leaders from across the spectrum of the civil and human rights community were in attendance, among them the Reverend Al Sharpton, president of the National Action Network, Kwesi Mfume, president and CEO of the NAACP, Wade Henderson, executive director of the Leadership Conference on Civil Rights, Raul Yzaguirre, president and CEO of the National Council of La Raza, Karen Naragaski, executive director of the Asian Pacific American Legal Consortium, Ira Glasser, executive director of the American Civil Liberties Union, Congressman John Conyers Jr., ranking member of the House Judiciary Committee, Ed Lewis, publisher of *Essence* magazine, and the Reverend Jesse L. Jackson, president of the Rainbow-PUSH Coalition, to mention a few.

Against the backdrop of growing outrage over the murder of Diallo, Hugh Price was intent on using the press conference to appeal directly to President Clinton to speak out boldly and forcefully on the issue of police brutality and misconduct. Speaker after speaker rose to underscore Price's appeal to the president. As executive director of the Center for Constitutional Rights, I used the occasion to call for a National Emergency March for Justice on April 3, 1999, Martin Luther King Jr. Memorial Weekend, in Washington, D.C. The call rang out across the nation, and people began to spontaneously organize to march on Washington.

In the corridor after the press conference, the Reverend Sharpton asked my opinion whether it was better to hold a massive rally to protest the death of Amadou Diallo at City Hall in New York or on Wall Street. Apparently, the Reverend Jackson was advising that City Hall was the better venue. The Reverend Sharpton was inclined toward a protest on Wall Street. For whatever it was worth, I agreed with the Reverend Sharpton, arguing that a massive demonstration on Wall Street, the capital of U.S. and world capitalism, would send a clear message to America's corporate and commercial elite that business as usual as it relates to police brutality would no longer be tolerated. The Reverend Sharpton also indicated that he was leaning toward engaging in civil disobedience by conducting a sit-down demonstration in the middle of Wall Street to block traffic and dramatize the demand for justice in the Diallo case. I told the Reverend Sharpton that if he decided to engage in civil disobedience, I would join him.

If New York City emerged as the epicenter of police brutality under the mean-spirited reign of Mayor Giuliani, it also became the eye of the storm of national protest that exploded across the country in the wake of the death of Amadou Diallo. On March 3, the Reverend Sharpton did indeed mobilize hundreds of people for a demonstration on Wall Street. At the appointed time, a select group of eleven people, including the Reverend Herbert Daughtry, a veteran of the anti–police brutality crusades of the 1970s and 1980s, Charles Barron of the Unity Party, a key activist in the Free South Africa Movement, and Wyatt Tee Walker, pastor of the Canaan Baptist Church in Harlem and former chief of staff for Dr. Martin Luther King Jr., locked arms with the Reverend Sharpton, walked to the center of Wall Street, and kneeled down for prayer. The police moved in and arrested the group for disorderly conduct and took us off to jail. The stage was set for a historic civil disobedience campaign in New York.

In the weeks and days leading up to the Wall Street action and thereafter, numerous coalitions of organizations, as well as women's and youth groups, staged large demonstrations at City Hall. At a meeting called by the Reverend Sharpton and hosted by the Reverend Daughtry at the House of the Lord Church in Brooklyn, the discussion turned to how to maintain the momentum of the movement following the success of the Wall Street demonstration and the other rallies and demonstrations that had occurred. Charles Barron and the Reverend Daughtry proposed that the leaders assembled launch a civil disobedience campaign modeled after the Free South Africa Movement with daily demonstrations and arrests at One Police Plaza in lower Manhattan, the headquarters of the NYPD.

I expressed skepticism that enough people could be mobilized to sustain the arrests on a daily basis. I suggested that, perhaps, a demonstration a week would be more likely to be sustained. The consensus was that to have maximum impact daily demonstrations and arrests were necessary, even if only a few people were arrested each day. Various pastors of churches and leaders of organizations, including the Center for Constitutional Rights, pledged to mobilize their constituencies to take a day at One Police Plaza. On March 9, the Reverend Sharpton, along with Charles Barron and the Reverend Daughtry, led the first group of protesters to One Police Plaza. With a multitude of local, regional, and national press on the scene, the group staged a sit-down demonstration blocking the entrance to the headquarters of the NYPD. They were arrested and taken to jail. The civil disobedience campaign was on. In the heart of winter, New York City was on fire and the nation and the world were watching.

On April 3, some five thousand people from across the nation gathered in Washington, D.C., for the National Emergency March for Justice/Against Police Brutality, the largest march there against police brutality in recent history. The march was endorsed by nearly a hundred local, regional, and national civil and human rights organizations and police reform advocacy groups, including the NAACP, the National Urban League, the National Action Network, the Southern Christian Leadership Conference, the Asian American Legal Defense and Education Fund, the National Council of Churches National Ministries Unit, the Malcolm X Grassroots Movement, the National Congress for Puerto Rican Rights, the National Conference of Black Lawyers, the National Lawyers Guild, and Jews for Racial and Economic Justice. The Reverend Al Sharpton, who traveled to the march with members of the Diallo family, Kwesi Mfume, Jaribu Hill, Ron Hampton, Liz Ou Yang, Walter Fauntroy, Jane Bai, Richie Perez, Will Harrell, Gabriel Torres, Mark Thompson, Joe Madison, Dick Gregory, Efia Mwangaza, Meghan Ortiz, and Martin Luther King III were among the leaders who addressed the rally.

At the center and in the lead of the march, however, were scores of family members of victims of police brutality who journeyed to Washington, D.C., from as far away as Arizona and California to tell their stories. There was massive press coverage of the march and rally, and the event was recorded and broadcast on C-SPAN. In addition to providing a voice for family members and victims of police brutality, the march was intended to demand action by the federal government to combat the scourge of police brutality and misconduct. The demands reflected a growing agreement among civil and human rights organizations and community-based police reform organizations around the nation about some basic steps that various branches of the federal government should take to achieve police reform and accountability. The following demands were articulated at the National Emergency March:

We demand immediate action from the President, Attorney General and Congress of the United States:

1. **President Clinton** should immediately speak out on this issue and empower a national commission to investigate the epidemic of police brutality and misconduct which is afflicting communities of color and poor communities across the nation.

2. **Attorney General Janet Reno**, under the provisions of the Omnibus Crime Bill of 1994, should issue a directive to the Justice Department to intensify pattern and practices investigations in communities with a high incidence of complaints of police brutality. In addition, we call on the Attorney General to press for the expedited investigation of ongoing civil rights cases and to hear appeals for the re-opening of cases which may not have received appropriate priority.

3. **The House Judiciary Committee** should immediately convene formal hearings to take testimony on the scope and breadth of police brutality and misconduct and formulate recommendations for legislation accordingly.

4. **The Congress of the United States** should:

a. Pass legislation to provide funds for the Justice Department to systematically collect data on police brutality as mandated by the Omnibus Crime Bill of 1994.

b. Enact legislation that would provide for independent federal prosecutors to investigate allegations of police misconduct where the use of illegal choke holds or deadly force results in the injury or death of the victim—**The Jonny Gammage Law**.[11]

Coupled with the massive civil disobedience campaign in New York, the National Emergency March helped propel the issue of brutality to the center of national focus and deliberations. Rose Ochi, the director of the Community Relations Division of the Department of Justice, attended the march as an observer. Other high-level officials of the Justice Department monitored the news coverage and watched the proceedings on C-SPAN. The moving testimonies of family member after family member telling the stories of the tragic loss of their loved ones made a powerful impression.

In the aftermath of the National Emergency March, the Southern Christian Leadership Conference, under the leadership of Martin Luther King III, moved to hold community-based hearings on police brutality in several cities across the country. Activists from around the nation joined in the demonstrations in Riverside, California, protesting the death of Tyisha Miller, a young Black woman who was shot twelve times by four police officers as she sat in her car at a gas station. On April 15, twelve days after the National Emergency March, a coalition of labor, religious, civic, and political leaders, spearheaded by former Mayor David Dinkins, Dennis Rivera, president of the Health and Hospital Workers Union, and the Reverend Al Sharpton, led a march of upwards of twenty thousand people across the Brooklyn Bridge in support of a ten-point agenda for police reform and accountability in New York.

In the face of escalating movement around the issue of police brutality and misconduct across the nation, the federal government began to act. In response to the February press conference convened by Hugh Price, President Clinton did, in fact, speak out on the issue of police brutality during one of his weekly radio broadcasts. The president directed Attorney General Janet Reno to begin a series of conversations about police brutality and police community relations with civil and human rights leaders, heads of community-based organizations, and officials in law enforcement. The Congressional Black Caucus held a hearing in Washington, D.C., and subsequently in New York, Chicago, and Los Angeles. The U.S. Commission on Civil Rights also conducted a hearing in New York. In June 1999, Janet Reno convened a national summit on police-community relations where President Clinton addressed the group and issued an executive order banning the use of racial profiling by federal law enforcement agencies. The president also participated in a roundtable discussion on police brutality and misconduct at the summit.

Within the Congress, Congressman José Serrano of New York, a member of the House Judiciary Committee, teamed up with Judiciary Chairman Henry Hyde of Chicago, an unlikely ally, to introduce a bill calling for the creation of a national commission to study the issue of police brutality and misconduct. John Conyers, ranking member of the Judiciary Committee, introduced a bill to ban traffic stops based on racial profiling. Congressman Conyers is also considering introducing a bill entitled the Law Enforcement Trust and Integrity Act, which would empower the attorney general to withhold Justice Department funds from police departments that engage in racial profiling and other forms of police misconduct.

The Justice Department, which has been pursuing a pattern-and-practice investigation of the NYPD since the Louima incident, has finally indicated that its investigation reveals a pattern of lax discipline toward officers implicated in incidents of police abuse. The U.S. District Office is sending signals that it may take legal action against the city if Mayor Giuliani refuses to enter a consent degree to remedy the problems uncovered by the investigation. In the meantime, under pressure from various quarters, the mayor and police chief have begun to hint at modest reforms in policing practices of the NYPD. However, no one expects serious changes in the NYPD in the absence of sustained pressure in the streets, the courts, and the City Council.

Certainly, no issue in recent memory has so stirred the passion of Black people and other people of color as the epidemic of police brutality and misconduct. On May 26, 1999, a grand jury in New York indicted the four police officers who shot Amadou Diallo, charging them with second degree murder. Daily demonstrations at One Police Plaza lasted twenty days and resulted in the arrest of 1,166 people from various races, ethnicities, and religions. All agreed to be arrested because they believed changes in the attitudes and practices of the police were necessary to the preservation of a wholesome and civil society. Whether real change will come to New York and the nation on this issue remains to be seen. What is clear is that a few cosmetic changes will not be sufficient to address the long-standing problem of police abuse in people of color and poor communities.

The reaction of people across the country to the death of Amadou Diallo and other cases of police brutality and police killings should serve as a wake-up call, a warning to public officials and policymakers that unless real change is forthcoming, huge sections of the American populace will completely lose faith in the legitimacy of policing authorities. If America is truly to become one nation under the law, "with liberty and justice for all," a new paradigm of policing must be developed. The government at all levels must be compelled to institute policies and practices that will restore faith and confidence in those who are entrusted with "protecting" our communities. What we need in this country is community-based, Constitution-compatible policing buttressed by public policies that promote social, economic, and racial justice.

Clearly, this suggests that the paramilitary "war" paradigm used by an increasing number of police departments in the United States must be eliminated. Racial profiling and the practice of conducting massive sweeps of inner-city communities that target, harass, and terrorize young people of color must end. There can be no room for the "us against them" psychology and the "blue wall of silence" within police departments that expect to command the respect of the community. The new paradigm of policing must be based on the principle that police are first and foremost servants of the people. Their job is to function at the behest of and in partnership with communities to carry out a special mandate to maintain peace and security consistent with the Constitution.

In accordance with this view, police officers must be educated and trained to see themselves as a vital part of the community, not outsiders under orders to "occupy" and "pacify" the community. Though ideally police officers should be required to reside in the jurisdictions they are responsible for policing, at a minimum units within the police force should be assigned to work within communities to become acquainted with the customs, cultures, and mannerisms of the people in particular neighborhoods. Police officers should be perceived as friends of the community, not its enemies. To achieve this goal, the composition of a police force should resemble the ethnic and cultural makeup of the communities where police are assigned to serve. In addition, it is essential that police officers receive antiracism and diversity training as an integral part of their education in police academies. Police officers must learn to conduct themselves with sensitivity and responsiveness in multiethnic and multicultural communities.

It is not enough, however, simply to train police to function differently in our communities as they pursue the mission of maintaining peace and security. The familiar slogan "No justice, no peace" is in reality a formula for crime reduction and the creation of wholesome and secure communities. Unless and until this nation makes a firm and irreversible commitment to ensure that all of the people who live in this society will enjoy access to the same social and economic rights—good jobs, quality education, housing, health care, clean environment—instability, violence, and crime will continue to be problems that no amount or method of policing can contain for long. As community-based organizations, civil and human rights organizations, and public-interest advocacy groups struggle against police brutality and misconduct, the fight to create a new paradigm of policing must necessarily be seen as a part of the broader struggle to create a more just and humane society. Therefore, the demand for police reform and accountability must necessarily be coupled with the demand for public policies that promote social, economic, and racial justice. Our goal must be nothing short of creating a just, humane, and peaceful society. If there is no justice, there will be no peace in these United States of America.

NOTES

1. National Lawyers Guild, October 22 Coalition, Anthony Baez Foundation, *Stolen Lives: Killed by Law Enforcement*, 2nd ed. (New York, 1999), 298.

2. Ibid., 195.

3. Ibid., 33.

4. Ibid., 207.

5. Allyson Collins, *Shielded from Justice: Police Brutality and Accountability in the United States* (New York: Human Rights Watch, 1998), 254–55.

6. National Lawyers Guild, *Stolen Lives*, 314.

7. David A. Love and Gabriel Torres, *Police Brutality and Racism in the United States: Race Convention Report to the United Nations* (New York: Center for Constitutional Rights, 1998), 17–19.

8. *A Chronology of Notable Events in the History of Africans in America and the Diaspora, 1600 BCE through 1980* (Kent, Ohio: Institute of African American Affairs, Kent State University, 1984), 123.

9. *New York Times*, May 28, 1997, Section B, p. 1.

10. *Daily News* (New York), June 1, 1997.

11. Document created by the National Emergency March Coalition, the Center for Constitutional Rights, et al., New York City, April 1999.

Biographical Notes

RICHARD AUSTIN was born in 1973 in Brooklyn, New York, to parents of Haitian descent. He received his B.A. in psychology from New York University and is currently a doctoral student in counseling psychology. Austin is an educator who has worked with young people for over ten years. As a grass-roots activist, he is a member of the revolutionary, people of African descent organization—Forever in Struggle Together (FIST), based in central Brooklyn.

DERRICK BELL has worked for over forty years on racial issues as a litigator, administrator, law teacher, and writer. He has taught full-time as a visiting professor at the New York University School of Law since 1991. He has also taught at Harvard, among several other law schools. His text *Race, Racism and American Law,* first published in 1973, is now in its fourth edition. Bell is also the author of a basic textbook on constitutional law. His publications aimed at a more general audience include *Faces at the Bottom of the Well: The Permanence of Racism, Gospel Choirs: Psalms of Survival in an Alien Land Called Home,* and *Confronting Authority: Reflections of an Ardent Protestor.*

CLAUDE A. CLEGG III is an associate professor of history at Indiana University at Bloomington. He specializes in African American history and is the author of *An Original Man: The Life and Times of Elijah Muhammad.* He is currently writing a book on African American emigration to Liberia.

STANLEY CROUCH is a native of Los Angeles, and has written poetry, essays, reviews, and plays for many years. He is the author of three collections of reviews and essays: *Notes of a Hanging Judge, The All-American Skin Game,* and *Always in Pursuit.* In 1993, he received a MacArthur Foundation grant. He is currently writing the scripts for *Jazz: The Music, the People, the Myth,* a television miniseries. Crouch is an artistic consultant for jazz programming at Lincoln Center and writes a twice-weekly column for the New York *Daily News.*

RON DANIELS was born in Beckley, West Virginia, and grew up in Youngstown, Ohio. He received a B.A. from Youngstown State University and an M.A. in political science from the Rockefeller School of Public Affairs in Albany, New York, and is currently completing his doctoral degree. Daniels was an independent candidate for president in 1992 and served as executive director of the National Rainbow Coalition in 1987 and as southern regional coordinator and deputy campaign manager for Jesse Jackson's presidential campaign in 1988. Daniels has been executive director of the Center for Constitutional Rights, a nonprofit legal and educational organization dedicated to advancing and protecting the U.S. Constitution and the Universal Declaration of Human Rights since 1994.

ARTHUR DOYLE was born and raised in New York City. After graduating from Morris High School in the Bronx, he enlisted in the Marine Corps. He joined the New York Police Department in 1965. He received his B.S. in criminal justice from John Jay College in 1974. During twenty-nine years in the NYPD, Doyle served as a youth gang investigator, community affairs specialist, and supervisor of the Runaway Unit. During his last six years, he was commanding officer of the NYPD's Youth Services Division, which encompassed all programs directed at young people. During his career in the NYPD, Doyle received fourteen commendations for meritorious and exceptional police acts. A man who does not shy away from going against the grain, Doyle retired as a lieutenant in 1993. In 1994, he was a Charles H. Revson Fellow on the Future of the City of New York at Columbia University.

FLORES ALEXANDER FORBES was a member of the Black Panther Party from 1968 to 1977. He received his B.A. from San Francisco State University and master's degree in urban planning from the Robert F. Wagner School of Public Service at New York University. He has also been a Patricia Roberts Harris Fellow at NYU and a Charles H. Revson Fellow at Columbia University. At night, Mr. Forbes works on his memoir entitled *An American Urban Guerrilla*. During the day, he is a professional urban planner as the deputy director of the Office for Land Use of the Manhattan Borough President.

ROBIN D. G. KELLEY is professor of history and Africana studies at New York University. He is the author of several books, including most recently *Race Rebels: Culture, Politics and the Black Working Class* (1994) and *Yo' Mama's DisFunktional!: Fighting the Culture Wars in Urban America* (1997). He is currently writing a book on the pianist-composer Thelonious Monk.

ELVIN MONTGOMERY is a New York–based management consultant, organizational psychologist, and dealer in African American history and cultural materials. He offers vintage, rare, research, or collectible materials in a wide variety of fields: social history, politics, slavery, music, entertainment, literature, sports, religion, popular culture, arts, and civil rights. Montgomery is a graduate of Harvard College and holds a doctorate from Columbia. He can be contacted at P.O. Box 1760, Manhattan Station, New York, NY 10027.

ISHMAEL REED is the author of nine and a half novels, four books of essays, four books of poetry, and five plays. He has published works by Victor Cruz, Calvin Hernton, Lorenzo Thomas, Colleen McElroy, Alex Kuo, Alison Mills, J. J. Philips, Amiri Baraka, Bill Gunn, Thulani Davis, and other distinguished authors. He is the publisher of *Konch*; www.ishmaelreedpub.com

KATHERYN K. RUSSELL is an associate professor of criminology and criminal justice at the University of Maryland, College Park. Russell received her undergraduate degree from the Univerity of California, Berkeley, her law degree from Hastings Law School, and her Ph.D. from the criminology department at the University of Maryland, College Park. Russell is the author of *The Color of Crime: Racial Hoaxes, White Fear, Black Protectionism, Police Harrassment, and Other Macroagressions* and is currently working on her second book.

PATRICIA J. WILLIAMS is a professor of law at Columbia University and a columnist ("Diary of a Mad Law Professor") for *The Nation* magazine. A graduate of Wellesley College and Harvard Law School, she is the author, most recently, of *Seeing a Color-Blind Future: The Paradox of Race* (1998).

Acknowledgments

Thanks to my editor and friend Bob Weil for helping me turn outrage, disgust, and sadness into a book, and to my agent Jennifer Lyons and my assistant Davarian L. Baldwin for their good work. My gratitude to The City College of New York, the Department of Media and Communication Arts, and the staff of Cohen Library for their support.

Once again, Ray Hicks's eleventh-hour assistance was invaluable. My family and friends offered their loving support, and Lynnie good humor as well, all much appreciated.

Finally, I appreciate the ongoing spirit and indefatigable energy of the countless ordinary people and activists whose consistent work for justice makes them extraordinary.